D0140095

Defining Student Success

WITHDRAWN

The Rutgers Series in Childhood Studies

The Rutgers Series in Childhood Studies is dedicated to increasing our understanding of children and childhoods, past and present, throughout the world. Children's voices and experiences are central. Authors come from a variety of fields, including anthropology, criminal justice, history, literature, psychology, religion, and sociology. The books in this series are intended for students, scholars, practitioners, and those who formulate policies that affect children's everyday lives and futures.

Edited by Myra Bluebond-Langner, Board of Governors Professor of Anthropology, Rutgers University and True Colours Chair in Palliative Care for Children and Young People, University College London, Institute of Child Health.

Advisory Board

Perri Klass, *New York University*

Jill Korbin, *Case Western Reserve University*

Bambi Schieffelin, *New York University*

Enid Schildkraut, *American Museum of Natural History and Museum for African Art*

Defining Student Success

The Role of School and Culture

TOURO COLLEGE LIBRARY
Kings Hwy

LISA M. NUNN

RUTGERS UNIVERSITY PRESS

NEW BRUNSWICK, NEW JERSEY, AND LONDON

KH

Library of Congress Cataloging-in-Publication Data

Nunn, Lisa M., 1975-
Defining student success : the role of school and culture / Lisa M. Nunn.
    pages cm. — (Series in childhood studies)
    Includes bibliographical references and index.
    ISBN 978-0-8135-6362-6 (hardback) — ISBN 978-0-8135-6361-9 (pbk.) —
ISBN 978-0-8135-6363-3 (e-book)
    1. High school environment–United States–Case studies. 2. High school students—
United States—Case studies. 3. Prediction of scholastic success—United States—Case
studies. I. Title.

    LB1620.5.N86 2014
    373.18—dc23   2013033864

A British Cataloging-in-Publication record for this book is available from
the British Library.

Copyright © 2014 by Lisa M. Nunn
All rights reserved
No part of this book may be reproduced or utilized in any form or by any means, elec-
tronic or mechanical, or by any information storage and retrieval system, without
written permission from the publisher. Please contact Rutgers University Press, 106
Somerset Street, New Brunswick, NJ 08901. The only exception to this prohibition is
"fair use" as defined by U.S. copyright law.

Visit our website: http://rutgerspress.rutgers.edu

Manufactured in the United States of America

12/17/15

For Garrett

CONTENTS

ACKNOWLEDGMENTS

This book would not have been possible without the high school students, teachers, and principals who were willing to share their experiences with me. Thank you for your candor and your trust. If you ever need a favor in return, please look me up.

As this is a book about school environments, I would be remiss not to acknowledge the graduate school that shaped me and my work. The sociology department at the University of California, San Diego (UCSD), has a culture of nurturing relationships between faculty and graduate students, and I benefited enormously from the environment there. Amy Binder is a true mentor and friend, encouraging my work and pushing my thinking in new directions. I owe many insights in this book to her challenging questions. John Evans kindly and patiently developed my scholarly potential. His wisdom and guidance have seen me through many an intellectual puzzle (and a few social ones too). I thank Akos Rona-Tas for his unflagging enthusiasm for my work. He helped me craft both a stronger project and a stronger me. I thank Bud Mehan for his support, generosity, and infinite expertise.

I owe many debts to people who have contributed to this book by reading drafts, offering comments, debating with me in hallways and coffee shops, and sharing their knowledge and ideas. I heartily thank Tim Hallett and Ruben Gaztambide-Fernandez for their excellent suggestions and helpful critiques. Steph Haggard, Mitchell Stevens, Mary Blair-Loy, Michael Evans, Stephanie Chan, and Erik Fritsvold have provided invaluable insights at various stages of the project. I thank Peter Mickulas at Rutgers University Press. In addition, I took part in many fruitful and inspiring conversations at Sociology of Education Association conferences, culture and society workshops at UCSD, and Ocelot Writing Group meetings as well as in the sociology of education classes I teach. Thank you, students, friends, and colleagues.

The sociology department at UCSD funded my work on this project with graduate research grants. My new institutional home, the University of San Diego, also funded this work with a faculty research grant. I am grateful to Michelle Camacho and Judy Liu for mentorship and support that have allowed this book to come to fruition.

For their love and encouragement, I thank my family: Monica Beith, Scott Beith, Nick Beith, Trevor Beith, Maria Evans, Rick Evans, Nick Moraitis, Betty Goldfield, Alan Goldfield, Bil Goldfield, Kelly Goldfield, and little Alana Goldfield. Thank you for your devotion to me. I dedicate this book to Garrett Goldfield, who reminds me everyday that true happiness is possible.

Defining Student Success

Introduction

Three High Schools with Three Distinct Ideas about School Success

Deshawn, a high school freshman, sits with me for an interview during his lunch break.[1] It's a Tuesday in January, but Deshawn is not at school. Instead, he is at his internship, where he works from 10:00 A.M. to 2:00 P.M. on Tuesdays and Thursdays, busing tables, running the cash register, and learning the ropes of food service at a popular lunch café in a busy suburban shopping and business district. Deshawn hopes to become a chef one day, and he sees this internship as a good step toward attaining his dream career.

His school, a place I call Alternative High, not only supports balancing school with internship work but actually mandates it. School days are scheduled on Mondays, Wednesdays, and Fridays only. Students are required to spend time in the world of work (usually unpaid) on Tuesdays and Thursdays. The goal of the internship program is to allow students to gain real-world knowledge and experience so that after graduation they have a clearer sense of what college and career paths they might like to pursue. In addition, they can tout their internship experience on their résumés when they apply for jobs.

From Deshawn's perspective, the arrangement is working well. As a teenager in a low-income, single-parent home, he certainly appreciates the free lunches after his shift. But he also takes his job experience seriously. He is confident that high school and job success go hand in hand, and he sees his internship as part of that relationship. "I want to become an executive chef," he tells me, "so that I can really do what I like. And so at home, I just try a lot of different things. I don't really go out [to eat in restaurants] because of money. Money issues, you know? I don't really go out there. But if it was like a box or something, I can do it. You know, I am learning from boxes. And I try to do as much of the cooking as I can because I am trying to determine if I do want to be an executive chef or not, or a pastry chef. You never know."

In his daily life Deshawn has very limited access to resources, but Alternative High has designed its mission around preparing him and other low-income urban youth for bright futures. The school prides itself on providing opportunities for students to discover their talents and passions and build futures around them. Deshawn takes advantage of these opportunities. Even though he is not actually learning any chef-level cooking skills, he is an eager intern and works hard at the lunch café. His attitude can be seen as a personal commitment to the ideal of hard work. Yet as I argue in this book, looking only at students' individual characters is shortsighted. We need to look at students' school environments if we want to comprehensively understand how their ideas and behaviors relate to the concept of success. In other words, to understand Deshawn's dedication to the low-skill labor of busing tables and running a cash register, we need to recognize that his high school actively fosters an ethic of hard work. At Alternative High, hard work is heralded as the essential ingredient for success in life. According to Deshawn's principal, "if the culture and the school environment [are] there, then students can get all As and [they] will have options as far as careers are concerned."

As the lunch rush dwindles to a handful of customers, Deshawn sits down to talk with me. Against a backdrop of clanking dishes, I ask, "Why do students go to school?"

"To learn how to work in our environment," he responds. "We usually learn how to be productive and how to be very businesslike in school. And after we have received a good amount of education, we are able to be really into our own working field. And we would probably be successful in that because of our education. And after college, usually you do get a good job because of the fact that you stayed in school rather than going and doing your own thing, you know."

Throughout our interview, he reiterates the idea that the purpose of school is to prepare students for the world of work. Rather than claiming that students learn facts and knowledge that will help them in their future careers, he emphasizes that school teaches students behaviors that they will need to be successful in their future jobs. One of the most critical behaviors, according to Deshawn, is turning in one's work on time: "In a real job you have to know how to meet deadlines; you have to do that. That's the reason why I need to go to school, so I know how to meet deadlines. And that's basically what we are doing. We're trying to get all the work in right, and meet it—meet the deadline."

Like many Americans, Deshawn is confident that hard work is the key to success. For him, this is as true in high school as it is anywhere else. His principal agrees: "When a task is given, you need to do your very best at completing the task. Completing the task may say, 'I got an A on this task because I did the check-off.' [She mimics checking items off a list.] You will have children who won't complete their work and may not get an A, B, or C. Getting less than a C simply means that you didn't manage your time, you weren't organized, and you didn't ask for help."

Notice that Deshawn's principal does not indicate that a lack of intellectual ability might be the reason—or even part of the reason—for why a student earns low grades. Similarly, when I ask Deshawn, "What does it take for a student to earn good grades in your school?" he responds, "A lot of dedication." Importantly, like his principal, and like many other students I interviewed at Alternative High, Deshawn does not believe that a person has to be particularly intelligent to do well in school. Instead, he believes that paying attention in class and completing homework are all it takes to earn good grades. "You don't have to necessarily be smart," he explains, "because the teachers teach you plenty enough to do what you need to do on your own. And it's a matter of whether you listen or not. Because, well, they can be smart, but if you don't turn your work in, you know, you are not going to be graded for your smartness." He later volunteers: "I really respect a person who can get their work turned in."

Deshawn's ideas about school success are typical of the students I interviewed at Alternative High, where I found a strong, consistent belief that everyone is smart enough to meet the demands of schoolwork. Anyone can do it, the students told me. It's all a matter of whether or not a person tries. Their attitude is common in U.S. society: some scholars refer to it as achievement ideology, while others call it American dream ideology.[2] Yet according to this ideology, hard work is only one way to achieve success. Natural or God-given talents offer another route. These two resources—effort and talent—are the focus of this book. Throughout, I distinguish among cultural ideas about success in which a person draws on talent to achieve goals, relies on hard work to achieve them, or uses a combination of the two. In terms of school success, I focus on high intelligence as students' most salient natural talent.

Deshawn's understanding of school success as being dependent on effort rather than intelligence is rooted in the particular way in which success is understood at his high school. Different schools create their own versions of larger cultural ideas, modifying and adapting those that are prevalent in wider U.S. society. These distinct understandings of school success have consequences for students. In the three high schools I have chosen to study, I focus on two types of consequences. First, I look at the ways in which students construct an identity for themselves—what I call their *success identity*. I find that, as students describe themselves, they draw heavily on their own school's definition of success. Thus, if Deshawn were to attend a different kind of high school, his ideas about both school success and himself would likely be different.[3] Second, I look at students' futures in higher education. Each school's belief about success is aligned with a particular tier of higher education. Finally, I argue that school-level beliefs about success serve as a mechanism for reproducing the existing social order in American life.

Like others at Alternative High, Deshawn uses behavioral criteria to judge how successful he is and to anticipate how successful he will be later in life. He asserts that his grades are based on these behaviors: "Usually my teachers come up with the report card for me with how good I've acted. . . . My way of doing things is really, like, strict. I put a lot of strict things on myself just to get things done ahead of time. And that usually helps the teachers understand that I am doing my job and I should get a good grade for that."

Notice that Deshawn does not claim that his grades are based on whether or not he masters the material in his assignments. Nor, he says, are good grades the result of high intelligence. Hard work and meeting deadlines explain who is successful and who is not: end of story. I ask him if he thinks it is easier to get great grades in school if a person is highly intelligent. He adamantly disagrees: "The person that's not so smart, you know, could be working harder than the intelligent person because the intelligent person might have their ego so high that they think a teacher knows them, that they don't have to turn in their work or something." In fact, he suggests that intelligence is irrelevant to success in school: "If you don't turn your work in, you know, you are not going to be graded for your smartness."

The second school in my study, which I call Comprehensive High, fosters a different understanding of what it takes to succeed in school. Although Comprehensive High students also emphasize the importance of effort, they present a more complicated picture of what effort means. I ask Flor, a junior, "If a student tries hard enough, can she make all *A*s in school?"

She responds, "No. Because I am trying really hard in chemistry right now, and I'm not even getting a *B*. I'll listen, but I just don't understand anything he's talking about. . . . Even if you do try, you might not get what you want."

Students at Comprehensive High echoed this idea again and again in interviews with me. Their understanding of school success included the notion that hard work has its limits. You have to be intelligent in a subject in order for your effort to pay off because you have to be able to understand the concepts. Students often described this limitation in terms of having "weak points." A weak point is a subject or two that a person is simply not very good at. In a class that is your weak point, you cannot expect excellent grades, no matter how much effort you put forth. The students I talked to at Comprehensive High accepted this as a fact of life.

Flor and I are drinking lattes in a popular coffee shop in a strip mall across the street from Comprehensive High. The atmosphere is crowded and noisy, but Flor does not seem to mind the bustle . She listens to my questions and answers each one thoughtfully. School has just let out for the afternoon, and the stress of her school day lingers over her as she talks. Flor explains that school success comes easier for students who are naturally intelligent, and she feels that students who are working hard toward good grades should not be blamed for achieving less school success: "If you want to get there, and you're trying but you just don't get there, then it's not like it's your fault that you can't get there."

Nonetheless, like most of the students I talked to at Comprehensive High, Flor does not downplay the importance of putting forth effort. As an example, she tells me about her own problems last semester. Her grades were disastrous: she received Ds in three of her six classes. Flor explains, "I wasn't expecting anything good, and so I know I got those grades for a reason. I got really lazy. It was the beginning of the semester, and I didn't do any of my homework, and so towards the end of the semester—or middle of it—I knew I had to do all of my homework and stuff, but then it was too late to raise [the grades] up dramatically." Since then, she has turned over a new leaf. Now she aspires to be successful in high school and go on to college. Yet although she is proud of her newfound effort and improved success in school, she does not expect to earn As, no matter how diligent she is. She simply does not think she is intelligent enough: "I'm not dumb or anything. It's just that, like, if I tried, I'd probably pull off being a B student—if I really tried."

Flor's principal also believes that a combination of effort and intelligence is necessary for school success. When I ask her, "What does it take for a student to earn good grades at your school?" she replies, "What we hope teachers would say [is] you need to be here. Attendance is huge. You need to participate in the class, ask questions, and be actively engaged. You need to complete the assignments you've been given. I would say those are probably the three things that would lead to success for the student."

At first, her remarks sound as if she is promoting straightforward effort, as the principal at Alternative High was. But when I ask her if a student should be able to earn all As if she tries hard enough, the Comprehensive High principal tells me firmly, "Oh, I disagree. Totally. If they don't master the content, they aren't going to pass the class." She draws on the term *academic ability* when she refers to the intellectual capabilities necessary for mastering course content, and she repeatedly emphasizes that grades are supposed to be a reflection of ability: "Hopefully, most of the grades that students are issued by the teacher have to do with their academic ability much more than their attitude or behavior." Yet she acknowledges that "effort is certainly involved" in getting good grades. Behaviors such as participating in class, being engaged, and completing assignments play a role in student success, but "as far as a teacher issuing a grade, it is supposed to be purely on academics."

I also studied a third school, which I call Elite Charter High. My interview with Daphne, a sophomore there, offers a telling example of the ideas about success that it fosters. Daphne and I sit down together one evening on large couches in the living room of her family's spacious two-story home. She has made sure to complete her homework early and has returned from martial arts practice in time to accommodate our interview. Her younger siblings are sequestered with her parents in another part of the house, so the room is quiet and calm. Daphne seems relaxed as she explains to me the purpose of school: "to enrich yourself, to open your mind to more things." This attitude is very different from Deshawn's, who believes that school teaches students to be "businesslike" and "meet deadlines."

Like many other students I interviewed at Elite Charter High, Daphne connects learning to a person's natural intelligence. When I ask her how we can recognize someone who is intelligent, she replies, "Well, in school: grades. They prove [it] easy." She goes on to describe how intelligence manifests in a person: "If they show a passion for something, then definitely they will have the knowledge of that, and there is intelligence there. . . . [If] they question—that's a big one—thinking about it can intrigue them enough that they ask about it, then they have the interest and they want to increase their knowledge of that, so there is intelligence there."

According to Daphne, people who are intelligent feel passionate about learning and are therefore motivated to pursue knowledge: "It's the trying to learn. If you believe in yourself, you go through it; then your intelligence will show more. . . . Trying to bring yourself to the higher level. Trying to bring yourself up instead of just staying at a plateau or going down. The human wants to strengthen themselves." In her view, intelligence is connected to an internal desire to learn, grow, and develop.

For many students I talked to at Elite Charter High, this general motivation to learn enhances school success. Because such students are excited about their schoolwork, they devote energy to it, which yields good grades on report cards. Thus, the school's cultural wisdom about success includes a distinct type of effort, characterized as *initiative*. Effort is not simple hard work, as it is at Alternative High and Comprehensive High. At Elite Charter High, successful students take an eager interest in learning. They take initiative.

I ask Daphne, "What does it take for a student to earn good grades in your school?"

She answers, "Self-motivation," which she explains as "definitely trying. Good study habits. Spending time doing the homework, getting it done. Presenting it in a needs-to-get-done fashion, no procrastination—where it is just like getting it done, not waiting until the middle of class to do it." Although Daphne's response sounds a bit like Deshawn's explanation of what it takes to earn good grades at Alternative High, her focus on internal drive speaks to the different understandings of success at each school. Daphne tells me that if a student is not getting good grades, the reason is likely a motivation problem, but her description of motivation is rooted in a desire to learn, not simply to complete assignments on time, as Deshawn emphasizes. She says, "It is a matter of finding what works for you. Like if taking notes helps you learn the material better, the effort has to be put forth there too. Finding how you learn the material, what works for you. If someone wants to try, wants to do their homework, wants to try hard—like if the teacher says, 'Read this,' they read it once, maybe twice if they need to."

Yet at Elite Charter High, initiative alone does not equal school success. At Deshawn's high school, students believe that "you don't have to necessarily be smart" to do well in school. In contrast, Daphne and others at her high school believe that intelligence is the essential factor in school success. Her chemistry teacher says, "I don't necessarily think that just effort is going to bring about an A. . . . There is a certain level of mastery. It's not just doing it . . . in order to be able to excel and get an A and all that stuff. The ultimate goal of it: they have to be able to not only do those skills but do them correctly."

Top grades demand intellectual ability. Daphne's chemistry teacher does think that effort can help but only in the form of initiative: "making sure the homework is done correctly, not just done . . . that kind of stuff where they actually take initiative in what they have learned rather than, say, repetition." Yet he acknowledges that initiative does not always work: "I know kids that try—they are very driven to do well and put a lot of effort in and sometimes they don't succeed. So I see it."

The local wisdom at Elite Charter High is that initiative can enhance success but cannot bring about good grades on its own. This sounds similar to ideas about success at Comprehensive High, and indeed there are similarities. Just as Daphne's chemistry teacher says that "a certain level of mastery" is required "to get an A and all that stuff," Flor's principal at Comprehensive High asserts that students must "master the content" in order to "pass the class." The key differences between these two schools lie in their conceptualizations of effort and in the level of success that each school deems to be acceptable. Elite Charter High prizes passion for learning and self-motivation in the form of initiative, while Comprehensive High conceptualizes effort as memorization and "regurgitation" of information on tests.

Moreover, while C grades are an acceptable minimum threshold of success at Comprehensive High, especially in courses that are a student's weak point, Elite Charter High students disdain Cs. One student tells me that she would "feel dirty" if she had Cs on her report card. Another says, "I'd hate myself if those were my grades," while still others assert that getting Cs would cause their friends to worry about them or ridicule them. At Elite Charter High, a *B* is the minimum threshold of acceptable success, and many students aim not only for *A*s but for *A*s in advanced courses.

As I will elaborate, the curriculum and school structures at Elite Charter High emphasize intelligence. Whereas Deshawn's school requires students to attend classes only three days a week, Elite Charter High has an accelerated course schedule that requires students to complete two more courses per year than typical high schools do (Comprehensive High, for example). While Deshawn's school serves primarily low-income students, many of whom will be the first in their families to graduate from high school or attend college, Elite Charter High serves primarily upper-middle-class families who expect their children to attend a "good college," not just any college, after graduation. Again, Comprehensive High falls in the middle, serving some middle-class students alongside a substantial number of low-income students. The mission of Elite Charter High is to prepare its students for elite college futures. To that end, its course offerings are loaded with honors-level and Advanced Placement (AP) courses, for which students can earn college credit if they pass the corresponding AP standardized exam. In short, Elite Charter High is an academically rigorous school whose reputation is built on providing an educational environment where "smart kids" can thrive. This environment fosters a particular understanding of what it takes to succeed in school: intelligence plus initiative.

Schools As Organizations

Following a line of scholars in organization theory, I treat each school organization in this book as an "inhabited institution."[4] In other words, I recognize that schools are not merely bureaucratic machines that produce educated students according to rules and patterns established for all schools. Instead, a school is a bureaucratic structure that is inhabited by a set of people. The principal, teachers, staff, students, and parents at one school are not identical to those at another school. Thus, they can adopt practices and change features of school life in ways that differ from one school to the next.[5] This helps us understand why different schools have different atmospheres, or school cultures. Beliefs about school success are cultural beliefs, and individual schools can develop their own distinct beliefs about success, just as any organization can cultivate a particular cultural belief that fits the sensibilities of the people who inhabit it. As Tim Hallett and Marc Ventresca argue, this line of scholarship helps us recognize that "institutions provide the guidelines for social interactions" but they also are "constituted and propelled forward by interactions that provide them with force and meaning."[6]

Inhabited institutionalism bridges two traditions of research in organizational studies: one that focuses on institutional environments and another that focuses on organizational culture.[7] My study links the institutional (widely shared cultural ideas about hard work, intelligence, and success) with the organizational (school structures and school-specific identity stories) while showing that individuals have creative responses to both. Viewing organizations as inhabited institutions highlights the ways in which local meanings are constructed by actors in local contexts. It means to look carefully at how actors interpret cultural ideas in local settings in ways that can support, shift, or even dismiss aspects of widely shared cultural explanations for success.

Taking an inhabited institutions approach to students' understandings of school success and the consequences for students' own identities lays essential groundwork in two ways. First, it requires an investigation of how organizational arrangements—in this case, school structures—matter to student identity. Second, it creates an expectation that students (actors) in different school environments might not imbue similar meanings to institutional features that are shared across schools. For example, grades might be understood differently at different schools or standardized test scores might be treated as important indicators of, say, intelligence in one school but not others. It also lays an expectation that each school's environment might differently interpret popular American beliefs about school success.

Thinking about a school in terms of the people who inhabit it, the people who make decisions about teaching and learning, and the people who respond to those decisions allows us to think critically about the transfer of cultural ideas in those organizations. It is important to look at the ways in which cultural ideas are modified and adapted at the level of the organization. This helps us understand how students at one high school have certain ideas about success, while those at another high school have radically different ideas about it. Most work that treats schools as inhabited institutions focuses on the work practices of school administrators and teachers, largely ignoring the students themselves.[8] My book, however, applies this approach to students. Other studies have interrogated how school administrators and faculty respond to organizational pressure to follow institutional myths or logics such as the "myth of accountability" under No Child Left Behind legislation.[9] Still others focus on how teachers balance curriculum mandates against classroom realities.[10] In contrast, I focus on how students respond to organizational pressure to pursue academic success as structured by teachers and administrators. Although I interviewed teachers and principals at each school, my goal in including their perspectives was to triangulate students' ideas and experiences in order to better understand the students' school contexts. With students at the forefront of analysis, I use inhabited institutionalism theory to demonstrate how widely shared cultural meanings about success are reshaped in schools through processes of local meaning making.

Cultural Ideas That Explain School Success

I define *school success* as broad academic success: good grades, high test scores, and other kinds of acknowledgment from teachers and classmates. But what does it take to succeed? As we saw with Deshawn, Flor, and Daphne, many people view school success as the product of hard work, intelligence, or some combination of the two. Throughout this book, I refer to these explanations as cultural ideas, but in fact they exemplify what cultural sociologists such as Mary Blair-Loy call *cultural schemas:* ideologies that are shared across a society. Blair-Loy explains that these ideologies are cognitive, moral, and emotional maps that provide individuals with guidelines to understanding the world and behaving within it: "[They are] shared cultural models we employ to make sense of the world. These schemas are frameworks for viewing, filtering, understanding, and evaluating what we know as reality. Constructed by societies over time, they gradually become largely unquestioned. Schemas are objective in the sense of being shared, publicly available understandings. They shape social structure, the patterns and activities of groups and individuals in institutions, firms, and families."[11] Blair-Loy's definition draws on William Sewell, Jr.'s, conceptualization.[12] Both Blair-Loy and Sewell, along with other scholars, advance cultural schemas as a framework for understanding how human action is culturally structured without being culturally determined. As cultural schemas are widely shared, this theory focuses on the ways in which individuals use and adapt schemas in their everyday lives.

I argue that organizations such as schools play a more substantial role in this process than either Sewell or Blair-Loy acknowledge.[13] Through my comparative study of three similar organizations that are similarly situated in terms of material resources, I demonstrate that individuals who are embedded in an organization—as students are in high schools—rely on the organization's interpretation of a given cultural idea rather than a more widely shared version of the same idea.[14] In this book I show that each school under study mediates its students' understanding of the wider cultural ideas of success in particular ways.

The Cultural Idea of Success-through-Intelligence

As I mentioned previously, my description of American cultural ideas about school success comes largely from a body of literature on achievement ideology and American dream ideology.[15] Although effort and intelligence are two parts of the same ideology of success, I separate them analytically so that we can more clearly see how school organizations cultivate their own modified versions of this larger American cultural idea. Each school in my study has a particular explanation for school success that focuses heavily on one route to success over the other or that combines the two in a specific way.

The cultural idea that I refer to as *success-through-intelligence* embodies the widely held belief that different people have different levels of intelligence. It posits a relatively uncomplicated relationship between intelligence and school success: the more intelligence a student has, the greater success he or she can have in school. Because native intelligence is, in this view, the mechanism through which a person learns, the strength of that mechanism hinders or boosts how effectively one can learn, which directly affects school success. Some people are smarter than others, and this is seen as a fair, natural inequality.

As a cultural idea, success-through-intelligence has long roots and in the early twentieth century received a scientific boost from IQ testing, which gave way in the 1940s to educational testing.[16] The scientific notion of the bell-shaped, or normal, curve lies at the heart of these tests, which assume that all naturally occurring variation in a population will be distributed along this curve. Since Sir Frances Galton in 1856, scientists have asserted that if we properly measure traits such as intelligence, then we should see that people have different amounts of it and that our differences should fall on a graph in the proportions of a normal curve, with most people clustering around the average. The bell-shaped curve supports the idea that some people are smarter than others and that this is what nature intended. Of course, such a line of reasoning applies only if you believe that we know how to measure intelligence properly. Yet by and large, Americans do believe it.[17]

The Cultural Idea of Success-through-Effort

At first glance, success-through-effort seems like a straightforward explanation. The harder people try, the more success they can achieve. In reality, however, motivation and effort are susceptible to outside influences such as families and friends. We know that a student's family can encourage (or even force) her to spend a great deal of time and energy studying or, conversely, prevent her from devoting much energy to her schoolwork. Similarly, some groups of friends spend their free time studying together, while others ridicule their friends and classmates for studying too much or trying too hard in school.[18] Yet in the popular understanding of school success, friends and family are generally left out of the picture. Instead, the onus of responsibility rests on the individual student: he or she must be motivated enough to put forth the necessary level of effort, which is construed as a feature of the individual's character. The definition of *enough* remains unspecified. For one person it might mean extra hours of

studying to prepare for a specific test, but for someone else it might mean drop-
ping friends, suffering ridicule, or avoiding a chaotic household.

Although both effort and intelligence explain school success, a student
does not have to depend on one rather than the other. The two cultural ideas
are compatible. Success-through-effort suggests that hard work can compen-
sate for limits to intelligence, barring any serious mental disability. According
to this logic, people with higher intelligence need to put forth less effort than
do people with lower intelligence. In American culture this inequity seems just
because most people view intelligence as a natural talent over which individuals have little control.

Another factor complicates the idea of success-through-effort: the availability of resources. For instance, Internet access, money for private tutors, and
transportation to a public library may influence students' ability to muster up
enough effort to succeed in school. Students may also have unequal access to
human resources, such as adults and peers who can help with homework. When
speaking of success-through-effort, most Americans tend to focus on the gap
students must fill between their native intelligence and school success. This
attitude is summed up by the popular adage "Where there's a will, there's a
way." Success-through-effort holds the student responsible for doing whatever
it takes to achieve school success. It only vaguely acknowledges effort's suscep-
tibility to obstacles of resources and motivation.

Organizations Modify Cultural Ideas

A school is a distinct organizational unit inhabited by a particular set of individuals. Even though all schools have classrooms, books, teachers, students,
homework, tests, parents, and neighborhood concerns, each school is its own
place with its own cultural atmosphere. No two principals in these inhabited
institutions make exactly the same decisions for their students, but neither are
they faced with exactly the same set of issues that influence their decisions.

By thinking about schools as individual inhabited institutions, we begin
to see how cultural ideas such as success-through-effort and success-through-
intelligence can be modified and adapted at the level of the organization. The
people who operate within a school refine cultural schemas to fit the circumstances and sensibilities of that particular environment.[19] Thus, local meaning
making is an interplay between wider cultural beliefs and existing school structures such as curriculum policies.[20] In the three high schools under study, I have
found that for the most part the people associated with a particular school share
beliefs about how to achieve school success. Cultural ideas are effectively produced in the space of the school. For example, at Deshawn's school, Alternative

High, local wisdom about school success draws entirely from the idea of success-through-effort and dismisses success-through-intelligence. As the principal asserts, "All our students here are brilliant." The issue is whether or not they work hard.

A fundamentally different explanation for school success prevails at Comprehensive High. While effort is important, it is not the only ingredient in the recipe for success. If your brain is not good at math, then you will never do well in it, no matter how hard you try. This attitude is a modified mix of the two cultural ideas. Unlike Alternative High, which ignores success-through-intelligence, Comprehensive High sees it as the foundational explanation for success. Nonetheless, success-through-intelligence is somewhat dependent on success-through-effort because getting good grades requires completing assignments, which means that students also have to do the work.

Elite Charter High's local wisdom about success is both similar to and different from Comprehensive High's. Both students and teachers at Elite Charter High believe that intelligence is the root of success, though effort can enhance it. Like Comprehensive High, the school draws heavily from the idea of success-through-intelligence. However, it modifies success-through-effort in a specific way: it reshapes it into initiative.

There is a debate among scholars over whether or not schools themselves make much of a difference in students' academic performance, their attitudes toward education, and their future aspirations.[21] My findings in this study complicate that debate by showing a more complex picture. While families' attitudes toward success certainly matter in students' lives, I find that the school environment also shapes students' ideas about success in ways that are independent of and additional to families. Nonetheless, there are undeniable links between schools and social class. In popular American thought, public education is often seen as a "great equalizer," meaning that through schools individuals have access to knowledge and preparation to compete equally in the job market, no matter what social class they were born into.[22] However, scholars of education have shown that schools actually contribute to social reproduction.[23] Similarly, my findings indicate that each school's cultural wisdom about intelligence and effort play a role in reproducing the social order. While most of the field's previous literature uses inhabited institutionalism to explain change, my study demonstrates that it also helps us understand the stability of inequality and social reproduction, even as the individuals within schools respond to their institutional environments in ways that are dynamic and fluid.[24] As Judson Everitt explains, "the fact that people contribute to the reproduction of existing institutional logics does not make the process through which they do so any less agentic."[25]

Consequences of Schools' Definitions of Success

This notion that we have widely shared American cultural explanations for school success and that school organizations adapt and refine those cultural ideas in particular ways provides the backdrop for understanding students' success identities. Individuals construct identities from available cultural ideas. This book focuses on how individual students see themselves as intelligent, hardworking, successful people—or, in some cases, as not-so-intelligent, not-so-hardworking, or not-so-successful people. As I've already shown, when the students I interviewed describe themselves, they draw heavily on the ideas about success that are prevalent at their own schools. However, just as school organizations do not simply absorb and reflect cultural ideas handed down from society, individual students adapt and refine their school's version of success when they apply it to themselves. Interestingly, when I ask them to describe other people, they tend to offer remarkably similar explanations for school success.[26] But when it comes to describing their own situation, they refine their explanation to better fit their own circumstances.

The distinct cultural ideas about school success that I find at each of the three high schools in my study have consequences on another level: students' college futures. We know that high schools prepare students unequally for life after high school, including preparation for college. Some high schools do an excellent job, and many of their students head directly to college after graduation. Meanwhile, other high schools have students with low standardized test scores, insufficient college preparatory courses to qualify for four-year institutions, and therefore low college-going rates among graduating seniors.[27] My study shows that even schools such as Alternative High, whose purposeful design is to ensure that students from underprivileged backgrounds have equal access to college preparatory education, may inadvertently reproduce the existing social order through their cultural ideas about school success. The problem is not that these high schools are doing something wrong but that higher education is stratified. Going to college is an important part of getting ahead in American society, but the type of college you attend affects how prestigious and financially rewarding a career you will likely have access to afterward.[28] Even though the three high schools in my study all endeavor to get their graduates into college, their results are not equal. The differences are particularly stark in terms of gaining admission to elite universities, where the future career rewards and life satisfaction are known to be the greatest.[29]

1

Alternative High

Effort Explains School Success

Alternative High is a small school. It is also a new school, opening just two years before I began my research in 2005. At the time I started my observations and interviews, the student body consisted of only freshman and sophomores, fewer than one hundred students in all. The school's design and mission is based on a school reform effort that was launched on the East Coast, although several dozen schools around the country now work from its model. These schools take a nontraditional approach to education, focusing in particular on ways to advance the prospects of inner-city students.[1]

While Alternative High is dedicated to helping students fulfill all the course requirements for college entrance, it is also designed to prepare them for the world of work. The explicit goal of the school model is to help students identify what they are passionate about and hone skills and goals that build from these personal interests. Students attend school on Mondays, Wednesdays, and Fridays but spend Tuesdays and Thursdays doing internships at local businesses, government offices, and the like. Typically students start work on these internships at about 9:00 A.M. and finish at about 12:00 P.M. This means that they have a good portion of those days to schedule as they please. School officials expect students to do schoolwork on their own during that time, but do not expect students to attend school after their internship hours.

Many students I talked to were thrilled with their internships and felt that new career fields had been opened up to them. One student was delighted to be interning at a law office; another was similarly excited about shadowing a police officer. However, I also saw cases in which students' internships did not live up to the goal of the program. For example, three students were interns at a private photography studio, and one complained to me that she had not learned anything about photography even though she had been an intern there for two years. She had sought out this particular internship in hopes of learning photography skills, perhaps even developing a portfolio to launch a career of her own. But rather than treating the internship as an apprenticeship, the owner of the studio scheduled his interns to answer phones while he was away from the office on off-site shoots. He did not have the them shadow him and learn as he worked. Thus, their internship, in effect, did little more than train them for low-level clerical work. Likewise, Deshawn, whom we met in the introduction, spent most of his internship working at the cash register and busing tables rather than learning kitchen skills that would give him a leg up in pursuing a career as a chef.

Students' internships are intended to be field sites where they can put their academics into action. Toward this goal, students keep journals on their internship work and, for example, record any math that they do in the course of their jobs. Students can earn credit toward their grades in any subjects that they practice in their internship work. The principal tells me, "We have to believe that learning outside of the school is powerful. . . . Internship provides a great opportunity for children to allow their brilliancy to come in." Of course, how well these academic and career goals are realized varies from student to student and site to site.

Alternative High promotes an image of itself as a place where students are able to discover their own strengths and work somewhat independently to achieve success in those strong suits. The school promises to hold students to rigorous academic standards while giving them opportunities to participate in the real world of work. Students are required to set their own academic goals (approved by the teacher) and prove that they have reached those goals by means of an end-of-quarter demonstration of their schoolwork. This is very different from assessment in traditional high schools, which typically involves a week of final exams. Nonetheless, these end-of-quarter demonstrations are every bit as stressful for students. They wear professional attire and create elaborate demonstration materials to exhibit their academic work. Posters and PowerPoints are common presentation strategies. Students' homeroom teachers are the primary judges of the demonstrations, but other teachers also watch and judge the work. Schoolmates and the general public are invited to attend and to offer written and verbal comments and criticisms, which the judges can take into consideration. Generally, the "public" does not include more than the students' parents and internship mentors, but in principle, students must be prepared to respond to comments from outsiders as well. During the period of my observations and interviews I attended ten end-of-quarter demonstrations and found them to be an excellent venue for practicing presentation skills, although they were relatively weak in terms of academic content.

Students at Alternative High perform poorly on some of the California standardized tests and at an average level on other state measures, though its academic performance index (API) is more than twenty points higher than the state average.[2] The school does not serve a particular neighborhood zone. As an alternative school in a large urban school district, it is able to draw students from any school zone within the district's boundaries. Students who would normally be assigned to their neighborhood high school can opt to attend Alternative High instead. "We are a school of choice," the principal explains. "We take fifty incoming ninth graders every year and any tenth, eleventh, or twelfth grader who wants to apply. It's first come, first served. The only students who have a guaranteed spot are those that already have a sibling here." Alternative High is a Title I school with a majority-minority student body. More than 50 percent of the students are socioeconomically disadvantaged, as defined by the state of California.[3]

Education's Role in Social Reproduction

Social reproduction refers to the way in which people who are born into families with advantages and privileges are often able to secure lives for themselves that include advantages and privileges. Meanwhile, people who are born into families that face disadvantages often remain in similarly disadvantaged positions throughout their lives. In many ways the idea of social reproduction is the opposite of the idea of the American dream, which is about moving up the social and economic ladder to become more successful than one's parents were. While some Americans are able to accomplish this upward mobility over the course of their lives, most people tend to remain on the same socioeconomic rungs of the ladder. Generation after generation, we reproduce the existing social order.

To understand how education facilitates social reproduction, scholars study differences both among and within schools. We know that public schools that serve more affluent neighborhoods tend to offer curricula and teacher instruction that promote more rigorous academic engagement than do schools that serve lower-income and ethnoracial-minority neighborhoods. This sets up students at more privileged schools for college and professional futures and students at less privileged schools for low-skilled jobs in the workforce.[4] Alternative High was designed explicitly to challenge this pattern by preparing low-income minority youth for promising futures.

Regarding curriculum tracking within schools, scholars often find a similar pattern. Lower-income and ethnoracial-minority students tend to be disproportionately placed in lower curriculum tracks, while middle-class, white, and Asian American students are disproportionately placed in higher curriculum tracks.[5] Thus, schools reproduce the social order by educating different groups of students with knowledge and skills that are appropriate for different kinds of adult futures.[6] This is why Alternative High does not practice curriculum tracking but gives every student access to the same curricular content.

In addition to the formal curriculum and the way in which teachers teach it, scholars pay attention to "hidden curricula" that tacitly teach norms and values.[7] They find that that working-class students are more often taught to value traits such as being on time, respecting authority, and following instructions—behaviors that workers need to be successful in low-skill jobs. Meanwhile, students from the middle and upper middle classes are more often taught to value skills such as creative thinking, problem solving, self-motivation, and assertiveness—abilities that managers and professionals need. Importantly, school administrators, teachers, and students do not necessarily reinforce these curricula in a conscious way. As Michael Apple writes, "a fundamental problem facing us is the way in which systems of domination and exploitation persist and reproduce themselves without being consciously recognized by the people involved."[8] Hidden curriculum can be invisible even to those who carry it out.

Of course, it would be wrong to see schools only as blind reproducers of the existing social order, as if their role were completely determined by inequalities in the types of jobs that the economy offers to American workers. Like Alternative High, many schools actively attempt to fight against these dynamics of reproduction: they "untrack" students and target low-income and ethnoracial-minority students for advanced, rigorous academics that will lead to successful college futures.[9] Similarly, the widespread program known as Advancement Via Individual Determination (AVID) supports minority students' preparation and enrollment in honors and AP curricula at Comprehensive High as well as in many other schools across California and throughout the country.

Connected to schools' role in social reproduction is the widely held notion that doing well in school pays off with a bright, successful future after graduation. Americans generally believe this truism, and schools themselves encourage it.[10] For many students, however, it is a false promise. They leave high school with knowledge and skills that are suitable only for low-level, often dead-end work. They simply do not receive the kind of schooling that qualifies them for ambitious careers or higher education (see chapter 7). Research also shows the many ways in which poor, working-class, and minority students themselves resist school messages about success. They recognize that, whether their report cards show As or Ds, their prospects as adults will likely be the same.[11]

In the course of my research, I looked carefully at how students create identities for themselves in the cultural environment of their own school.[12] None of the students I talked to resists messages about the positive benefits of school success. Each endeavors to do well in school and contends that school success is a good and valuable pursuit. The schools work to support this attitude.

Alternative High, for instance, seeks to redress the systematic inequality of U.S education, and in many respects it succeeds. Students are drawn to the school because it is committed to doing things differently from traditional high schools. Many of Alternative High's students were underperforming in their middle schools and came here in hopes that more individual attention from teachers and the relative freedom of attending school only three days a week would yield better academic results. While the academic content of the lessons I observed was relatively low, I certainly saw that most students at Alternative High are challenged by their curriculum and that their homeroom teachers hold them accountable for improving their skills in each subject.

School Is Like a Second Family

During the three days a week that students are at school, they spend the entire day in their homeroom class with their homeroom teacher. This fosters a tight-knit community among classmates and the teacher. Jimmy, a student ambassador who is assigned to greet campus guests such as myself, explains, "We don't like to call it homeroom; we like to call it a family." Many times I heard teachers, students, and the principal compare homeroom units to being "like a big family." Students such as Sherie, an African American sophomore, enjoy this aspect of school life tremendously: "I mean how many schools do you know where you get to know your teacher on this level? And all your classmates, they are like a big dysfunctional family; that's what I always say. I love school. I come here and have fun."

Homeroom teachers are generally responsible for English and history curricula. Most other subjects are taught by part-time staff members, some of whom are retired instructors from a nearby community college. When it is time, say, for a chemistry lesson or a Spanish lesson, that teacher comes to the students' classroom rather than the other way around. Students see their subject-specific teachers just once or twice a week. There are no honors classes, every student in homeroom participates in the same subject lessons, and homerooms are not stratified into ability groups. For science and math subjects, the majority of the students' work is accomplished via online programs, which offer some internal "help" features for students as they complete assignments on their own. Students also have the option to visit their teachers during assigned office hours.

Monique, an African American sophomore, says that she would prefer to have "more one-on-one time" with her teachers: "The only time we get to see our teachers is maybe the hour and a half when he or she comes in and then if they have an office when they're actually in their office to talk to them. Because they're usually with another class, so we're kind of stuck. So it's either you look on the website, if that's what we're using, and try to figure it out from what they give you, or you just skip it and in some cases like for math you can't skip it. You have to learn it or else [the online math program] won't let you go to the next level." Most of the students I spoke with felt that office hours were either inconvenient, intimidating, or both. As in Monique's case, this generally meant that students got little help on their homework assignments from their subject-specific teachers.

Because they have a stationary homeroom class, students are able to make the classroom space their own in a variety of ways. Many rooms are adorned with personal photos of students, their families, their non-school friends, and their romantic interests. Even during lunchtime, each cohort of twenty or so classmates plus the homeroom teacher stays together, confined to an enclosed patio adjacent to the cafeteria. During my classroom observations, I came to agree that the groups have family-like rhythms and dynamics. Arguments, bickering, and avoidance strategies are common, but everyone seems to know what to expect from everyone else. This is especially true in the sophomore class, which had already been together for a year and a half when I observed them. They are the group that Sherie calls "a big dysfunctional family." Each student seems able to carve out a comfortable place for herself in the space of the classroom. At the same time, everyone is more or less aware of what the others are doing. Importantly, this means that one's work and study habits are visible to everyone in the "family."

As in family life, spending time together in a bounded space can help develop nurturing interactions among individuals. For example, one morning the chemistry teacher asks the class a question, and Lupe says the answer out loud. The teacher looks around: "That's right. Who said that?"

Lupe sits silently and does not identify herself. Her classmate Sheena bursts out, "Go on, girl! Lupe! It's the first time she's spoken up in homeroom since freshman year!"

Lupe blushes and nods toward the projector screen: "The answer is written right up there."

Pointing to the text on the screen, the chemistry teacher smiles excitedly: "That's right! Why do you think I do this?"

Although homeroom families often give positive, public support to one another in ways that affirm individuals both academically and personally, not all interactions are so cheerful and encouraging. On another day, half an hour after the class returns from a schoolwide awards ceremony for internship mentors and their students, Sheena calls across the classroom, "Hey, Keesha, you used to be a wacked-out intern? Is that why you got 'Most Improved'?"

Keesha bristles. Seemingly offended, she turns away from her computer to face Sheena (and most of the rest of the class, who are all working at the computers that line the classroom walls). She calmly explains, "I had to improve my public-speaking skills for my internship. Now I'm not quiet anymore. That's why I'm 'Most Improved.'" Still looking hurt, she turns back to her computer.

When I observed this interaction, I couldn't tell if Sheena intended to be hurtful or just playful. But this example shows that, as in any family, interpersonal dynamics can be supportive in some instances and insensitive in others. This is true even when the same person is involved.

In every class at Alternative High, students spend a portion of their day doing independent study. During this time the homeroom teacher keeps an eye them, but for the most part students are allowed to do as they please. They walk freely around the room, choose which assignments to work on, and decide how long to spend on a task before moving on to something else. During my observations in two separate classrooms, I noticed a fair amount of chatting with neighbors, text messaging on cell phones, organizing of personal photo albums, and so on. All of this was tolerated during independent study. I found the environment to be comfortable, although it was somewhat distracting for students. They worked at their own pace, collaborated with classmates, and had the teacher available to answer questions. The period stands in sharp contrast to the more rigid, sit-in-your-seats environments of Elite Charter High and Comprehensive High. To be fair, however, I should point out that students in the other schools are not less distracted; they are just more discreet about it. To me, Alternative High's homeroom environment was much like any work environment where colleagues are also friends.

As part of its educational mission, Alternative High does not practice curriculum tracking.[13] Keeping students integrated fosters the family environment of each homeroom, and the school day is designed to have enough flexibility to accommodate students' individual learning speeds without stratifying the curriculum. Students are separated by grade level, however. Because there were only ninth- and tenth-grade groups at the school during my research, I observed in one ninth-grade homeroom and one tenth-grade homeroom so as to make comparisons within the school. I found the pace and atmosphere of both classes to be remarkably similar.

The one markedly different dimension is racial tension, which is evident in the ninth-grade class and not in the tenth-grade class.[14] This is perhaps due to the fact that the ninth graders are newer to the environment of Alternative High. Many of the African American students attended nearly all-minority middle and elementary schools, where building relationships with white students was not explicitly part of their schools' educational objectives. Now the students find themselves in a small, intimate setting where they are expected to get to know one another and build a family-like community.

The ninth-grade class is comprised of twenty students: four white, one Asian American, seven African American, and eight Latino. The tenth-grade class has similar proportions. Several of the African American ninth graders seem distrustful of and often disinterested in their white classmates. The fact that the white students are also more economically well off than most others in the class probably adds to the tension. The twenty white students who attend Alternative High are drawn from far-reaching suburban corners of the urban district. According to the 2000 U.S. Census, the median home value is 228,000 dollars in the neighborhoods where these white students live, compared to between 131,000 and 166,000 dollars in the neighborhoods where the African American and Latino students live.[15] This also means that white and non-white students have little chance of being neighbors.

Everyone Is Smart Enough to Succeed; Effort Is What Really Counts

Students at Alternative High assert that school success requires effort. Unlike students at Elite Charter High and Comprehensive High, many here are hesitant to affirm that intelligence is necessary for school success. Instead, they are confident that anyone has enough ability to perform well in school. Moreover, the students I interviewed at Alternative High do not describe effort as enthusiasm, passion for learning, or initiative. Rather, they use the language of behavior to characterize the meaning of effort in school.

To understand how students at Alternative High perceive school success and the types of people who can attain it, I showed them report cards as part of our interview. I asked them to imagine that each belonged to a student at their school, someone whom they did not personally know. Then I asked them to describe the owner of the report card. I listened carefully to how they chose to articulate the cultural ideas of success-through-intelligence and success-through-effort, with the goal of finding out how these ideas are refined and modified at Alternative High. I also listened carefully for any identity stories that might emerge.

Discussing the low-performance report card in figure 1.1, Samantha, a white sophomore, shares a typical reaction: "I guess everyone can do better. I don't know, maybe the teacher is horrible, but they probably sit in the back, talking during class." Although Samantha does not approve of this low report card, she does not imply that the low grades are at all due to the anonymous student's limited intelligence. Instead, she and other students at Alternative High link low grades almost exclusively to student behavior. As Samantha's comment illustrates, one such behavior that comes up again and again in the interviews is not listening in class.

Alternative High students emphasize that attending school is a key behavior in achieving school success, but simply showing up is not enough. Deshawn, the African American freshman whom we met in the introduction, says that

FIGURE 1.1.

Anonymous Report Card of a Low-Performing High School Student

PE	B	2 absences	2 tardies
Woodshop	B	2 absences	0 tardies
Math	C-	2 absences	0 tardies
Science	C-	2 absences	0 tardies
English	D	2 absences	2 tardies
History	C	2 absences	0 tardies

to get good grades "you don't have to necessarily be smart . . . because teachers teach you plenty enough to do what you need to do on your own. And it's a matter of whether you listen or not. Because, well, [a student] can be smart, but if you don't turn your work in, you know, you are not going to be graded for your smartness." Deshawn's and Samantha's comments are typical. Students I interviewed at Alternative High stress that listening to the teacher during class and turning in schoolwork are two of the most critical ingredients for success.

Just as low intelligence does not explain low school success at Alternative High, neither does high intelligence explain high school success. This is strikingly different from the perspectives of students at Elite Charter High and Comprehensive High, where students say that achieving As requires a certain level of intelligence. Discussing the high-performance report card in figure 1.2, students at Alternative High tend to discount the notion that high intelligence is necessary to receive such great grades. When I ask Martín, a Latino sophomore, whether a person has to be intelligent to receive these grades, he responds, "Well, I mean you don't have to be, like, a super genius. Like, I mean you can be like a regular student . . . with, like, a regular mind and you can still get straight As because I mean, even like when you just—what's it called?—when you just do your work? Sometimes, um, teachers give you credit for it." Clearly Martín understands school success, even straight As, to be products of effective school behaviors such as completing one's assignments.

His homeroom teacher, Mrs. Williams, agrees. When I ask her what it takes to earn good grades at Alternative High, she says, "You have to be committed to doing the work that is put in front of you. Just doing the work—for my philosophy—if a student comes and they turn their work in every day, no matter what it is." Mrs. Williams sees this as the key to not only high success in the form of good grades but also to minimal success. Simply turning in assignments will ensure a passing grade: "And if it is not the highest-quality work, they know they will pass with at least a C-minus."

FIGURE 1.2.

Anonymous Report Card of a High-Performing High School Student

English AP	A-	0 absences	1 tardies
Physics	A	0 absences	0 tardies
Trigonometry	B+	0 absences	0 tardies
Student government	A	0 absences	0 tardies
Drama	A	0 absences	0 tardies
History AP	A	0 absences	0 tardies

Martín does not currently enjoy straight *A*s, yet the route to attaining them doesn't seem problematic to him. He boasts of having had straight-*A* report cards in his previous years in school. He presently holds *A*s and *B*s alongside two *C*s and one *F*. He is unsatisfied with these grades but explains that recently he was able to purchase a laptop computer for use at home, which will make it much easier for him to complete his online math and science assignments after school and on Tuesdays and Thursdays after his internship. He is confident that as soon as he turns in his unfinished work from the previous quarter, he will be able to raise his grades.

According to Martín, achieving high grades definitely does not require intelligence. Good school behaviors, such as completing homework, will result in effective learning. He says that doing class assignments pays off because "even if you don't understand [them] thoroughly, over time you . . . will start understanding because you are actually reading [them] and, like, putting in answers, so you will start learning it eventually. So when the tests come in or sort of stuff like that, you start catching on." His understanding of the relationship between effective behaviors and school success is typical of the students and teachers I interviewed at his school. At Alternative High there is a pervasive belief that simply making the effort to read the class material and fill in answers on assignments leads to effective learning and school success.

This belief follows the logic of the cultural idea of success-through-effort. At Alternative High, effort is defined as enacting effective school behaviors. Importantly, it also requires that a student decide to take control of his or her behaviors. Ensuring school success is a personal choice: you can sit around watching TV, or you can do your homework. This is a striking difference from the perspective I found at Elite Charter High, where students tend to conceptualize effort as a motivation arising from an innate curiosity about the world, a desire to learn new things. At Elite Charter High, taking initiative in one's own learning is also linked to intelligence. It is more than simply a choice; it is a feeling of "enthusiasm," as one student says. Alternative High students, on the other hand, conceptualize effort as concrete behaviors that a student must choose to enact. According to sociologist James Coleman, we can expect each school to have its own particular "value climate"—in other words, its own set of norms, its own cultural atmosphere.[16] At Alternative High that value climate is heavily focused on effort.

Motivation Comes from External Sources

Doing homework instead of watching TV is a choice, but it is not one that students at Alternative High believe that you should have to make on your own. Sometimes it is hard to muster up the motivation to get your work done. That is where family and friends come in. The intimate classroom environment is more than just a backdrop for students' beliefs about school success. It contributes to their widely held attitude that a critical ingredient of school success is support from other people. Monique, an African American sophomore, says, "I think everybody is smart; they just need a little more help or support. Because some people, you just need to give them a little push or a kick and they rise back up. I have a friend who had an F in chemistry, Spanish, everything. Gave her a kick and she's all the way up to the Bs and Cs. I think she may even have an A now."

Several students at Alternative High express similar sentiments. They, too, believe that students rely on friends and family to keep tabs on them. These supporters help ensure that students do not slide away from behaviors that bring school success. Often support comes in the form of punishment for lapses in effective school behaviors. Several students mention parents who motivate them with punishments for poor grades, incentives for good grades, or both.

Homeroom "family members" also keep one another in check, and the homeroom teacher is a central support. Mrs. Williams says, "If I get somebody that won't push themselves, I'll push, push them. And once they see the results of it, they will start to push themselves." Many students appreciate the way their homeroom teacher keeps a watchful eye on their efforts and accomplishments. Reina, a Filipina sophomore, explains, "A teacher who cares has personal goals for you, pushes you. My homeroom teacher cares. It matters to her if you reach your goals. She cries for us if we don't do it."

Importantly, each homeroom teacher has control over students' grades in all of their subjects, even those taught by other faculty. The rationale is that the Spanish teacher, for example, only interacts with the students once a week or so. Because he or she has little opportunity to get to know students individually, this teacher can only grade them based on their assignments. Alternative High promotes a philosophy of individualized learning and comprehensive evaluation of not only how much students have learned in their subjects but how much responsibility and maturity they develop and exhibit over the course of the term. The principal explains, "Children don't learn in the same manner. And they don't go at the same rate. So we have to give kids many different ways and many different opportunities to learn and to grow." Thus, an important aspect of evaluation is how much responsible effort toward learning the student puts forth, not just how well the student masters the material.

The homeroom teacher takes the grades provided by each subject-specific teacher (for example, a C in chemistry) and then adjusts the grade based on her assessment of the student's effort in that subject. In our interview, the principal reinforces the idea that recognizing student success requires individualized assessment. She asserts that success becomes visible "if you work hard and you are given opportunities to present how you learn in a different manner—that all twenty-five children aren't lined up in these little desks, and all twenty-five children have to take the same test, and that's the only way you are going to be graded."

Students I interviewed trust Alternative High's personalized approach to grading. Jaynah, an African American freshman, says that if her homeroom teacher were to grade her and her best friend "at the same rate," it would not be fair. "Because she sometimes gets stuff faster than I do, and that wouldn't be right because maybe I just hadn't gotten it yet or something like that." Jaynah's comments illustrate how thoroughly success-through-effort trumps success-through-intelligence at Alternative High. Jaynah is confident that she can learn anything that her best friend can learn; it may just take her a little more time and effort. She believes that her best friend's higher intelligence should not be allowed to be an advantage in school, and this idea is supported and legitimated by Alternative High's approach to evaluating students' work.

Additionally, students such as Deshawn feel that it is crucial for teachers to know their students personally so that they can factor students' outside-of-school circumstances into their expectations for each student's work. He says, "If a teacher knows that student, then she will know why they got that grade, why they may have failed that class, based on . . . what she thinks, and what she knows about them. Therefore, she can probably, like I said, give them a little sympathy and grade them a little more higher." This is important for Deshawn personally because he does not have Internet access at home, which puts him at a disadvantage compared to his classmates in being able to complete online assignments on time. (Math and science classes are all online, as are most research sources for English and history assignments.) He does not live within walking or biking distance of a public library, so accessing the Internet requires finding someone to drive him to the library or staying at school until his work is complete, which is not always easy. He relies on public buses to get home, and the city bus service is spotty at best.

The school intends the homeroom teacher to be a continual observer and participator in classroom life. She gets to know each of the students in terms of both their individual rates of mastering material, as Jaynah indicates, and outside-of-school circumstances that boost or hinder their ability to accomplish schoolwork. This makes the homeroom teacher a prime figure of support, a person who can easily recognize when students need a "kick." Mrs. Williams is particularly effective at encouraging the entire class to take responsibility for keeping each other on track for school success. One of her strategies is to make poor grades public information among the members of the class. In multiple interviews with sophomores from this homeroom group, students talk about classmates who are working to improve unacceptable grades.

Tammy, a white sophomore, makes a typical comment when she discusses the low-performance report card in figure 1.1: "I know that if they apply themself, maybe they could get their grade up. . . . If they work hard, I mean I am pretty sure that they can get good grades. I mean, like, four people in my class have Ds and they raised them up. Like, Samuel right now is turning in all his work, and he's going to get good grades." Tammy knows this information because Mrs. Williams is in the habit of routinely announcing students' effort problems. It is common to hear her tell the class, for example, "Don't forget, guys, that your reading journals are due on Friday—especially Samuel, who has an F right now on that." By making the group keenly aware of whether individuals such as Samuel are choosing effective school behaviors to rectify their poor grades, Mrs. Williams strategically ensures that her students can help keep each other on track.

School Structures Emphasize Effort

The homeroom is a central structural feature of classroom life at Alternative High. Reina says that her homeroom teacher "sees everything and hears everything. . . . She has been with us for almost two years now. She really knows us." As I've said, the homeroom teacher plays an important role in fostering the belief that effort is the key to school success. By knowing her students' individual strengths and weaknesses, she can adjust her expectations for each person. This puts students into a better position to realistically achieve school success—if they try hard enough. Their work is not evaluated on a rigid set of criteria that is only reachable through high intelligence, as students at Elite Charter High and Comprehensive High often perceive their work to be. Mrs. Williams tells me, "Yes, I do believe that any student—even if they aren't the smartest kid, they may have come in from middle school with all Cs —but if they really, really, really struggle and want it and focus and work hard, they can get all As."

Although effort is the main criterion for success, students still have to get the answers right. However, Alternative High offers structural support so that they can arrive at the correct answers at their own pace. The principal explains, "We have a built-in support system with tutoring before and after school . . . [and] when you submit your work on time and you don't get an *A, B,* or *C,* you can resubmit it and work toward a higher grade." For example, students must rewrite their history essays again and again until they receive an acceptable score. Sometimes this means multiple rewrites over several weeks of the term. Students are not let off the hook until they succeed in writing a good essay. The underlying logic of this policy matches Alternative High's belief about success: it is impossible to fail one of these assignments just because you are not smart enough. The only way to fail a history essay is not to complete a revision or never to turn in the first draft. The school structures assignments so that failure has only one cause: lack of effort.

In this environment, it is not surprising that students believe that intelligence is largely irrelevant to school success. Their attitude illustrates how the organizational structures of a school affect the ways in which the people who inhabit it respond to broader cultural ideas. The Alternative High community embraces the cultural idea of success-through-effort so tightly that members completely dismiss success-through-intelligence.

Additions to Success-through-Effort

Alternative High is an inhabited institution.[17] The students, the teachers, and the principal modify success-through-effort to fit their particular circumstances and sensibilities. They share a collective understanding of school success that is fostered at the organizational level; it is not taken directly from wider cultural beliefs about success. I spell this out because it clarifies the critical role that school organizations play in shaping students' ideas and expectations for their own success.

As I have shown in this chapter, the inhabitants of Alternative High add two tenets to success-through-effort, a modification that demonstrates how savvy they are to the complicated dynamics of this cultural idea (see the introduction). First, they understand that teachers play an important role by reconciling performance expectations for individual students. As Jaynah and Deshawn have explained, grading all students by the same expectations is seen as unfair and misguided. The principal elaborates on the school's philosophy: "If we talk about differentiated learning, differentiated instruction, you have to look at the whole child. What is the child's background? What is the child's environment that they are coming from? I may come from an environment that has provided every opportunity for me since conception. There may be another student over here that because of environment, finances, or whatever hasn't had the same opportunities, but that doesn't mean that they don't have a brilliant mind. . . . [Our school model] says that every child is gifted and talented and bright in something."

Second, school inhabitants understand that individual students are not entirely responsible for their own effort. They recognize that students need to rely on people who care about them, who will help students keep up their motivation and effort. As Monique says, "I think you always need somebody to help, either, like I said, the teacher, a friend if they are good enough, somebody at home."

The organizational arrangements at Alternative High create and encourage some of students' reliance on support. These arrangements include intimate class sizes and long hours in a single shared space, where students are encouraged to think of their homeroom teacher as a source of feedback about their effort and of motivation to stay on track. Their homeroom classmates become a version of a family that keeps tabs on each member's effort toward school success. While success-through-effort lays the onus of responsibility on each student's own shoulders, students at Alternative High distribute that responsibility among trustworthy others. School success is not something that one accomplishes entirely alone.

These two modifications of success through effort allow Alternative High to better reflect and promote its educational goals. It is a school that seeks to challenge the pattern of social reproduction through education. A vital aspect of its mission lies in making academic success possible for a traditionally underserved population of students.

2

Fearing Failure at Alternative High

Students at Alternative High are very concerned about avoiding failure. In this way they are different from students at the other two schools I studied. At Elite Charter High, the topic of failing a class rarely came up in my interviews; instead, students are focusing on how to reach the highest levels of school success. At Comprehensive High, where C grades are the minimum level of acceptable success, students worry about proving that they are "at least average." But at Alternative High, the minimum level of acceptable school success has a much vaguer threshold, so it's important for students to avoid any association with failure. Not only do students worry about F grades, but they also don't want to appear too close to failing, which they typically describe as getting Ds or "too many C-minuses." The school administration seems to agree. A few years after I conducted my first wave of research, Alternative High instituted a "no-D policy." Mrs. Williams thinks the change "makes sense because what college that you are applying to wants to see Ds on your transcript? So you either push for a C or you fail."[1]

Many of the students I interviewed at Alternative High come from poor, working-class, and/or immigrant families that have a harder time paving the way to school success than do the more affluent families of the students I interviewed at Elite Charter High.[2] Many will be the first person in their families to graduate from high school, and most will be the first to graduate from college, should they follow that path. Achieving a high school diploma is an important and weighty goal for these students. Many have friends and family members who have failed or dropped out of school. Failure is a very real possibility in the lives of these students, and they worry about it.[3]

Constructing Success Identities from Identity Stories

Most Alternative High students have a success identity in which they see themselves as smart, hardworking, successful people. Others have a different success identity: they see themselves as not very smart or successful. All of these students draw on the ideas that circulate in the cultural environment of their school as they make sense of who they are. As I discussed in chapter 1, the cultural wisdom here is that effort, not intelligence, is the key to school success. This idea shapes the way in which students see themselves and others.

The concept of identity stories is a useful analytic tool for thinking critically about how students construct their success identities. According to sociologist Ann Westenholz (who prefers the synonym *field stories*), people use identity stories to describe kinds of people (but not actual individuals) who are character types within a particular organization. Identity stories are widely shared among actors in a specific organizational context, and they are relevant to the particular circumstances, experiences, and concerns of the organization.[4] As a construct, identity stories are similar to what Jenny Stuber calls "mythical figures" in her study of privileged college students' understandings of their class position.[5] Westenholz demonstrates that identity stories help people make sense of larger cultural schemas—what I am calling cultural ideas.[6] People identify types of characters that embody attributes and concerns that matter in their organizational environment. These identity stories become available cultural types against which individuals negotiate their own identities.

In the case of my three schools, identity stories provide a framework for student self-definition. That is, the students decide for themselves whether or not they are at all similar to the character type in an identity story. Importantly, the identity stories are vividly different in the three schools. This makes sense, given that each espouses its own version of success-through-intelligence and success-through-effort. Because each school has its own set of character types that embody the worries, hopes, fears, and attitudes that matter to this cohort, students' self-understandings become largely limited to the available cultural ideas. None of the students I interviewed describe themselves or their school success in a way that is dramatically different from their school's local wisdom about success and that environment's prevailing identity stories.

Given students' concern about avoiding failure and the school's heavy focus on effort, it is not surprising that the most salient identity stories I find at Alternative High involve character types who fail in effort by cheating or not trying. Students here are sure that poor grades happen to people who do not put much effort into their schoolwork. They believe that no one is going to hand them a high school diploma just for being smart, that even a highly intelligent person has to work for success.

Unlike Elite Charter High students, for example, who often view good grades as evidence that a person is highly intelligent, Alternative High students are skeptical of grades, which they suspect might inaccurately represent a student's true intellectual abilities. For instance, a person with poor grades might be smart, just not trying very hard. That idea is embodied in an identity story that I call *smart-but-not-trying*. Likewise, a person with good grades might have gotten those As and Bs by cheating—another inaccurate representation of true ability. Because this high school sees trying hard as morally valuable, students consider getting good grades by cheating to be a moral fraud. Their worry surfaces in a second identity story at Alternative High, which I call the *cheater*.

The *Smart-but-Not-Trying* Identity Story

At Alternative High, nearly all the students I interviewed suggest at one point or another that "everyone is smart." They do not endorse the notion that everyone is smart all of the time or equally smart in every subject. Rather, they tend to identify actions that are "a smart thing to do" and others that are not. For instance, when discussing the owner of the low-performance report card (see figure 1.1), Sheena says, "I would ask this person, 'Did you ask for help? Because then if you didn't ask for help, then that was dumb on your part because you should ask for help' . . . but I wouldn't say that they are stupid . . . but I would be, like, 'You are kind of dumb because you should ask for help and you could have brought those grades up.'"

Like Sheena, most Alternative High students are reluctant to say that poor grades are due to low intelligence. Rather, they invoke the identity story of *smart-but-not-trying*. This identity story surfaced again and again during my interviews. Oriana, a Latina freshman, asserts, "Just because you are smart doesn't mean that you have to get good grades, which probably means that you aren't trying . . . but you are smart." Likewise, when I ask Jaynah (whom you met in chapter 1) if we can tell whether a poor report card signals low intelligence, she responds, "I really can't say if they are smart. Because they can be smart and they just aren't trying."

Smart-but-not-trying is not an enviable character. He or she is not making responsible and respectable decisions. Yet as the previous remarks make clear, few people are willing to admit that this person is completely stupid. By acknowledging that behavior, not intelligence, is the cause of poor performance, the identity story allows the student to salvage some dignity. The smart-but-not-trying identity story is far less offensive to students at Alternative High than the cheater story is. Her troubles could easily be the result of a failing support network or a temporary behavior glitch. This character could begin to put forth effort in school at any moment, and then she would be able to prove that she is an intelligent, successful person.

The *Cheater* Identity Story

At Alternative High, a *cheater* is specifically someone who copies work from a classmate or the Internet (although the Internet rarely offers ready-made answers to fit a given class assignment). Concerns about *cheaters* often surface when students respond to the anonymous report cards (see figures 1.1 and 1.2). Reina, whom you met in chapter 1, offers a typical perspective when I ask her if high grades indicate that a student is intelligent: "What if they were cheating? People in my class cheat and get good grades."

Reina is very proud of her 4.0 grade point average (GPA), and she feels that she works hard to achieve perfect grades. (Because Alternative High does not have curriculum tracks, it does not offer AP or honors courses. Therefore, students cannot earn a GPA higher than 4.0.) Recently, she was offended and frustrated to discover that some of her classmates had been copying her work without her knowledge: "I just found out that all year last year the students who didn't go to internships, who came to school instead, would steal my chemistry folder and copy it every week because I had it there [on Thursdays] for the teacher to check." She adds furiously, "And they got good grades that way!" Apparently the chemistry teacher never caught on, even though the cheaters were copying Reina's work word for word into their own notebooks.

Even students who do not claim to be victims of cheating invoke the *cheater* identity story. When I show Tonyah, an African American and Filipina freshman, the high-performance report card in figure 1.2, she responds with admiration. Yet like Reina, she's also suspicious. Immediately she tells me, "It looks pretty. Because there is a lot of *As* and there is only one *B*—but you never know. Because they may have been copying. I know a lot of people who used to copy in my class." Tonyah goes on to admit that the previous year, as a middle school student, she herself engaged in cheating. "We would make sure that we would sit by the smart people," she giggles, "so it was just like [*whispering*] 'Can I see your answers?' It was funny because some people in the class actually paid them to copy off of their tests." Judging from her description of her disastrous middle school report cards (one year she got into so much trouble with her grades that her father refused to allow her any Christmas presents), her cheating exploits did not garner much school success. Nonetheless, the *cheater* is such a pervasive identity story at Alternative High that even Tonyah suspects that the high grades might be due to copying rather than to legitimate effort.

A Teacher Calls Monique a *Cheater*

The *cheater* identity story is reinforced at Alternative High in multiple ways, including through teacher expectations. During my classroom observations I witnessed a striking example of an exam-prep teacher who *expected* her students to be *cheaters*. During their sophomore year, students prepare for and take the California High School Exit Exam, which everyone must pass in order to receive a high school diploma. It is standard practice for students to take the exam during their sophomore year so that anyone who does not pass the first time has two more years to study and retake it. To help the sophomores pass the exam on their first attempt, a special writing teacher works with their classes, and their math curriculum is geared specifically toward exam concepts and learning objectives.

One Wednesday, the exam-prep teacher returned graded essays to the students and reviewed common mistakes with the group. The essay prompt had asked students to write about a famous person they admire, a type of question that the teacher said is typical on the exit exam. The teacher had an overall unfavorable view of the group's essays and had compiled a list of eight pitfalls in their collective work, which she detailed in an unmistakably dissatisfied tone of voice. To help the students get accustomed to the scoring rubric, she had scored each essay according to the exit exam's number system.

Two students received a *P* rather than a score, so they raised their hands to ask what it meant. Publicly invoking the *cheater* identity story, the teacher stridently announced that *P* was not a score at all. It stood for *plagiarism*, and plagiarized essays would receive *Fs*. There was some confusion among students over the term *plagiarism*, but once they had figured out the meaning, Monique, one of the two students in question, loudly contended that she had not copied her essay. In response, the teacher gave Monique a heavy dressing down in front of rest of the class. "I am not naïve," she said, telling students that she could recognize plagiarism when she saw it. It was "obvious" to the teacher that Monique had copied information, although the teacher had given explicit instructions that the essays were to be written "off the top of your heads, without any research."

Monique had written about Harriet Tubman. "You gave her birthday and the year she was born!" the teacher told Monique in an exasperated voice. According to her, Monique could not possibly have known such details without research. She insisted it was too well written and too informative and therefore must have been copied. She refused to listen to Monique's protests about remembering the information from a report she had written during the previous term. The teacher was resolute that the grade would stand. From my standpoint as an observer, it seemed as if she had come into the class prepared to be lied to or bullied by students, and now, as planned, she was standing her ground. According to Jeanne Oakes, teachers often take this approach when readying themselves to face low-curriculum, difficult classes.[7]

On the next school day (Friday), Monique spoke to her homeroom teacher about the situation. Monique reported that her mother was very upset about the F, and Monique felt she had been unfairly accused of copying the essay. The homeroom teacher willingly allowed her to write a second essay about a different famous person. Overall, however, the homeroom teacher supported the position of the exam-prep teacher, saying to Monique, "Look, I know you. I know you are good writer, and I know that you did a whole report on Harriet Tubman just last quarter. But she doesn't know you." In other words, the teacher encouraged Monique to write a less-polished essay rather than demonstrate that she is indeed capable of writing an excellent, detailed essay "off the top of her head."

In this situation, not only the public accusations of the exam-prep teacher but also the more subtle response of the homeroom teacher worked to reinforce the *cheater* identity story. The homeroom teacher might have assured Monique that when she takes the real exit exam, the essay portion will be written on the spot so that she cannot be accused of copying anything. Instead, she cemented the notion that people in authority are likely to expect Monique to be a *cheater* and that Monique can manage this notion only by altering her performance to fit within believable boundaries.[8] Monique, for her part, did not accept the exam-prep teacher's insinuation that she was a *cheater*. Although she was unable to convince the teacher that she had unfairly accused her of plagiarism, she did what she could to defend herself in front of her classmates.

Monique still does not view herself in any way as a *cheater*. In our interview she tells me that she spends nearly forty hours a week on homework. Often she's still working at one in the morning, when her mother forces her to put her books away and go to bed. Monique invites me into her family's living room to show me the posters that she has made for each of her end-of-quarter demonstrations. She stores them behind the piano, where she can access them easily. As she pulls out each one, she demonstrates pride in her handiwork and her academic accomplishments. She spends several minutes admiring one particular poster depicting the *Twilight* fiction series she had read and presented on. Because I have not read the *Twilight* books, she gives me a thorough summary and suggests which volumes I might like best. As she shares her learning with me, she shows genuine delight. She is pleased with her school success and basks in its positive reflection on her character. She enjoys the moral satisfaction that comes along with her hard work. In fact, she is so secure in her hard-earned achievement that being publicly accused of being a *cheater* has done little to tarnish it.

Family Support and Success Identities

The common assumption at Alternative High is that anyone can get good grades if she tries hard enough, yet not every student I talked to believes that this wisdom applies to her own case. Tonyah and Natalia are among the students who are not convinced that dedicating enormous effort to their schoolwork will automatically yield good grades. These two freshmen struggle to understand some of the concepts and assignments they encounter in school. While such students claim in general that effort is the key to school success, they do not exert much effort themselves in subjects that overwhelm them intellectually because they do not believe their attempts will pay off. Their rationale sounds much like the cultural wisdom about school success that I found at Comprehensive High: intelligence limits the effectiveness of effort.

In their behavior and descriptions Tonyah and Natalia draw on the *smart-but-not-trying* identity story, using it as a refuge for their doubts about their intellectual abilities. They do not invoke identity stories that resemble those I heard at Comprehensive High, nor do they take comfort in the notion that "everyone has a weak point," as do their counterparts at that school. Instead, they rely on an identity story that is available at their own school and try to use it in a way that protects their self-worth. Of course, it is difficult for a student to come out and say that she is not smart. It's hard to admit this to oneself, let alone to other people. So I've drawn my conclusions about these students' feelings from very close readings of expressions, word choice, volunteered explanations, and immediate reactions to interview questions.

At Alternative High, there is no virtue in not being smart. Nor is there any virtue in not trying. Thus, students such as Tonyah and Natalia do not happily describe themselves as intellectually incapable of school success. If nothing else, the belief that school success is "all about effort" is too strong at Alternative High for a student to be able to contradict it entirely. Yet feeling intellectually inadequate also elicits shame, as Tonyah and Natalia illustrate.[9] For example, when I ask Natalia whether her grades "give a good picture" of her intelligence, she responds, "Well, not always because, like, in science I could probably do better, but I'm just not putting the effort into it." At such moments during our interviews, each young woman asserts that she could probably receive As and Bs if she really dedicated her time and energy toward schoolwork. Sometimes both also claim that they are smarter than their poor grades reveal them to be. However, at other moments each acknowledges that she feels intimidated and overwhelmed. "I don't get this, I'm not going to do it," Tonyah says about her math. Neither student puts much effort into subjects that are hard for her. When faced with assignments, they often do not understand what to do or how to do it.

Tonyah and Natalia are useful examples because they come from two very different home life environments. While Tonyah has a contentious and emotionally distant relationship with her father (her parents are separated), Natalia has a warm and nurturing relationship with her parents and siblings, especially her mother and her older sister. While Tonyah receives mixed messages from the adults in her life about whether or not she is "dumb" or has what it takes to graduate from high school, Natalia is continually reminded that she is amazingly intelligent and has a bright future. Clearly, even though families contribute to students' understandings of themselves, they continue to rely heavily on the identity stories and cultural ideas about success that are available at their school.

Tonyah and Natalia Use *Smart-but-Not-Trying* As a Refuge

To all appearances, Tonyah and Natalia exert little effort in subjects that they find challenging. This means that their classmates and teachers may see them as *smart-but-not-trying* rather than as genuinely not smart enough to perform well. *Smart-but-not-trying* is not a virtuous position, but it is preferable to being exposed as unintelligent.

School success is frequently a point of contention between Tonyah and her father, who is raising her as a single parent. Although she seemed to have turned over a new leaf in her last year of middle school and is keeping it up during this first year of high school, she has a history of purposefully failing in school as a way to act out against her father.

My brief encounter with Tonyah's father illuminates her home-life frustrations. When Tonyah schedules our interview, she suggests that we meet somewhere other than her home, and we agree on a library near her school that has private study rooms. In the morning her father drops her off at the curb where I am waiting to meet her. He is talking on his cell phone and does not pause in his conversation as Tonyah gets out of the car and shuts the door behind her. They do not exchange verbal or nonverbal goodbyes: Tonyah simply gets out, and he drives away.

She and I quickly realize that she has forgotten to have her father sign the permission forms for the interview, so she calls him on her cell phone to ask him to return to the meeting place and sign them. She does not reach him and decides not to leave a message. Yet just as we are about to give up on the interview, we see his SUV pull back into the parking lot. It seems that he had registered her call even though he did not answer it. He is still engaged in his phone conversation but lowers his window so that Tonyah can communicate with him while he continues his phone call. She silently hands him the forms and a pen through the window. He signs, rolls the window back up, and drives away, never exchanging a word with either Tonyah or me. In fact, he never even glances in my direction. In most of my fieldwork in classrooms and in locations where I interview students, I have felt decidedly conspicuous, a researcher looking in on others' everyday lives. In this instance, I feel entirely invisible.

My short exposure to Tonyah's father that morning adds credence to her descriptions of him as emotionally distant. She also claims that he is difficult to get along with. We talk about him during our walk from the curb to the library and throughout the interview. I remark, "He seems like a very busy man," and she tells me that he routinely picks her up from school very late in the afternoon or even in the evening: "This one time, he didn't even come get me until seven!" When she complained, she says his response was unsympathetic: "You have homework to do, nothing else. The library is a good place for it."

Tonyah's tense relationship with her father is complex. Although she says he does not offer much encouragement, he does provide strong external support for her academic success. Two years earlier, when she entered middle school, she "went on strike" from schoolwork: "It was science and math and language and I got an F in those, and my dad he just had a heart attack. He was, like, 'How could you do this to me?' and I was, like, 'Um, I did not want to go here [to this middle school].'" Tonyah giggles. "I had an F-minus-minus-minus-minus." Her laughter betrays a rebellious sense of pride that her "strike" was so successful. However, the next year, her punishment for poor grades convinced her to try harder in school. She recalls, "He didn't get me anything for Christmas because I had gotten bad grades. So that, like, really affects you."

Tonyah's home life has additional strain at the moment because her aunt and the aunt's adult sons are also living with Tonyah and her father. The crowded space creates extra stress for Tonyah. Moreover, she describes her aunt as an unkind person. The aunt's negativity affects Tonyah even during the school day, when they are separated. She tells me,

> Everybody always has a crazy person in their family, and my Aunt Maggie—it is, like, pressure because everything gets to you. Like, my Aunt Maggie, she is just, like, pure evil. She talks about everybody. She talked about me, [*Tonyah growls*], she talked about me, like, right in my face, like, I was driving in the car with her, she would just be, like, "Yeah, you're, you're going to drop out of school," and blah, blah, blah. And I was just, like, "Yeah, okay." But then it is, like, you go to school and you want to have fun, but all that stuff that has happened at home gets to you. And then, I don't know, it's weird because then you bring it up in school. I don't know. It's complicated.

As a freshman at Alternative High, Tonyah is taking academics more seriously than she did in middle school. However, pursuing school success is not always easy for her. Her home life looms over her experiences at school. In our interview, she expresses anxiety about her father's disapproval, her aunt's low expectations for her, and her track record of failing on purpose. All contribute to the pressure she feels to prove that she is capable of achieving school success.

Another aspect that complicates Tonyah's pursuit of school success is that she does not perceive herself as very smart. She is not confident that effort will actually yield good grades, especially in subjects that are challenging for her.

LISA NUNN: On an intelligence scale, a smarts scale, from one to ten, where would you fall?

TONYAH: Uh, I would say a six.

L.N.: When you were just thinking about which number to choose, what crossed your mind that helped you figure out which number was the right one?

TONYAH: Because I'm not, I'm not, like, dumb, you know. Hello, I'm not dumb. But I'm not, like, a brainiac. I don't know mostly everything. I know I have to try and work at it, and even if I try and work at it, I still don't get the material. And it's hard.

Throughout our interview, Tonyah describes herself as unable to achieve good grades. Importantly, she does not depict herself as unwilling to try hard, but she admits to garnering only minimal success even when she does try hard. For example, when I ask her whether she thinks that students can make all *As* in school if they try hard enough, she immediately responds, "No, I don't."

I ask, "Why not?"

She answers, "Because I've tried. I've tried before, and I didn't get any *A*. Like, with my math right now—no, with my science. The way that that webpage is set up, it's hard. And I have tried and I have gotten, like, a *D* in science." She quickly shifts the discussion and begins bemoaning the heavy workload at Alternative High: "Now it's, like, you have to be kidding me because there is so much work that we have to do, and it is, like—they make it seem like we don't have a life here because they give us, no seriously, they give us all these assignments and I am just, like, 'Oh, my gosh.' But I would rather go here than a normal high school because if I go to a normal high school I know that I am going to have a lot of work . . . and have to worry about all the other kids at school—no."

Because Tonyah does not have a history of trying her best in school, we might reasonably be skeptical of her willingness to dig in and get her work done. It is tempting to read her descriptions of the difficulty of her coursework as convenient excuses that explain away her low effort and subsequent poor performance. However, a close look at her responses indicates that she believes that she unable to grasp course concepts easily, and this self-perception works as a de-motivating force. For example, when she looks at the low-performance report card (see Figure I.I), she disagrees with my suggestion that the student might be trying his best but may not be smart enough to understand the concepts being taught. Tonyah retorts, "No. They may be smart enough; they may just not want to do it. Because that's how I was in math. I was just, like [*she makes a sound of exasperation*], I don't get this; I'm not going to do it. So then I got my report card and my dad started yelling at me, and I was, like, 'oop,' changed my mind."

Although Tonyah portrays herself in this story as *smart-but-not-trying*, a key point in her description is that she decides to stop trying after realizing "I don't get this." Her father convinces her to apply herself, and her increased effort seems to have improved her grade enough to satisfy him. However, she also admits: "I've tried before, and I didn't get any A." Effort has helped her grade, but it does not seem to have helped her perceive herself as possessing much intelligence.

Tonyah dons the *smart-but-not-trying* mask at several points in the interview. For instance, when I ask, "Do you think that your grades give a good picture of how intelligent you are?" she answers, "No, I don't think that they do. Because I could slack back most of the time. I could just be in class, you know, acting like this [*hides her head*], and then I just doze off." Notice that she uses the word *could.* She does not come out and say that she makes a habit of either slacking off or dozing.

In classroom observations I note that Tonyah is generally engaged in lessons and follows the norms during independent study time. This includes some studying but also some chatting with neighbors and some staring into space—what I describe in my field notes as "mostly working." However, on a couple of occasions, I also see her employ the strategy of visibly not trying in an effort to mask feelings of incompetence. For example, one day during group math instruction, her body language changes from intent listening, to an expression of confusion (narrowed eyes, cocked head), to complete disengagement. At this point she begins shuffling through her backpack and distracting herself with items on her desk and at her feet; she is clearly not listening to the math instruction. Tonyah's confusion about the math lesson seems to prompt her to give up on trying to follow the teacher's explanation. Instead of raising her hand for clarification, she enacts behaviors that visibly signal that she is not paying attention. They invite her teacher and her classmates to expect her to do poorly on the subsequent math assignment.

I note another example in a morning class discussion. The homeroom teacher asks the group an open question, and Tonyah calls out an answer with gusto. Many other students call out answers at the same time. The homeroom teacher briefly acknowledges Tonyah's response (which was the loudest), tossing a curt "no" in her direction. The teacher then turns the group's attention toward a quieter classmate's correct answer. Tonyah's perky body language deflates. She immediately disengages from the group discussion, even though a moment earlier she was avidly interested in the topic. She begins to elaborately rearrange her neck scarf and rebutton her jacket. It is clear that she is embarrassed at having shouted out a wrong answer. After she finishes rearranging her clothing, she turns around in her seat and stares off into space. Her behavior is an unmistakable signal to the rest of the class that she is not only not participating but also not listening. Her open display of disengagement is likely to be noticed in this case because the homeroom desks are arranged in a circle to facilitate the class discussion, meaning that everyone can easily see everyone else

Tonyah's classmate Natalia also uses the *smart-but-not-trying* identity story as a mask for not actually feeling very smart. Natalia enjoys more emotional support and encouragement at home than Tonyah does, but she has doubts similar to Tonyah's about her own intellectual talents. When I meet Natalia at a coffeehouse near her home, her mother and older sister, age twenty-three, arrive with her. Her mother greets me warmly, and I watch her inspect me as if she is determining whether she feels comfortable leaving her fourteen-year-old daughter with me. Mother and sister politely refuse my offer to drive Natalia home after the interview. They prefer to wait for her in the car, although they assure me that they are not in a hurry and we can take as long as we need for the interview.

On the whole, Natalia's mother and her sister seem happy that she has been chosen for a research interview; the sister playfully chides her not to "get any of the answers wrong." Before they leave the coffeehouse, Natalia's mother discreetly asks her daughter in Spanish if she has enough money with her to buy coffee. Then she turns to me and jokes in English that this coffeehouse is Natalia's favorite place in the world. It is no surprise to her that Natalia has chosen it for the interview location.

Toward the end of the interview, when I ask Natalia who in her family knows her the best, she decides the answer is a tie between her mom and the sister who waits outside in the car. She also lives with her father, an older brother who is twenty-six, and another older sister who is nineteen. When I ask Natalia where her mom and sister would place her on the one-to-ten intelligence scale, she says, "Seriously, my mom would give me a ten; she thinks that I'm—" Here Natalia seems at a loss for words.

I suggest, "Really smart?"

She giggles, "Yeah. And my sister, probably like a nine." These are higher numbers than the "six or seven" that Natalia has given herself on the scale earlier in the interview. This disparity indicates that her relationship with her mother and her sister is a positive influence on her self-perception. These two family members give her complimentary information about her intellectual talents, even if Natalia does not take it to heart.

Natalia struggles in some of her subjects but not in others, and she indicates in the interview that her limited ability to easily understand the material creates the struggle. She also admits to not trying very hard in those difficult subjects. However, like Tonyah, she demonstrates that the trouble she has in understanding assignments causes her lack of motivation. This link becomes clear when I ask her to describe the relationship between effort and intelligence in her own school performance:

LISA NUNN: How much of your grades is based on your hard work or effort, and how much is based on your intelligence or ability to get the material? Is it a fifty-fifty balance?

NATALIA: Well, in math, it depends on my effort. Because how fast I get it—I don't get math, like, really fast.

L. N.: So it's all effort for you?

NATALIA: Hmm, well not all effort, probably, like, seventy-five . . . no, I'm not that slow [laughs]. It's probably, like, sixty-forty.

L. N.: That's for math. Is it also true, more or less, for your other subjects?

NATALIA: Well, for English, I mostly understand all the assignments they give us and everything, so I put effort into it because I know how to do it. So it's, like, "Okay, just let me get it done." But then, like, math, I kind of, like, wait it off, and I'm, like, "Oh, whatever."

L. N.: So is English more like fifty-fifty, or is it even more on the smart side?

NATALIA: I get it, so I like to do it. That's, like, the best grade that I have. I have an A.

Natalia's description of herself—that she lacks motivation because she lacks intellectual talent in math—sounds much like the cultural wisdom at Elite Charter High: that highly intelligent people often feel naturally enthusiastic about learning. However, Natalia's explanation does not actually align with Elite Charter High's explanation for school success. There, motivation to work hard is seen as an internal motivation, a desire to learn and achieve. On the contrary, Natalia's "I know how to do it. So it's, like, 'Okay, just let me get it done'" suggests that she is choosing to do her work, a behavior that will yield school success according to the cultural wisdom at Alternative High. Her responses do not indicate that she is inspired and excited about learning new things. Even though she does "like to do it," she does not say she spends extra time learning more on her own, which would be characterized as initiative at Elite Charter High. Instead, her understanding of her lack of motivation in math is rooted in her high school's cultural ideas about school success.

Just "get[ting] it done" is problematic for Natalia in subjects such as math. She finds it difficult to muster up the energy to work on assignments that involve concepts that she does not clearly understand. As I discuss in chapter 3, being good at some subjects but not others is a common situation for students at Comprehensive High. There, students see this situation as a fact of life. They tend to simply accept the fact that they receive lower grades in subjects that they are "bad at." This is not cultural wisdom that Natalia has ready access to at Alternative High. Here, students express faith in the idea that everyone is smart enough to succeed in all school subjects. Natalia is supposed to be able to do well in math, just like everyone else.

By not trying her best, Natalia might be mistaken for *smart-but-not-trying*, and she does occasionally borrow this identity story during our interview. For example, when she is discussing the low-performance report card (see figure I.I), she shifts into describing her own situation: "Probably I could get *As* and *Bs*, you know what I mean? But, you know, the effort I put into it." I ask if she means that she doesn't put in enough effort to get such high grades, and she responds, "Well, I think I could put [in] more effort, but I don't know. I probably could get *As* and *Bs*, but I don't. So I don't put [in] that much effort, I guess." Listening closely to this answer, I conclude that Natalia does not seem convinced that *smart-but-not-trying* accurately fits her. Her word choice—"probably," "I think," "I don't know," and "I guess"—illustrates the tension she experiences between her sense of her own abilities and the prevailing cultural wisdom at her school.

The identity story *smart-but-not-trying* offers a ready explanation for Alternative High students whose minimal efforts result in low grades. It is a plausible reason for poor academic performance, one that fits neatly within local understandings of the relationship among effort, intelligence, and school success. However, *the story* does not capture the self-identity of students such as Natalia and Tonyah, whose motivation to try hard in school is thwarted by frustration over their limited intellectual facility in some subjects. *Smart-but-not-trying* may not be a virtuous identity, but it is preferable to identifying oneself as intellectually incapable of good grades.

Identity Stories and Inhabited Institutionalism

Natalia, Tonyah, and Monique illustrate how individual students make differing use of identity stories as they construct their own success identities. Identity stories are frameworks of meaning that students draw on in creative ways. Individuals do not simply adopt an identity story for themselves wholeheartedly. Instead, they craft their success identities by negotiating with existing identity stories: rejecting one outright (as Monique does with the *cheater*) or posturing with one (as Natalia and Tonyah do with *smart-but-not-trying*). As we will see in the following chapters, students at Comprehensive High and Elite Charter High are similarly inventive and resourceful in the ways in which they alter and refashion the identity stories that exist at their schools,.

Inhabited institutionalism theory helps us see how actors within school organizations modify and adapt macrolevel cultural ideas of success.[10] By extending inhabited institutionalism to identity construction, we can understand these same dynamics at the micro level. Individuals craft self-identities by creatively reworking organization-level ideas as they apply those ideas to themselves. Both processes demonstrate the agentic ways in which people make sense of the circumstances and realities of their school environment or their own lives, even as cultural ideas bear down on them from above.

3

Comprehensive High

Effort Is Helpful, but Intelligence Limits School Success

Comprehensive High's campus covers a city block. The main entrance opens off a busy thoroughfare, and the school is sandwiched among large six-lane boulevards that feed miles of strip malls, restaurants, supermarkets, auto repair shops, and the like. Although Comprehensive High is considered a suburban school, the surrounding landscape does not have the quiet residential peacefulness that many suburban schools enjoy. I interviewed few students who live close enough to walk there. In the school parking lot, each car must pass through a guard gate where security personnel check student and faculty parking passes and verify visitors' permission to enter. Fences border the campus. To a visitor, the place has the feel of an industrial complex more than a suburban school. Inside, however, its single-story classroom blocks, open-air walkways, and outdoor eating pavilions make it feel much like any other southern California school.

Comprehensive High is a majority-minority school, meaning that the student body includes more ethnoracial minority students than white students; and its student body is roughly in line with California state averages. Slightly more than 50 percent of the student population is Latino. (The state average is 42 percent.) With such a large proportion of Latinos, Comprehensive High also has a higher-than-average proportion of English language learners: over 20 percent compared to 15 percent across the state. Its proportion of white students nearly matches the state average of 37 percent, and African Americans and Asian American students together comprise another 10 percent (roughly half of state averages for those two groups).

However, the school's ethnoracial diversity is not spread evenly across socioeconomic categories. On the whole, white students at Comprehensive High are more affluent than Latino and other minority students are, although nearly

45 percent of the student body is socioeconomically disadvantaged (as defined by the state), which is slightly higher than the state average of 40 percent.[1] The median home value in the area is 203,000 dollars, according to the 2000 U.S. Census.[2] Nonetheless, I found wide disparity in the homes of students I visited for interviews. White students in my sample tend to live in fairly large, spacious homes in newly constructed subdivisions, complete with perfectly landscaped lawns. In contrast, Latino students I interviewed tend to live in older neighborhoods in homes in various states of disrepair, with nonfunctioning cars crowding driveways and front yards. Still other students, both Latinos and whites, live in cramped apartment complexes scattered around town.

Comprehensive High has undergone considerable organizational change over the past several years. This is common for schools that are scrambling to avoid sanctions and meet standards exacted by No Child Left Behind legislation. In the five years that bookend my research, the high school has had three principals. Additionally, the district built a new high school nearby to relieve Comprehensive High's overpopulation problems. As a result, the student body fell from slightly more than 3,100 students to fewer than 1,500, and the staff shifted from 130 teachers to 65. The new school opened the year before I began conducting my research, and many of the students I interviewed at Comprehensive High have been reflecting on the changes in their own school, which is now half its original size. In general, they are happy with the smaller size, and many mention that gang activity on campus has diminished sharply. Several recall that fighting was common during every passing period and that gang members defended territories on various parts of the campus. During my weeks of observation, I saw neither fights nor obvious gang activity, although I did witness visible tension among groups of students who encountered each other between classes and at lunch.

In terms of academic performance, Comprehensive High is a fairly typical California high school. Its California Standards Test (CST) scores hover a few percentage points below state averages in English, science, and social science, although its math scores are nearly 15 percent lower than the state average. However, the percentage of tenth graders passing the California High School Exit Exam, including the math component, is slightly higher than the state average.

To compare students at differing academic levels, I selected an eleventh-grade AP English class and a tenth-grade college-preparatory world history class for my observations and interviews. The principal told me that all Comprehensive High students are now enrolled in college-prep courses that meet the state university entrance requirements. Thus, the school no longer has a designated general track. This is one of many new curriculum developments that this principal brought with her when she arrived in 2004. Students and teachers I talked to are still adjusting to these strategic attempts to boost the school's academic profile. But even though the principal is actively trying to improve its reputation, the school still does not have a clear mission for preparing its students. Unlike Alternative High and Elite Charter High, Comprehensive High does not have what Burton Clark calls an "institutional saga," a story of itself and its mission that gives an educational institution character and distinction.[3] Simply it does the best it can to educate its students according to state and federal guidelines.

Both the English and history teachers warmly accepted me into their classrooms and gave me permission to be as active or as passive as I preferred. In all three schools I studied, I worked to maximize observations and minimize intrusions, choosing a side table in the front of each room and busily taking field notes during class time. I said nothing, unless a teacher or student explicitly solicited my opinion. This rarely happened at Comprehensive High.

The school has recently switched to a modified block schedule. In a traditional block schedule, students attend, for example, math class only on Tuesdays and Thursdays, when they meet for a two-hour math period. However, at Comprehensive High only some days are block days. Students attend all six of their classes on Mondays and Fridays for 57 minutes each. On Wednesday they attend half of those classes for 120 minutes each, and on Thursdays they attend the other half for 120 minutes each. On Tuesdays students begin the day 43 minutes later than they do on the other days and spend 51 minutes in each of their six classes. As is usual in high schools, this schedule was altered frequently during my three weeks of observations to accommodate pep rallies, assemblies, tests, and other interruptions. Although I found the schedule dizzying, the students and teachers I interviewed seemed generally content with the arrangement.

The purpose of a block schedule is to allow teachers to engage in more intensive instruction, but I cannot confidently claim that the teachers achieve this goal in either of the two classes I observed. The AP English class certainly spends long uninterrupted stretches on reading texts or writing essays, yet the teacher often begins instruction ten minutes or more after the class officially begins and ends instruction ten minutes or more before the bell rings. Clearly, maximizing time is not a central concern for this class. In contrast, the history teacher carefully budgets his class minutes. He also schedules in a mid-block break, presumably so that students don't have to sit still for two straight hours. In addition, he segments class time into discrete activities that are often largely unrelated to one another. This approach seems to be a carryover from the pre-block days. Instead of scrapping his tried and true lesson plans, he simply retrofits them into longer class periods. Yet even though the block periods are not as fruitful as they could be, the principal expresses confidence that the modified schedule has increased the academic rigor of her school.

AP and General Curriculum Are Separate Worlds

Although every Comprehensive High student now takes classes at the college-prep level, the students I interviewed see an important difference between being "in AP" and being in "regular classes." Because AP classes at the school are understood to be reserved for highly intelligent people, this distinction appeared to be a status marker for students, I also found striking differences in the atmospheres of the two classes I studied. Based on my observations, I am not convinced that the academic content of the AP English class was significantly more advanced than the academic content in the college-prep world history class. Some students I talked to expressed a similar impression. For instance, Shannon, a white freshman in honors curriculum, says, "Honors is basically almost exactly the same as regular non-honors, except without the smart kids."

Nonetheless, the two classes have very different academic atmospheres, in part because of the teachers' method of delivery.[4] In addition, the students themselves have a great deal of influence over the classroom context. At Comprehensive High, most students and teachers seem to agree that AP classes should be oriented toward open discussion because the students have keen insights to offer. In contrast, they feel that the college-prep classes should be more lecture-driven and include structured tasks that help absorb new information rather than open a forum for discussion and debate.

Mrs. Brookings allows students in her AP English class to call out answers and contribute to class discussions as she loosely manages their interactions with each other and the material. This pedagogical style effectively fosters debate and group effort, but the free-moving conversation very often whirls beyond the teacher's control. Whenever Mrs. Brookings turns her attention away from the students, vigorous chatting erupts, and she has to exert visible effort to get the class back on track. However, in academic tasks, the students collaborate well, building on each other's comments in discussions and refining definitions or concepts with a sense of team spirit. Of course, in any classroom with such an open dynamic of interaction, students who are shy or reserved end up being left out almost entirely. Typically, a few students do most of the talking, and in this class a junior named Stephanie tends to dominate the verbal space of the classroom.

Students engage in side conversations as well as participating in teacher-led discussions. In addition to the typical gossip and schoolwork complaints, these side conversations often cover current politics, national news scandals, and the like. For example, one morning as students wait for the dismissal bell, Stephanie, Erin, and Sue are critiquing Hillary Clinton, and I hear Stephanie assert that "she better not run for president" in the next election. On another day, when the students have been reading a selection by Mahatma Gandhi that includes his photo, Brett leans over to his neighbor and says, "Gandhi looks like he needs to eat a big steak." Todd, who overhears the comment, takes the opportunity to show off his knowledge of Hinduism: "But if he killed or ate a cow, he'd be disgraced forever." These worldly-wise topics and this debate-style interaction are noticeably absent from the college-prep world history class.

At Comprehensive High, AP courses are seen as classes for smart kids, and students at all three of the schools I studied view discussions of topics such as politics and history to be signs of a person's high intelligence. Yet as Shannon has already noted, the honors students at Comprehensive High don't believe that AP and honors content is dramatically different from college-prep content. Yvonne, a Latina junior in AP classes, says, "A lot of people think that people who are smart, the AP kids, have it tougher, but I have found that it is actually easier . . . because people look at the book, and it is really thick. And the students exaggerate about how much work there is in AP, when really we get like three months to complete the big assignments." Thus, while AP classes may or may not be more academically challenging than college-prep classes, students view them as spaces in which intelligent students congregate and engage in casual discussions about "smart topics." This creates a separate environment in which AP students negotiate their success identities. They are able to see themselves as smart, just by virtue of being enrolled in AP classes. Even students who were receiving Ds or Fs in their AP classes when I interviewed them still consider being "in AP" to be a distinguishing aspect of their identity.

The relatively small AP English class is comprised of twenty-two students: ten white, seven Latino, four Asian American (including one Korean immigrant), and one African American. There are eight males and fourteen females. The composition of the world history class more closely reflects the school's student body. Out of thirty-seven students, fifteen are white, twenty-one are Latino, and one is Asian American. There are twenty males and seventeen females.

Not only does the world history class have a different ethnoracial composition, but pedagogically it is a different world. The teacher, Mr. Rockport, is punctual about beginning and ending his lessons. During the eight-minute break on block days, students are free to wander the room, though few of them do. Instead, they talk loudly, sleep on their desks, eat snacks, listen to iPods, text-message on cell phones, or goof off with classmates who sit near them. This teacher has little trouble getting the lesson going again after the break; the students are generally quiet and docile and follow his instructions. Whenever they become too disruptive or inattentive, Mr. Rockport uses the break time as leverage, threatening to take away minutes from their break if they do not immediately settle down and resume the rhythm of his lesson. This is a surprisingly effective technique, perhaps because he follows through on his threats and warnings. During my observation period, he twice removed minutes from students' break time.

This class is not discussion-based. The teacher disseminates most information with handwritten transparencies on an overhead projector. He supplements this approach with lectures. Mr. Rockport often asks students factual questions. Most of these questions review material he's already presented—for instance, he asks students to recall dates or names. Occasionally, the teacher invites students to participate in his delivery of new material. For instance, one day he asks, "Why do you think they called it the cold war?" When a student calls out, "Because it was fought during the winter!" Mr. Rockport corrects the response. The student is surprised that his answer was not right, but the teacher assures him that it was a good guess.

Students sometimes raise hands or call out semi-unrelated questions in the middle of teacher presentations. This happens during Mr. Rockport's description of Nazi policies in Germany, when he explains that not only Jews but also other populations considered undesirable or inferior, including homosexuals, were sent to concentration camps. Sandra calls out incredulously, "You mean they had people like that even way back then?"

Mr. Rockport responds, "Yes, there have been homosexuals all throughout history."

Sandra says, "I didn't know that!" In his characteristic style, Mr. Rockport immediately resumes his lecture on Nazi camps without responding further to Sandra. He is willing to field questions but is quick to return to his lesson agenda. The class includes no open discussion and no student-driven debate.

Unlike AP English, the world history class does not run on the assumption that students bring important ideas and insights to the material or that knowledge is gained by dissecting and critiquing ideas. Instead, both teacher and students seem to believe that a teacher's role is to deliver knowledge and a student's role is to acquire that knowledge. While the class features little open interaction, the teacher also spends much less time straying from academic topics, and no student personalities dominate the verbal space. These differences may partly stem from the difference in class size. It is more difficult to keep a lesson on track if thirty-seven voices are free to openly contribute to the presentation of material.

Mary Metz's study of curriculum tracks tells us that we should expect to see exactly these differences between these two classes.[5] She found that higher curriculum tracks tend to work from a philosophy of teaching and learning that is rooted in the idea that students make meaningful contributions. Both teachers and students expect these classes to be discussion-based. Meanwhile, lower curriculum tracks tend to work from a philosophy of teaching and learning that is rooted in the idea that teachers are experts who have knowledge to share. Both teachers and students expect top-down management and stricter discipline. In the world history class, there is little opportunity for students to publicly display their intelligence or effort because there is little, if any, group performance.

At Comprehensive High, AP and college-prep classes feel like separate worlds. However, most AP students are enrolled in at least one college-prep class and thus experience both spaces. Despite this overlap, these students retain the status distinction of being "in AP" and have concerns regarding grades and intelligence that strictly college-prep students do not share. I will discuss these concerns in chapter 4.

Education at the Intersection of Race and Class

Education in the United States is not a monolithic or uniform social good that is delivered to all students in all schools evenly, and students themselves live out these differences. Schooling is always raced and classed; that is, students who are members of different ethnoracial groups or different socioeconomic classes experience the schooling process differently from one another.[6] As I discussed in chapter 1 and will take up again in chapter 7, students from lower- and working-class backgrounds and those from ethnoracial minority groups systematically suffer educational disadvantages. They also comprise most of the students at both Comprehensive High and Alternative High.

It is critical to understand how social statuses such as race and class compound the disadvantages in individuals' lives. A working-class white student does not experience school in the same way that an African American or a Latino working-class student does, even though they share working-class status and may attend the same school. The African American or Latino working-class student faces a double disadvantage, and the school itself can exacerbate the situation. In other words, an African American or Latino working-class student who attends a largely white, middle-class school will not have the same school experience as a comparable student who attends a majority-minority school in a working-class neighborhood.

As in every other school, education at Comprehensive High takes place at the intersection of race and class. However, while Alternative High was specifically designed to fight patterns of educational disadvantage (for instance, by offering the identical academic curriculum to all its students), Comprehensive High remains more traditional, stratifying both its curriculum and its student body. These dynamics play out in students' academic lives and their understandings of success. They also have very personal and emotional responses to their experiences in school, which shape their sense of who they are.

Teaching to the Test

At Comprehensive High, both the AP English class and the world history class rely on what I call correct-answer–oriented pedagogy. As a close observer of both classes, I can say that this approach seems to be effective: students walk away from their class sessions having learned something new. Nonetheless, instruction and discussions are tightly focused on guiding students to understand how they might respond correctly to test questions as opposed to gaining a more open-ended comprehension of the subject matter. To be fair, I should say that I collected my observational data during the spring, when teachers must concentrate on helping students prepare for the CST and AP exams. However, even after the CST tests were over, the pedagogy remained the same.[7]

In the AP English class, correct-answer–oriented teaching is ubiquitous: almost all of the presented material is directly related to the AP exam. For example, one morning as a student begins reading aloud a passage by Thoreau, Mrs. Brookings stops her after the opening sentences. "What is this called?" she asks. "What did he just do?" Students seem unsure of the correct answer is, and they fidget quietly. Once she is sure that no one is going to volunteer an answer, Mrs. Brookings continues, "For the AP test, you would have to know that he opens with a paradox." She does not proceed into a discussion of the literary or philosophical meaning of Thoreau's paradox or the meaning of the excerpt in general. Instead, she asks the student to continue reading aloud, and in the discussion that follows she focuses on the types of literary devices that are commonly used at the beginning of literary works.

In the world history class, Mr. Rockport is also correct-answer–oriented in his presentation of material and similarly focused on student success on standardized exams—in his case, the CST. He diligently covers material that students can expect to find on the state's tenth-grade history exam, and he continually reminds them of the importance of memorizing the material so that they can recall it for the test.

Better test scores are not the only goal of learning at Comprehensive High, but they are an important one, and the principal tells me that she is determined to improve the school's standardized test scores.[8] Two years earlier, before she became principal, she conducted a "needs analysis": "I spent three months talking to staff, students, parents, going into classrooms, looking at test scores. . . . It became very clear to me from the feedback I was getting from all sources that the school was very underperforming. . . . [The kids] were as bright . . . as anyplace, but the test scores were terrible." Thus, the administration supports the classroom teachers' exam focus. As Mrs. Brookings says, "I don't really buy into the CST . . . [but] next year I am going to have to because I have a college-prep class which is *all* about that. . . . The CST is still a big deal, you know."

Intelligence Limits the Scope of School Success

According to students at Comprehensive High, school success is the result of both intelligence and effort. While many feel certain that effort plays a greater role than intelligence (an attitude similar to that of students' at Alternative High), most buy into the notion that intelligence is a determining factor in an individual's level of school success. In this view, students with limited intelligence will attain only limited school success, whereas students with high intelligence have more opportunities for significant school success, thanks to AP courses' weighted grades and the potential for earning college credit.

Sandra is a Latina sophomore who takes college-prep classes. I show her the low-performance report card in figure 1.1 and ask her to describe the anonymous student to whom it belongs. Her first reaction is "It looks like they are *kind of* trying." When I ask her to explain which details on the report card signal that this student is "kind of trying," she tells me that "the Cs and D, the grades" hint that the student is not putting forth his or her best effort. I ask if someone might get these grades who is really trying her best or if anyone who puts in a reasonable amount of effort should receive higher grades than these. Sandra ponders for a moment and then says, "That's a hard question because sometimes I've been like this, and I've tried really hard and can't get grades that great, and then when I try really hard in other subjects, then I can. So probably [the anonymous student] is having a hard time in some of the material that's being covered in class." Like students at Alternative High, Sandra implies that with greater effort the anonymous student would have had higher grades. Yet she is unwilling to declare that effort alone might be all the student needs to improve his or her grades. She expresses a common perception among students I interviewed at Comprehensive High: grades can be limited by a student's limited intelligence.

Sandra describes her own experience of "trying really hard" yet not "get[ting] grades that great" but notes that this is true only in some classes. Effort in other subjects pays off. Among students I talked to at Comprehensive High, this is a familiar condition. As Diana, a white sophomore in college-prep classes, asserts, "everyone has a weak point." While students at Elite Charter High and Alternative High also express an awareness of individual strengths and weaknesses in particular subjects, none of those students think it is acceptable to do poorly in weaker classes. In contrast, students at Comprehensive High perceive a relationship among intelligence, effort, and school success. Flavia, a Latina junior in AP classes, explains that a student's school success is restricted to the limits of her intellectual abilities, especially in "a particular class you have never been very good at." The principal shares this belief. When I ask if students can earn all As if they try hard enough, she responds, "Oh, [I] disagree! Totally. Because if they don't have the content—because I can try real hard, but if I just don't have the—I'm terrible at languages. And I can try really hard to speak German, but if I can't figure it out and I can't articulate it and I can't answer questions on a test, I am going to fail the class, no matter how hard I try."

At Comprehensive High students use the language of "caring about school" and "wanting to do well" to describe the motivation behind effort. In this they are similar to students at Elite Charter High. However, students at Comprehensive High do not describe caring about school as initiative inspired by passion or enthusiasm. Instead, they tend to focus on future life goals. As Kathleen, a white sophomore in college-prep classes, says, "you have to work for what you want. You can't go [through] high school with Ds. Unless you want to actually not go anywhere in life."

At the same time, the Comprehensive High descriptions of effort focus on concrete student behaviors, an attitude that echoes the students at Alternative High. Yet unlike their counterparts at Alternative High, these students do not perceive effective school behaviors as a straightforward path to school success. As the principal also makes clear, intelligence plays a substantial role in the equation. Stephanie, a white junior in AP classes, affirms, "You can try as hard as you can and put in as much effort as you can and still not understand the material." Using the language of cultural ideas, I characterize the dominant belief at Comprehensive High as success-through-intelligence combined in a particular way with success-through-effort. In other words, trying hard only brings success in subjects that you are already "smart in."

School Structures Give Conflicting Messages

At Comprehensive High, curriculum tracking supports the notion that intelligence matters in school success, and recently the school administration restructured its AP course offerings to reinforce the institutional belief that "everyone has a weak point." Students at who are eligible for AP coursework can now choose from eight available AP courses (compared to twenty-two at Elite Charter High). In addition, the school now bundles the AP courses in math/science and language/history. Thus, if a student is interested in taking an AP math course, she must also enroll in the corresponding AP science course. Likewise, if a student wants to take AP English, he must also take AP history. The result, as the principal proudly tells me, is that students are enrolling in more AP classes.

Although students express some frustration about the bundling (for instance, what if an individual is interested in English but not history?), in general they accept the structure as sensible. They agree that if someone is good at math, she is likely to be good at science, but they would not assume that same person is also good at English and history. They often mention the popular explanation of a right-brain/left-brain split in intellectual abilities as the rationale behind the structure of AP course offerings. However, few of the students who offer this explanation are sure which side of the brain corresponds to which ability, a confusion suggesting that they are agreeable to this line of reasoning rather than convinced by a specific theoretical perspective.

While it is possible to enroll in both bundled sets during one year, many students I interviewed prefer to focus on one side of the brain, so to speak; that is, they tend to take only one bundle of AP coursework. The structure of available courses certainly reinforces and contributes to the assumption that "everyone has a weak point." Even if a student is willing to sign up for four AP-level classes and thus circumvent the imposed choice, she must then manage what the school sees as a very demanding course schedule. The structure of bundled courses prevents students from pursuing advanced instruction in the specific subjects that interest them most, an experience that might lead more students to believe that they are good at a wider variety of topics.

The school organization by no means fosters the belief that intelligence is the only route to success. Intelligence simply sets the upper limit for how much school success a student can reasonably expect to attain. Other structural features of school life encourage students to see success as dependent on effort. Trying one's best is a necessary part of getting good grades and respectable test scores. For example, the school calendar is loaded with benchmark, or practice, CST exams that students are required to take throughout the school year. The rationale is that the more times students attempt the test, the more familiar they will become with its demands and the better their final score will be when the real CST comes around in spring. Each time a practice test is administered, students benchmark their progress. This is success-through-effort logic: by plugging away at a test regimen, a student can improve her scores and reach higher levels of success. To encourage students to take the practice tests seriously, many teachers use them as part of students' course grades

Yet in other aspects of their assessment, students hear a conflicting message. As the principal explains to me, student grades should not reflect effort:

> What is supposed to happen is that it is really—as far as a teacher issuing a grade—it is supposed to be purely on academics. But of course, wrapped up in the academics is their participation, their attendance, their effort is certainly involved in that. There are some gifted kids who can answer questions on a test and write well quickly so they don't have to put a lot of effort into it. But hopefully, most of the grades that are issued by a teacher have to do with their academic ability more than—*much* more than their attitude or behavior. Those things are *not* supposed to be involved in issuing someone's grade. There is a place on the report card where a teacher can mark effort, conduct, participation, that kind of thing. So it is supposed to be strictly separated.

The principal's explanation of effort is a bit confusing. On the one hand, effort "is wrapped up in" a student's academic success. She indicates that participation, attendance, and effort all contribute to the ability to get good grades. Yet effort is "supposed to be strictly separated" from a student's grade. In the end, correct answers on tests and strong writing skills seem to be all that matter. Effort is not the key to success; "academic ability" is. Yet the principal does not discount effort completely. In another part of our interview she says, "Although most students who try very hard—certainly that contributes to their success. If they come in and get extra tutoring from the teacher, if they get tutoring after school, or they study for hours at home or whatever if the content is difficult for them. That's all going to contribute to their success. But that is not going to be the thing that the teacher is going to say, 'Well, you are just a nice person and you try real hard, so you've got an A.' Uh-uh. Not going to happen."

Unlike her counterpart at Alternative High, the principal does not express confidence that any student who tries hard enough will be able to master the course content and earn As. She describes effort as a worthwhile endeavor "if the content is difficult" for a student, but it is "not going to be the thing" that ultimately earns an A. Her view contradicts the logic of success-through-effort, but only partially. Hard work will contribute to some level of success, but it does not guarantee highest success.

There is another feature of school life that sends a conflicting message about whether or not effort is a key to maximizing school success—what students describe as the "lazy" teaching practices of teachers who "don't care." Although I did not witness such practices in either of the classes I observed, I did hear about them during my interviews with students. Shannon, for instance, describes her honors science class: "The teacher never checked the homework. I could write, 'The cows went moo,' and she wouldn't notice. . . . You can write anything and show her—you go like this [*she pantomimes flashing a piece of paper for the teacher to check*], 'Okay. Good job. Next person.'" When I ask Flor, a Latina junior in college-prep classes, whether or not she likes school, she says, "It all depends on the teachers, and I really don't like some teachers. It seems like they don't care, so then I don't want to care, you know? But the teachers I do like are enthusiastic; they make it funny. So those are the ones that I usually look forward to in school." I ask her how often she has teachers who don't care, and she replies, "I only have two teachers that [I am] not liking this year."

Of course, at any school some teachers are favorites and others are less popular. What struck me was that students seem to feel cheated by the teachers whom they describe as lazy or indifferent. Flor discusses her chemistry teacher: "When he asks, 'Do you have any questions?' and you'll say, 'Yeah,' and he'll say, 'Okay, read the book,' then you're, like, okay, that didn't answer my question." Students also complain about teachers who assign meaningless busywork, which they often do not bother to grade. For Comprehensive High students, these classroom experiences give them a conflicted attitude about effort. Hard work certainly does not pay off in assignments that are never graded, and it rarely pays off when a student tries to master material by reading the textbook on her own without teacher feedback. At the end of the day, students come away with the impression that effort only matters sometimes.

Lazy Teaching Practices Inspire Cheating

In their interviews with me, students criticized many Comprehensive High teachers, but a few names came up again and again among multiple students. One was the science teacher whom Shannon has just mentioned. This teacher is famously unfair. Claire, a white freshman in honors classes, is presently finishing up a class with this teacher: "She is very unorganized. . . . She would tell us to do notes on a chapter and they're due, whatever, tomorrow. So people would write. She never read them, ever. People would write about their dogs and stuff: 'I have a dog. His name is—.' I mean, really. Really, seriously, it would be about their dog or maybe talking about what they had for cereal for breakfast. She's weird." Claire finds this teacher's homework habits not only "weird" but disgraceful. In a tone of disappointment and dismay, she tells me, "I'm, like, 'She is never going to check it, is she?' And she never did. Not the whole entire year. She never caught a single person."

During interviews, students generally offered similar details about this teacher, telling me that students write nonsense and turn it in as homework. At first I suspected that the tale was a popular school legend, but then I found that even students currently enrolled in this teacher's courses describe her behavior in precisely the same terms. Several said that her predictability makes their homework burden much lighter (they never feel that they have to complete it), yet at the same time they expressed deep dissatisfaction with their low accountability. Like Claire, they want to be held responsible for their work. Kristie, a white freshman in honors classes, is highly critical: "She is not really interested in [her job]; she doesn't really care. . . . If she did care, the class would actually be learning something. . . . This is coming from an honors class, and I just think it is pathetic to see this happening. . . . I guess it is understandable that she has a life outside of school, but how hard it is to read just a little bit of the [homework] questions and make sure? Maybe just one random question from a person's paper just to make sure [the answers] are real." Students feel that their effort is not taken seriously, which undermines the notion that they can maximize their school success by trying hard.

In interviews with me students indicted many other teachers for similarly lax and ineffective teaching behavior. Their complaints typically focused on two commonplace practices. One, as the science teacher illustrated, is assigning homework and not grading it. A variant of this practice is assigning weekly essays, worksheets, or chapter notes, which the teacher collects. However, instead of responding to all of them, he or she selects only a handful at random to actually read and grade. Students are particularly incensed when those scores factor heavily into their final grades. The approach is problematic because students receive no helpful feedback on how to improve their work over the course of the term. It also means that neglecting just one assignment might cost the student dearly in the end. As Claire explains, "you do, like, 500 million [worksheets], and let's say you don't do one. If she luckily picks that one, it goes as you missing a fifth of your homework instead of being like a millionth, because she gives a *ton*."

The students I talked to at Comprehensive High feel slighted by such practices. They sense that these teachers do not care enough about them to bother reading the assigned schoolwork. Students often respond to this injustice by reducing their own effort and dedication in these classes. Not only do they submit outlandish answers on assignments that are sure never to be read, they also commonly copy each others' work, even to the point of arranging in advance who in the group will write the first essay, the second essay, and so on. Not all students cheat, of course, but those who do tend to feel justified because they are simply matching the teacher's own level of involvement. At Alternative High cheating carries social and moral penalties for students, but at Comprehensive High it is acceptable and has no social stigma. There is no *cheater* identity story at this school because students believe that a teacher's unfair grading practices and laziness warrant a parallel response.

Students also dislike a second practice: when teachers require classmates to grade each other's tests. It is easy to understand why a teacher might use this option. In-class grading dramatically reduces his after-hours workload, which is a burden even at the best of times. In a few minutes a class can grade a batch of papers that might take hours for a teacher to grade on his own. However, students view this practice as yet another sign that he does not care enough about them to hold them accountable for their learning.

Multiple-choice or math tests are most likely to be graded by classmates. When using this approach, a teacher typically asks students to pass their test answer sheets to another student. That student is supposed to write her own name on the sheet she is grading so that the teacher can keep track of who grades whom. The teacher then reads aloud the correct answers as students score the tests. But Kristie explains how easily this system can be abused: "Well, we are supposed to switch, but I always just make up some fake name and write it on the side of the paper—[the name of] who is grading my paper—and then just grade my own and fill in all the answers." As I noticed during my classroom observations, some students simply chose to trade test sheets with a friend. Although I was not close enough to witness any students "helping" their friends get the correct answer, I did notice how easily they could have done so.

Effort Only Matters Sometimes

In classes run by lazy teachers, students are not rewarded for diligent effort and good learning habits. They can receive good grades by cheating or turning in nonsense homework, and there are no obvious negative consequences for doing so. Mrs. Brookings, the AP English teacher, admits that this is true: "The kids also seem to—.Um, they don't always do their own work. And that makes me a little bummed out." But even in classes with a engaged teacher, effort may only get a student so far. If a class is your "weak point," trying hard will not necessarily enable you to master difficult material. As Flor says, "I'm trying really hard in chemistry right now, and I'm not even getting a B. I'll listen, but I just don't understand anything he's talking about. The only things I can do, probably, is the homework and the lab work and labs, but when it comes to tests I can't do it all. Even if you do try, you might not get what you want."

These conflicting messages reinforce a specific combination of the cultural ideas of success-through-intelligence and success-through-effort. At Comprehensive High students believe that school success has an upper limit and that each student's limit is different because each person's intelligence is different. The smarter you are, the more potential you have for school success. Working hard in school can help a student get closer to her personal success limit, but effort alone will never break through that boundary. Students' experiences with lazy teachers strengthens their understanding that effort only matters sometimes. Intelligence, on the other hand, always matters.

4

Separate Worlds, Separate Concerns

AP versus College-Prep Track at Comprehensive High

Comprehensive High's Academic Performance Index (API) score at the time of my research was slightly higher than 700 but nearly a hundred points below California's goal of 800 for all its schools.[1] By comparison, the state's average API that year was 687, meaning that the school's standing was a bit higher than average, although it remained well beneath the state goal. As I mentioned in chapter 3, the school is close to state averages in terms of racial composition, percentage of the student body that is socioeconomically disadvantaged, and percentage of the student body that comprises English language learners. In other words, Comprehensive High is an average California school, which may contribute to students' resounding concerns about the notion of average. In their interviews with me, I learned that, for them, *C* grades are outward markers of average academic performance. They mark an average person who has average aspirations and who will achieve average success. And average success is acceptable at Comprehensive High.

The *Average Joe* Identity Story

When I arrived on campus to begin fieldwork, the administration, not surprisingly, did not tout the school's average characteristics. Rather, the principal emphasized the progress it had made in increasing its API score and the structural changes implemented to enhance learning and academic performance. Nonetheless, in interviews, students at Comprehensive High continually returned to the notion of average, using it as a reference point for talking about school success. In 2012, six years after my classroom observations and interviews, I ask the principal about this tendency. She responds,

That is very interesting because one of the things I noticed when I did this needs analysis [in 2003–4, just before she became principal], it was so obvious everywhere, . . . in the events that they put on, in the attitudes of the kids, in the expectations of the teachers and the parents, that average or mediocre was okay. "That is what we are; we are a mediocre school." . . . That was one of the impetus to make a lot of the changes. . . . The image that was being projected to the community was "we can't really do any better than this. This is about as good as we can get."

In interviews, students use *average* to gauge individual success but do not apply it to their school as a whole, which is how the principal describes her first impression of Comprehensive High. Some tell me it is important to demonstrate that one is at least average and not below average. For others, it's more critical to prove that one is above average rather than simply average. In all cases, however, the point of comparison is with an identity story that I call *Average Joe*. This identity story features a student who receives Cs but not Ds in her academic classes. Ds indicate that a person is below average. Thus, an Average Joe doesn't carry an overall C average (a 2.0 GPA), which would allow a student to receive a few unacceptable Ds counterbalanced with a few As and Bs. In his discussion of the low-performance report card (figure 1.1), Doug, a white junior in college-prep classes, explains this distinction:

DOUG: He's passing all the classes at least by minimum, but it's not what you'd normally want to pass by.

LISA NUNN: What would you normally want to pass by?

DOUG: At least a C.

L. N.: Why is a C better than a D?

DOUG: Because it shows that you are average. Even average at least shows you're not one of the people that doesn't try. It's better being average than below average; that's logical.

Doug's attitude is very common at Comprehensive High. In fact, when he says that the minimum desirable grade is a C, he expresses a more precise threshold than I at first recognized. I had assumed that he was referring to all variations of a C, including C-plus and C-minus, which is why I contrasted Cs and Ds in my follow-up question. However, I came to discover that at Comprehensive High the dividing line between acceptable and unacceptable grades lies precisely between Cs and C-minuses.

Kristie, a white freshman in honors classes, is instructive on this point. Responding to the same report card, she asserts, "A D in English I also think is unacceptable because most teachers will at least give you a decent grade in writing, at least a C. . . . and a C in history—again, it just depends if they are interested in the subject. I don't think that is as bad. And also because it is steady. It's not like a C-minus where you are close to getting a D. The C is more in the middle. So it's not like you are about to go right downhill. I think that's okay." Whether they are in college-prep or AP courses, students at Comprehensive High continually refer to Cs as minimally acceptable grades and C-minuses as below acceptable.

Of course, it is possible that an *Average Joe* might receive an occasional B or an A, particularly in elective or physical education classes, which are considered easier than core academic ones. However, *Average Joe* is a steady Cs kind of character. Another characteristic of the identity story is that this person cares about her future to at least a minimally acceptable degree. As we heard Kathleen say in chapter 3, "to work for what you want, you can't go [through] high school with Ds. Unless you want to actually not go anywhere in life." She condemns the D on the anonymous report card as "bad" and "unacceptable." According to Kathleen and others at Comprehensive High, receiving Cs rather than Ds signals that an *Average Joe* does want to make something of her life, even if her aspirations are not higher than average.

The *Trained Dog* Identity Story

A second identity story at Comprehensive High emerges almost exclusively in interviews with AP and honors students. I call this identity story *trained dog.* This is a student who enjoys great school success simply by knowing how to execute assignments and tests according to a teacher's criteria. René, a Latino junior in AP classes, describes this identity story in his response to the high-performance report card (figure 1.2). When I ask him if the anonymous student seems intelligent, he replies, "The problem with doing that from a report card is that it's so hard because they could be book smart, know how to take a test, be like a trained dog, and know the answers, and know what to give—but when asked themselves they may not know exactly what to do." Unlike students at Alternative High, who suspect that this anonymous student might have cheated to get such good grades, René posits that the student might have achieved legitimate yet not highly respectable school success by mastering school skills as a dog masters tricks. For René, memorizing material to score well on tests does not count as admirable intelligence. It is not as valuable as deeper learning, even though it is clearly tied to test performance.

At Comprehensive High, a truly brilliant student is called a *genius* and is a highly admirable character. However, she is often described in superhuman terms, making this an irrelevant identity story for most students. When students describe themselves to me, they do not invoke the *genius* as a point of reference. However, the character does enter the conversation now and then when they describe other, usually hypothetical people. For example, when I ask

Kathleen which is more important for good grades, understanding the material or working really hard, she replies, "I think working really hard. . . . Not a lot of people are born geniuses, they have to work for it." As an identity story, the genius is something of a myth at Comprehensive High.[2] It is reserved for a person who is so amazingly intelligent that she expends hardly any effort yet receives excellent grades. Only one student I interviewed, René, claims to actually know a *genius:* "One of my friends is just, like, genius level; she passed AP calculus during the summer between eighth and ninth grade and she is, like— she could graduate right now." Yet even this example is portrayed as somewhat superhuman: how many people can pass an AP calculus exam after having only finished middle school?

Although the students I interviewed do not negotiate the identities of most acquaintances against the *genius* character, AP and honors students at Comprehensive High do invoke the *trained dog* story when they describe themselves and fellow students. Claire, a white honors freshman, offers a similar response to René's when I ask her whether the anonymous student in figure 1.2 seems to be intelligent: "I would say that they are smart, but I definitely think that if you—I don't believe so much in being smart or stupid. I believe that if you go to class and you're there and you're paying attention, it's not a matter of how smart you are; it's a matter of how well you know the information that the teacher is telling you and you can regurgitate it onto a test and get an *A*. So I think it's not a matter of being smart." Taking a moment to figure out her thoughts about the role of intelligence, in the end she asserts that, for a trained dog, shallowly acquired knowledge is not intelligence at all.

Mrs. Brookings, the AP English teacher, acknowledges that some classes demand a trained dog performance, though she does not indicate that her own class is one of them. When I ask her what it takes for a student to earn good grades, she responds, "In my class in particular they have to be a good writer. But I also think that—I have seen that kids have to be good memorizers. Unfortunately." She laments that her students are grade-driven rather than genuinely interested in learning: "Kids take the AP classes because they want the weighted grades, and they don't have the passion . . . not just wanting to do well for the *A* but wanting to do well because they got satisfaction from understanding. . . . They become robotic. It's not as great." The difference she articulates between having passion and being a robot is similar to the difference that students describe between having "real" intelligence and being a *trained dog.*

The *trained dog* is an identity story born of the cultural idea of success-through-effort: any student can achieve school success by trying hard enough. This character does just that: she tailors her effort, trying precisely hard enough to fit the criteria of assessment. Wider approaches to learning or deeper acquisitions of knowledge are not necessary to school success, and thus the trained dog does not pursue them. She lacks creativity and a vivid personality. I suspect that this negative portrayal of legitimate school success is a response to the correct-answer–oriented teaching styles I observed at Comprehensive High. It is not surprising that students such as René and Claire, who consider themselves to be intelligent, might prefer to view high intelligence as the lively, dynamic root of curiosity and creativity rather than a dull mechanism for producing correct answers. Perhaps they disdain *trained dogs* in part because they are frustrated by teachers who channel intellectual curiosity into correct-answer formats. This also helps explain why the identity story exists chiefly among honors and AP students, not among college-prep students.

Conflicting Logics of Effort and Intelligence

Claire's immediate response to the report card in figure 1.2 is an acknowledgement that *A*s in AP courses are evidence of high intelligence. Her first impression is not that the anonymous student is trying hard; instead, she calls the student "smart," a response that clearly links to the cultural idea of success-through-intelligence. However, as she continues to consider the grades on the report card, she rather aggressively abandons success-through-intelligence in favor of the logic of success-through-effort. A breath or two after she recognizes that the student is smart, she claims that anyone can master the skills to achieve an *A* and claims that she does not "believe in being smart or stupid."

Claire's awkward mishmash of explanations might arise in part from the conflicting messages that the school as an organization sends to students (see chapter 3). In many of my interviews at Comprehensive High, students offer similarly confused explanations about effort and intelligence. In this light, we can see how the *trained dog* identity story both embodies and resolves these conflicting logics. At a school where success is understood to be limited by a student's intelligence level, high-achieving students feel threatened by the idea that someone might achieve high success without having what René calls "real" intelligence.

René's Creativity Makes Him Smarter Than a *Trained Dog*

The *trained dog* is a story of success predicated largely on rote efforts such as memorization and regurgitation of information, and at Comprehensive High success-through-effort alone is incongruent with widely held beliefs about what it takes to get good grades. Yet even as the *trained dog* identity story seems to conflict with these beliefs, it resolves the tension. A *trained dog* is not unintelligent. Rather, the intelligence he possesses is the wrong kind of intelligence because it does not inspire awe or envy. The identity story supports the notion that it is possible to be highly intelligent but not receive excellent grades.

René takes personal comfort in this notion. In our interview, he draws on multiple sources of information about his abilities: family, friends, teachers, and grades. The tensions he experiences in his success identity are rooted in ideas that are specific to Comprehensive High. He perceives himself as possessing a level of real intelligence as opposed to a *trained dog*'s mere book smarts. He sees himself more along the lines of what his principal calls a "creative thinker":

> There are some students—and we find this a lot with high-performing students—they love the rules and regulations. They want to know *exactly* what you want them to do. They love to be successful within a structure. And then there are other students, who will probably be more successful in life, who are very bright but, um, free thinkers, creative thinkers who hate the restrictions of a regular everyday schedule. . . . The book-smart kids are easy to recognize. They are the ones sitting in the front row with their highlighters out, with their stickies, and they are raising their hand a million times and they can't wait to get that assignment so they can get it done first. But then there is that other kid I was talking about . . . [who may] not be as concerned that much [with] what their grade looks like but be more interested in the creative process.

Although the principal paints such students in a positive light, suggesting that they "will probably be more successful in life," René is not so sure. This creates a tension in him because he feels intelligent yet his current grades show only mediocre success, which makes him doubt that his intelligence is all that high. Moreover, the principal believes that creative thinkers are not "concerned that much [with] what their grade looks like," but René is deeply concerned about his grades.

René is currently enrolled in two AP classes and one honors class (out of six total classes). At his school, the fact that he is taking half of his classes at AP/honors level means that he is smart. However, in our interview, he expresses disappointment because this year he is receiving the lowest report card grades of his high school career. He says, "Up until now I've had, like, almost straight As, except for the one B in [physical education], and then my freshman year I had straight As; sophomore year I had straight As except for a semester [when I had] one or two Bs." René is proud of his academic history, which is partly why his current grades distress him. Until now, his excellent grades have always reinforced his identity as a highly intelligent person.

At the time of our interview, more than halfway into the spring semester, René is holding a C in his math class (trigonometry-free calculus) and a C in his Spanish II class. These grades discourage him. In fact, the C in his math class is the first he's ever received, and he has been unable to raise the grade this term, despite his efforts. "It's a harder year," he explains. "It's the hardest one, and the one thing I don't like about it is it's the year that colleges look at the most, so I've been told." But even though René worries that his C in math will not look good to colleges, he does not discuss any strategies for rectifying or making up for it in other parts of his college application. His vague anxiety implies that he is not entirely confident about the little information he does possess about college admissions.[3] Instead, his feelings are anchored in the pervasive cultural wisdom of Comprehensive High, which views Cs as acceptable grades. Of course, many high-achieving students at the school hold themselves to higher standards, but they also tend to acknowledge that Cs are average and thus tolerable. C-minuses cross into unacceptable territory, where René is not in danger of going. Yet he continues to muse about his grades: "I don't know. It's not really too bad, I mean as an average, but since that's the year that colleges look at the most, so—" His voice trails off, giving me the impression that he's unsure whether or not disappointment is an appropriate response.

When I ask René where he would fall on 1-to-10 intelligence scale, he tells me he'd most likely be an 8. Still, he's not sure: "I'm definitely not a 5 because my grades—well, with grades, I've never been average, so I'm higher than that. But I've never had totally straight As all the time, so I wouldn't say that I'm a 10. But that's by book smarts, and if maybe for *real* intelligence, . . . I'd say I'm definitely more intelligent than average, but honestly I don't know what number I'd be past the second half. I'm somewhere in the second half, but don't know where I'd really fall."

Although he has difficulty pinpointing his own intelligence outside of school assessment, René believes that there is a critical distinction between real intelligence and the book smarts of a *trained dog*: "I don't remember who said it, but it was like: you're not really—those who are the most intelligent are those who realize how much they don't know. It *is* that way. Because there are different kinds of intelligence, because there is the book smart where you can read things and grasp the concepts and stuff, or there are those who can come up with a concept—those who get the bigger picture with bigger ideas." As he tries to articulate his success identity, René has difficulty reconciling the tension between these two types of intelligence. He wants to believe that he "gets the bigger picture with bigger ideas," but he also falls back on a belief in book smarts. Later in the interview he tentatively explains that his grades are an accurate reflection of his intelligence level because "it's not so much that I'm not trying, it's that I don't get it, which I guess shows that I'm not so smart in [math class] maybe."

Part of René's trouble is that his Cs are incongruent with what other people in his life believe about him. He tells me that his family and friends consider him to be very intelligent:

I have always had this reputation of being really smart and really, like, good at everything almost in a way. . . . It's, like, everyone—so I don't even know, even when I don't do so good in school, it's, like, people don't even see that. It's weird, they're just, like—I don't know, I don't know how to say it, it's almost like they don't see it or they don't believe it. Not so much that they don't believe it, but that they don't see it. They only look at the good, at what I'm doing. Almost. So I always have this reputation of being so smart, so good at stuff.

I ask him how he feels about this reputation, and he says, "I like it. It's a positive reputation, so I guess that's good. Maybe sometimes it's not so deserving, like when I'm not doing well [in school], but people tend to look past that." Again, René's rationale returns to grades, which he uses as evidence of his intellectual abilities. He characterizes people's high estimation of his cognitive talents as "not so deserving" in light of his lower grades this year. Thus, for the moment, he treats his grades as a more powerful indicator of his abilities than he does the assessment of people who "know me the best."

Grades, family, and friends are not the only sources of information that he draws on when he constructs his success identity. His teachers also play a key role. René considers himself to be a "favorite" of at least two of his current teachers. He believes that they like him because he is a good student with an exceptional, creative intellect. He is president of the school's art club, which garners him special treatment and privileges from the art teacher: "He doesn't care what I do, or whatever project I want to do, or some of the things I want to use or whatever. He won't let just, like, anyone do that."

René also believes that he is a favorite in his AP English class. Although my field notes do not mention any special treatment from the teacher, he is confident that he is among her favorites. Of course, his impression of their relationship is much more important to his success identity than whether or not my field notes confirm it. He says, "In English, me and the two girls who sit next to me, the teacher kind of likes us three a lot. She'll ask questions about how we feel about certain things, and she likes talking to us more. I don't think she grades easier on us, but she gives us more of a chance. She'll let me finish up something I didn't finish."

Interestingly, the special privileges that René believes he receives as a favorite can be seen as freedom from the constraints of a being a *trained dog*. In the case of the art teacher, René's good standing releases him from requirements for particular assignments. While the rest of the class might be instructed to compose an art project with certain materials or within certain limitations, he has permission to expand the boundaries of the assignment to accommodate his creative appetite. In AP English, René enjoys leniency in finishing up assignments, but even more he seems to relish the sense that the teacher takes him seriously. By soliciting his opinion and engaging him in personal conversations, Mrs. Brookings makes him feel like a person who has interesting insights, one who is not a *trained dog* or a memorization machine. In René's descriptions of his school success, these experiences are evidence that his teachers see him as a creative, intelligent, and interesting person. They allow him to see himself as smarter than a *trained dog*.

Stephanie's Verbal Acuity Makes Her Smarter than a *Trained Dog*

René's classmate Stephanie also feels superior to *trained dogs* but for very different reasons. A white junior in AP classes, she is his opposite in terms of current academic performance. At the moment, slightly more than halfway through the spring semester, she has a 4.17 GPA and the best grades she has received in all her years of high school. Stephanie explains that she has not always performed well in school. "I'm horrible in math, and I really don't like to do anything with that," she tells me early in our interview. She constructs her success identity around her strong suits—verbal communication and social interaction skills—and disavows the importance of math and science coursework. She does not see these subjects as critical to overall intelligence and success because "book smarts" and "memorizing things" are less valuable than the ability to "work with people" and "function out in society."

However, Stephanie is not entirely able to shield her success identity from the negative effects of her low academic performance in math and science. Last year, her final grade in algebra II was an *F*. She argues that she did not deserve it: "The teacher, towards the end of the year, decided she wasn't going to help me anymore because she didn't feel that I wanted it enough." According to Stephanie, this behavior was unfair: "I don't think it's her job to decide whether or not I wanted it or not. Rather, it's her job to teach the students to make sure they understand it." She claims that the teacher refused to give her individual help before or after school, which prevented her from passing the class. "How I feel about math in general, it's just hard for me to understand and hard for me to grasp it. I'm not saying that in her class that maybe I would have definitely had an *A* [but] . . . I didn't ditch class. I did all my homework. She just decided." However, Stephanie was able to retake the course over the summer and received an *A*.

Stephanie's math struggles are key to the tension she experiences in her success identity. In other classes she is able to leverage her outgoing personality and verbal agility to highlight her intellectual talents. She engages in class discussions and regularly initiates witty interactions with the AP English teacher. In this way she sees herself as much more intelligent than a merely "book smart" *trained dog*. Nonetheless, she acknowledges that her math difficulties limit not only her overall school success but also how intelligent she can assess herself to be. At Comprehensive High, there is a strong belief that "everyone has a weak point," so it might seem easy for Stephanie to accept this in herself. Yet because she is confident that the excellent grades of *trained dogs* do not reflect genuine intelligence, she feels a discord in her understanding of what grades do mean: "My history teacher, I know, definitely factors in effort and attitude. . . . It's nice to know that he recognizes that and . . . [adds] in how much you're involved. Because you can have people who really understand the material, but they never say a word in class. So they are not really involved in what is going on in the discussions, but maybe are really good at memorizing things. It doesn't really mean they understand in history how certain things have affected people."

In addition to being skeptical of students who are "really good at memorizing things," Stephanie emphasizes that "effort and attitude" and being "involved" are evidence of authentic learning and understanding. But what she describes as *involvement in class,* I characterize in my field observations as "verbally dominating class discussions," which I note that she does regularly. From Stephanie's perspective, such behavior demonstrates that she is engaged in learning the material. She thinks it is fair for teachers to count it alongside test performance to reward students like herself for being smarter than a *trained dog.* She says that her most recent history grade would have been a *C*-plus based on her test scores alone but that her participation raised it to a *B* and that she currently holds an *A.*

Stephanie constructs her success identity on measures of intellectual skills and effort that are not amenable to typical academic tests. While she reports spending only a modest amount of time doing homework outside of school (between one and a half and three hours a week), she describes herself as a hardworking student, focusing on what she calls "effort" during the school day instead of in her homework. Thus, despite having a relatively poor academic history, she bolsters a positive success identity. Likewise, she equates intelligence with verbal performance in non-school arenas. When I ask whether she feels smarter in her life inside or outside of school, she responds,

> My life outside of school, definitely. Like, my parents' friends—I love it when they come over for dinner and we'll have big conversations about things and they'll listen to me talk. . . . I like . . . working with people, getting to talk with people outside of school. . . . I know that people tell my parents [flattering] things, like about my sister and I, and my friends will tell me, and it just makes me feel a lot better than "Oh, I just got an A on my test," which really does make me feel good but at the same time it's, like, that's a grade, but this is what real people actually think.

Stephanie treats outside-of-school know-how as the most important indicator of her intelligence and success. Despite failing algebra II last year and her average-percentile score in math on the last CST exam, she claims, "I am plenty good in normal things I need to do in math. I mean, I could go out and be an accountant, and I'd have no problem. I know how to do stuff. A lady who works up the street, I helped her with mortgage stuff, and I know how to do all that. I've got a very successful career in something very involved in math even though I did very poorly in algebra II."

Later in the interview, she explains the relationship she sees between verbal skills and success in life: "Learning how to work with people is, I think, the most important [thing] anyone can do. I think how to work with people in a group successfully, learning how to be a leader, public speaking is very important, and I think learning how to give a first impression is probably the most important thing." These skills are not book smarts; they are outside the expertise of a *trained dog*, but Stephanie is certain that they vital. "If you make a bad impression—say, you're going on a job interview and the person doesn't read you very well: you're kind of quiet, you're not really open in talking—you don't get the job." Because she is more concerned about success in life beyond school than with success in school, she is able to maintain a positive success identity, including pride in her intelligence, despite her mediocre academic performance in previous years. Although she currently holds a 4.17 GPA, her cumulative average is much lower. She admits that last year she did not even reach a 2.0.

Yet despite her self-confidence, Stephanie is conflicted about the meaning of grades. She is aware that book smarts—and the good grades that come with them—have a payoff too. When I ask her whether or not intelligence matters in life, her response equates intelligence with good grades:

> It's going to matter to college. It's going to matter to the people hiring you. . . . Your grades are everything to your life. If you get poor grades and don't get into college and you don't get a great job, you can be struggling your whole life—unless you invent something great. Whereas people who get really good grades and are involved in their community or involved in the school and stuff, you're going to do really good in college and get a really good job, be successful—not that success comes with happiness, but, like, you're not having to worry about certain things all the time. You're a lot happier, spend more time with your family. I think it does measure success in life, intelligence. You have to be intelligent—or at least be able to get the grades to . . . [indicate] that you're intelligent—to prosper in life.

Although Stephanie says that her parents and friends would rank her intelligence at 9 or 10 on a 1-to-10 scale, she disagrees. "I would probably be an 8 because of math. I'm not very good at math, and I know it's something that is important in high school and something I know I'll have to take in college. So that's unfortunate." Here, she factors in school success, despite her certainty throughout our interview that book smarts do not reflect genuine intelligence. Her current college plans also reflect a modest view of her intellectual abilities: she plans to attend a local community college for two years and then transfer to a University of California campus. She is confident that starting out at a community college is the right first step, but her plans are a bit surprising because she does not face the financial obstacles that typically drive students to begin their higher education at a community college rather than a four-year institution. Presumably, she sees her low cumulative GPA as an obstacle to admission at a four-year college. Because her AP classes are clearly not a strategy to impress elite college admission boards with her high school transcript, I assume that she enrolls in AP English and history courses for more personal reasons: to counterbalance her poor performance in math and validate her success identity as a smart person.

Raul and Mackie Embrace *Average Joe*

I presented René and Stephanie side by side to demonstrate how individual students negotiate their own identities against available identity stories in order to fit unique concerns and dilemmas. Both of those students feel smarter than a *trained dog*, but that is where the similarity ends. They are from different ethnoracial and socioeconomic classes; one has the best grades of her life this year, while the other has the worst; and they experience completely different tensions in their success identities. While both resolve their tensions by favorably comparing themselves to *trained dogs*, they do so in distinct ways. Verbal involvement in class and being able to "function out in society" are not at all important to René's success identity. For Stephanie, however, they are the quintessential factors that prove she is superior to *trained dogs*.

Not all students at Comprehensive High show such concern with the *trained dog* identity story. Others, such as Raul and Mackie, draw more heavily on the *Average Joe* story as they construct their success identities. Both are among a handful of college-prep students I interviewed who largely embrace this story. When I asked Raul, a Latino sophomore, "In your mind, what is a good report card?" he told me he is pleased with his 2.56 GPA: "For me what I think—as long as I have above a C, I'll be good." Later, as we discuss standardized tests, he makes it clear that he likes to be the one who opens his scores when they are mailed home.

RAUL: If I see they are good grades, I'll give them to my dad. If they're not, I'll throw them away.
L. N.: What's good for you?
RAUL: Average.

Students such as Raul express contentment with average school performance, which on report cards usually takes the form of *C*s (at a minimum) and on CST exams a score ranked "proficient" (a test-specific term that among Comprehensive High students equals "average"). In general, they believe that *C*s show effort on their schoolwork and indicate an acceptable level of school success.

Another of these students is Mackie, a mixed-race sophomore, whose favorite subject is math because it is "easy" for him. He says he is always able to complete his math assignments during class. He reports sitting down for homework in his other subjects "maybe two times out of the week" for "twenty minutes to half an hour." Mackie's most recent report card boasts two *B*s and four *C*s, and he says that he is satisfied with these grades: "They were pretty good. I liked them. They were like *C* or above, so that's pretty good." Throughout the interview, he refers to the dividing line between *C*s and *C*-minuses as the difference between acceptable and unacceptable grades, thus espousing the widely shared understanding at Comprehensive High.

Mackie's parents seem to share this perspective. He tells me that, during the previous year, they punished him for poor grades.

MACKIE: They grounded me and made me do my work. So I got my grades up and they let me back out.

L. N.: How high did your grades have to be before you could go out again?

MACKIE: *C*s or higher. That's average.

Since then he has been able to maintain a *C* minimum on his report cards, and he feels pleased with this progress. He admits that his parents did a good thing by grounding him "because if they didn't do that, I wouldn't be able to graduate and get all my credits and stuff." Mackie acknowledges that he will need a high school diploma in order to get a decent job after graduation, though he also understands that higher education is the real key to a good job: "You need to go to college after that, but you still get better jobs if you get a high school diploma." When I ask if he has concrete plans for college, he responds, "I'm planning to go, like, part time. I don't want to go, like, full time. I won't be able to finish my work. It's too much." Mackie is hoping for a career in professional skateboarding, though he is unsure whether this will materialize. Still, after high school, he plans to "try to get into skating; I'll get some sponsors so they could put me into contests, and I would try to go pro after a while." At the same time he expects to be attending community college because "you need an education because, like, if something goes wrong, then you have to have a backup plan." Mackie's future plans are well aligned with the *Average Joe* identity story, which includes a desire to make something of your life, including working at a decent, respectable job. Though his aspirations to be a professional skateboarder are glamorous, he plans to turn to something else if he cannot earn an adequate living from it.

At first glance, Mackie does not seem to experience much tension in his success identity. He complacently embraces *Average Joe*. He's comfortable with the hour or so a week he spends on homework to earn acceptable school success. He describes his four Cs and two Bs as "pretty good" and tells me, "I liked them." Mackie places himself at 6 on the 1-to-10 intelligence scale and says that the person in the world who knows him best, his mother, would place him at 7. He believes that others would place him at "6 or 7," so there is fairly strong congruence in his perception of how smart he is. This seems fitting for an *Average Joe* at Comprehensive High, where modest intelligence is understood to garner modest school success.

However, the relationship between school success and intelligence is not quite straightforward for Mackie. He explains that he places himself at 6 "because I haven't tried in a lot of my classes." His view of his intelligence seems to be tangled with his opinion of his effort. While he is happy with his grades, he says, "I think they're lower than . . . [they] could be." If he were to try really hard, he believes he "could get better grades." This is probably true. Last year when he was grounded, he was able to improve his grades simply by buckling down when his parents "made me do my work." It is reasonable to think that his grades might improve even further if he were to spend more than an hour a week on schoolwork. According to this logic, by working harder in school and earning better grades, Mackie might be able to see himself as higher than a 6.

Like René and Stephanie, Mackie uses his grades to help him assess how intelligent he is. He is an *Average Joe* who might perform better and feel smarter if he were to try harder in school. Still, this does not seem to create tension in his success identity. However, a potential tension does emerge when he talks about intelligence more broadly. When I ask Mackie if intelligence matters in life, he agrees that it does but is unable to immediately articulate why.

L. N.: Does intelligence matter? Is it better to be more intelligent in life?

MACKIE: Yeah.

L. N.: Yeah? What's better? What does it get me?

MACKIE: Well—I don't know.

L. N.: That's okay. Can you think of anything that's better about it?

MACKIE: Just knowing more stuff, just knowing, like, what's going on. If you don't know anything, it sucks.

L. N.: So if you took brain vitamins tomorrow and got smarter, how would your life be different?

MACKIE: [*pause*] I'd probably, like—I don't know, probably think about stuff more. [*his voice brightens*] Like, about skating, I'd probably be, like, "I don't want to do this, I want to do something else," and stop skating. I don't know. It would probably be different; . . . it would be way different. If you know more stuff you'd just probably change a lot more.

In other words, while Mackie is content with his *Average Joe* school success and life aspirations, he imagines that he would not be so content if he were more intelligent. He does not express anything in our interview that suggests that he feels conflicted about this situation. Nonetheless, I describe it as a potential tension because of the way in which he views his effort as evidence of his intelligence. Not only does he indicate that he is a 6 because he does not try very hard in school, but he also tells me that he believes a person can become more intelligent by working at it: "Start doing your work a lot more, then you learn more stuff. Read more books and you know more stuff." Here, he defines *intelligence* as acquired knowledge (although at other moments during the interview he uses other definitions). Thus, we might describe Mackie as a person who is settling for *Average Joe* but feels capable of working his way to higher success. For the moment he does not express discontent, yet he imagines the possibility.

5

Elite Charter High

Intelligence plus Initiative Bring School Success

Elite Charter High is located in an upper-middle-class, largely white, residential neighborhood. Although it is a high-performing school with much to be proud of, it is not the star of its district. Another high school upstages it dramatically in terms of academic performance, placement of graduates in elite colleges, and state-of-the-art facilities. As one might expect, the district boundaries around what I will call Superstar High enclose some of the most valuable real estate in the state (and the country), meaning that funding and social networks from its parent base allow the school to maintain and build its reputation and standing. It is a public school to which wealthy parents in the area consider sending their children as an alternative to private education.

During our interviews, students at Elite Charter High often refer to Superstar High in their discussions of their own high school experiences. However, few claim to have friends who go there (which would give them some inside knowledge), so they rely on stereotypes and well-known facts. I commonly heard comments such as "Well, it's not like everyone here gets a new Porsche for every *A* they get on their report card like they do over at Superstar High." While the Elite Charter High students are, by and large, proud of their school, they are also quite aware that they are overshadowed by a "better" high school populated by wealthier and more privileged teenagers.

This is not to imply that Elite Charter High students struggle economically. Most of them do not. According to the 2000 U.S. Census, the median home value in its portion of the school district is just under 340,000 dollars (compared to 445,000 dollars in the Superstar High area).[1] The state of California classifies only 5 percent of the student body as "socioeconomically disadvantaged."[2] In addition, most Elite Charter High students come from well-educated homes: 91 percent of students have parents who attended college, according to self-reported student data provided by the school.

Because it is a charter school, Elite Charter High has more freedom than non-charter schools do in its approach to structuring education. It makes use of this freedom in two key ways, both of them designed to foster students' intense engagement with academics. First, the school operates on a four-block schedule. This means that, each semester, students take only four classes as opposed to the standard six. School days are organized as four class periods, each an hour and a half long, with an additional twenty-five minutes of homeroom time twice a week—an opportunity for the homeroom teacher to build relationships with a single group of students and keep tabs on their progress. The rationale behind block scheduling is similar to Comprehensive High's: that longer periods allow students to engage closely with class material without disruption. Additionally, only three of the four classes each semester are core academic classes. This allows students to focus on a few subjects in depth rather than spread their mental energy across several diverse subjects. Elite Charter High boasts that the material covered in a single semester at its school is equivalent to a full year of material at a typical high school. This belief is reflected in its course credit distribution as well. Students earn eighty class credits in a school year for completing eight courses, while other high school students earn sixty for completing six courses over the year.

Second, Elite Charter High does not have sports teams or the accompanying cheerleading squads, pep rallies, homecoming dances, and so on that embody school spirit on many American high school campuses. For this reason, it appeals to students who dislike the popularity contests driven by athleticism and beauty that are common features of typical high school social environments.[3] Such environments largely exclude bright students who are interested in academics and excel in schoolwork, but Elite Charter High provides a social atmosphere that allows "smart kids" (in the words of James, a junior) to be who they are without any social stigma attached.[4] At Elite Charter High being smart is seen as cool.

A Place Where AP Is King

Elite Charter High's administration focuses on rigorous academics, and my observations of classroom life support James's assertion that this school is a place where "smart kids" can pursue academics without social stigma. I chose to observe an AP chemistry class and a college-prep chemistry class, with the intention of creating a balanced interview sample between AP and non-AP students, as I did at Comprehensive High. In addition, I planned to talk to students whose academic lives and identities are aligned with each track. I soon found, however, that only one of the students I interviewed from the college-prep chemistry class, Mitchell, actually thinks of himself as a non-honors/AP student. Even though all the others are taking college-prep chemistry, at least one of their other classes this semester is at honors or AP level. At Elite Charter High, a student's academic bragging rights are not based on whether or not she takes honors/AP courses. Rather, it is a question of how many she takes and how many As she can get in them. A typical Elite Charter High student is at least partly an honors-level student: more than 60 percent of juniors and seniors take an AP exam, and many more take honors and AP courses.

This is not to say that every student is enrolled in these classes. Mitchell, a junior, has never taken any. So in order to gain a comprehensive view of the school, I decided to observe in a third classroom. To accommodate my request for a non-college-prep course, the principal arranged to have me observe the remedial English class. It is comprised of only eight students: five are Latinos who are categorized as English language learners, and three are white males who suffer from learning disabilities or struggle with reading and writing. None is enrolled in honors courses or plans to be, according to the remedial English teacher, Mrs. Belfry. Three of the eight students agreed to be interviewed. All are English language learners, and two are planning to attend college after graduating from high school, though neither seems aware that she will not have a high school transcript that qualifies her for most four-year schools. Of course, that does not preclude them from attending a community college, so their aspirations for higher education can still be realized.

The voices of these remedial English students and details of their classroom life are largely absent from my chapters on Elite Charter High because, as Mrs. Belfry acknowledges, this class is "a separate universe" within the school. Only 2 percent of the student body comprises English language learners, and Mrs. Belfry explains that Elite Charter High has never provided them with a "sheltered or scaffolded or leveled class based on language ability" before this year: "We don't have the population here for that," though other schools in the district do. According to Mrs. Belfry, the school is "just beginning to accept the notion that there are students coming into our school who lack basic literary skills." The class I observed was Elite Charter High's very first language class geared toward such students. In the ten years since the school opened, "our school, being a school of choice, . . . somehow got away with not servicing language learners." This class seems to be the exception that proves the rule at Elite Charter High.

The school's general population can be characterized as high-performing. The school's API score is more than 130 points higher than either Alternative High's or Comprehensive High's. In my interviews, students in the AP and college-prep chemistry classes described a climate of fierce competition over grades and test scores. The AP chemistry teacher, Mr. Fischer, expresses dismay about this dynamic: "They compare each other's grades all the time. And they base their self-worth off of how well they are doing in the course *all the time*. It's what they do." In a place where "smart kids" are free to revel in their academic prowess, high achievement seems to have become an arena for competition as well as jealousy and heartache, as I will describe later in this chapter.

Intelligence Is Requisite to Success

At Elite Charter High, the local wisdom about school success posits that intelligence is critical and requisite to earning good grades. In some ways, this is similar to what I found at Comprehensive High: effort alone is not enough. When I ask Mrs. Jones, the college-prep chemistry teacher, whether she believes that students can earn all As if they try hard enough, she responds, "I would disagree. Because there is always going to be some academic component . . . in chemistry [and] if you can't master that language, you know, you are never going to get an A on the test. It is just not going to happen. You can easily get by with a C simply because there are opportunities to show what you know, but I don't think just effort is enough. That basic 'A for effort' is just— ninth graders sometimes come in with that attitude but they learn quickly that it doesn't work here."

Students echo Mrs. Jones's assertion that that the intellectual ability to master course content is essential to earning As. Rebecca, a white sophomore who is taking three honors and AP courses this semester, tells me, "Last year I had geometry honors, and that was probably one of the hardest math classes ever. I was probably studying for it three hours a night last year . . . and I still walked out of that class with a B-plus even though I tried. . . . I mean I had tutoring; I went to all of the after-school stuff; everything. And I just couldn't get it to an A."

Chase, a white junior enrolled in one AP course this semester, is taking Mrs. Jones's college-prep chemistry class. On his most recent report card he had a B in both chemistry and pre-calculus, despite studying for seven to eight hours a week: "You know, first semester, chemistry was kind of hard for me and pre-calc still is. So I think a B is about right. I was hoping for an A, but I think . . . [a B] reflects well where my knowledge is in the subject." Chase does not feel conflicted about his B grades because he recognizes that he has not successfully mastered the content in those two courses. Importantly, at Elite Charter High Bs are seen as the minimum level of acceptable school success, as opposed to Comprehensive High, where Cs are the minimum. Chase is typical of students at his school when he asserts, "I think that if you put in the effort, you can get at least a B in all the core [academic] classes."

At first glance, this tenet sounds strikingly similar to the cultural wisdom at Comprehensive High: that a student must have the intellectual ability to do well in a class, even though trying hard can help bring one's grade up to some extent. However, ideas about achieving success are actually quite distinct at the two schools. The key difference lies in each school's understanding of effort. Unlike Comprehensive High students, Elite Charter High students do not express a belief that effort only matters sometimes. Instead, they are convinced that effort is an important part of achieving school success. Further, when they describe the kind of effort that successful students engage in, they depict it as much more than simply completing homework or memorizing concepts correctly for a test. At Elite Charter High, the effort that helps a student earn top grades is better described as initiative.

Initiative: A Particular Type of Effort

Like Mrs. Jones, Mr. Fischer, the AP chemistry teacher, does not believe that hard work is enough to garner *A* grades, but he does think that it plays a role: "I don't necessarily think that just effort is going to bring about an *A*. I do think that effort along with correct coaching, assessment of coursework, you know, assessment of progress can bring about an *A*." When I ask what he means by "assessment of progress," he replies, "Just coming back to the kids and saying what they did right and what they did wrong. And then remediation by the teachers, by the students, by the parents. Making sure homework is done correctly, not just done. That test problems that are missed are reviewed, . . . that kind of stuff, where they actually take initiative in what they have learned rather than, say, repetition."

Both chemistry teachers use the word *initiative* to describe the approach that successful students take in their schoolwork. This is how Mrs. Jones defines the word in her interview: "Somebody who is thinking about what is going on in class outside of class. Like a student who will come up to me and tell me, 'On the way in I was listening, my mom was making me listen to NPR,' or whatever, 'and I heard *this*.' Or they bring in a newspaper clipping. Or they ask me a question: 'I heard something somewhere about *this*, what does *this* mean?'" Initiative involves going above and beyond classroom tasks and becoming genuinely interested in the subject matter. Yet it also means a willingness to work hard. When I ask Mrs. Jones to describe students who earn great grades and truly deserve them, she says, "Those particular students, certainly they have a natural, innate ability in science. And they are really interested in the topic. So they ask questions; they help expand their own knowledge and help expand the knowledge of those students around them. And they also put the time and effort in whenever they struggle." She does not shy away from asserting that her top students are highly intelligent: they have "natural, innate ability." However, they also clearly show initiative. They are "really interested," ask questions, and expand "their own knowledge." Importantly, they are also motivated to work through any problems they have in understanding the material.

Although the students I interviewed do not consistently use the word *initiative*, their descriptions of the role of effort in earning good grades mesh with their teachers' definitions of the term. For example, in response to the high-performance report card in figure 1.2, Rebecca says, "It looks like they are challenging themselves more with the AP courses and the physics . . . and it also shows that they strive for excellence. They are working hard." For Rebecca, *A*s in AP courses do not come easily. She reports spending twenty hours a week on homework outside of school, and such striving for excellence does not always pay off with *A*s. Nonetheless, she portrays herself as a student who takes initiative in her schoolwork: "[In geometry last year] I had tutoring; I went to all of the after-school stuff; everything." This is the kind of effort that befits a successful student at Elite Charter High, and Rebecca wants very much to be successful in school: "Honestly when I'm doing a project, I'm not thinking, 'Oh, I just want to make this look nice.' I'm thinking, 'Oh, I want that *A*,' you know. So I'm thinking more on the level of intelligence and getting a reward for that hard work."

Adam, a white junior who is taking three AP classes this semester, offers a description of initiative that goes a step further than after-school tutoring: "If the success [that you are aiming for] is an *A*, then there are a lot of things you need to change. Not just the way you study, or the way that you come to school on time. You have to change how late you go to bed, how you eat, and then how you let the emotions take control of you." In contrast with Adam's comprehensive picture of what a student with initiative must be willing to do to achieve school success, Mr. Fischer's depiction is limited to the realm of school. I ask him to describe students who earn great grades and truly deserve them.

> It's a kid who came in and said, "Well, I tried these problems and I got these five and I didn't get these two, three, or seven," it doesn't matter [how many]. "Here's what I tried and I don't understand why the book answer is not what I'm getting." And then they review those questions; they come back and say, "Well, now I'm on these. I'm struggling with this portion." Then come test day they get a 98 percent or a 103 percent because they have tried every possible avenue. So it is an effort thing, but it is also—my definition—an intelligence thing where they are reviewing their skill set, saying, "What is it that I do well? What is it that I can't do well?" and focusing on what they can't do well. Only because they put the time in to see what they don't know.

Intelligence and Initiative

Mr. Fischer sees initiative as a version of effort that goes beyond repetition of concepts and skills. It entails a high level of motivation to learn and master course material and the willingness to try "every possible avenue" to bring one's skills and knowledge up to the *A* range. For him, initiative is "an intelligence thing" in addition to involving hard work. Several of the students I talked to agree. Denise, a white sophomore who is taking two AP classes this semester, explains what she looks for when she is trying to figure out how smart a classmate might be: "It's in how much they want, really. I mean, like, I don't watch people and say, 'Oh, they're dumb.' But if they tried hard in school and, like, did their homework and actually got interested—it's not just doing your homework and studying for tests, but *wanting* to know more about the subject." For Denise, intelligence is evident when a person takes an eager interest in learning new things: "When I think of intelligence, I think of how knowledge—or how curious you are." In her eyes, "wanting to know more about the subject" is part of trying hard and doing homework.

Some students such as Denise perceive a tight connection between intelligence and initiative, while others describe the connection differently. Kevin, who is currently enrolled in two AP classes, says, "The more you do your homework, the more you actually try to understand instead of just trying to [get] it down, you end up getting a better grade on the test . . . but also, I guess, intelligence has a big role in there because you still have to be able to understand and learn and listen. . . . That helps you absorb everything and . . . ends up helping you study more and you get enthusiastic about the class because you actually know more about it." His explanation of hard work is entwined with a feeling of enthusiasm about the topic, something that is not entirely separate from intelligence.

Later in our interview, when I ask whether highly intelligent students have it easier in school, Kevin agrees that they do but not because they have to work less hard. He says that intelligence can be seen in a person's attitude and approach to schoolwork:

> Intelligence . . . [is] your motivation toward something—like, the more motivated you are toward something, the better you will achieve, the better your attitude is, and therefore the better your quality of life will be. . . . Academic kids, I would say that almost everything becomes more easier right when you [start talking about] that group because right away . . . your mindset is always positive. You always want—like the glass is half full, that sort of mindset. So once you go into a class, like, no matter what it is, you're always thinking positively, thinking of the things you are going to be able to do. Maybe [you will] be creative in an art class or

excel and do long math problems in a math class. . . . You are always kind of looking toward things that you can do and what you will enjoy out of it . . . and the subpoint under attitude would be confidence, which is a form of attitude, which also helps you succeed a lot.

Kevin understands that high intelligence fuels a "positive mindset" as well as motivation and enthusiasm for learning. In his eyes, these feelings make school an enjoyable and positive experience. They are also the driving force behind initiative.

Kevin's characterization of intelligence and initiative is fairly common at Elite Charter High, but not everyone sees them exactly as he does. Daphne, an AP classmate of Kevin's whom we met in the introduction, believes that high intelligence is evident in people who "show a passion" for learning about a topic. In her view, questioning the world around oneself is also evidence of high intelligence: "Thinking about . . . [a topic] can intrigue . . . [a person] enough that they ask about it, [and] then they have the interest and they want to increase their knowledge of that, so there is intelligence there." Although this passion might translate into effort in school, Daphne sees a looser relationship between intelligence and initiative than Kevin and Denise do. When she tells me what it takes to earn good grades at her school, she talks about "self-motivation," which can be characterized as initiative: "It is a matter of finding what works for you. Like, if taking notes helps you learn the material better, so the effort has to be put forth there too. . . . If someone wants to try, wants to do their homework, wants to try hard: like, if the teacher says, 'Read this,' they read it once, maybe twice if they need to."

Her comment seems to separate initiative from intelligence level. In fact, intelligence is absent from her explanation of what it takes to earn good grades. When I ask her whether students can earn all *As* if they try hard enough, she responds, "Yeah, definitely." However, later in our interview, when she is talking about outside-of-school activities, she makes it clear that "trying to learn" is an unmistakable sign of intelligence.

DAPHNE: Certain kids go to the beach, just lie on the beach, don't do anything. I like volunteering at the Nature Conservancy Center. I like teaching, volunteering, teaching people about the animals. So that's the thing. . . . That's an intelligence, [and] there's the motivation again. . . .

L. N.: It sounds like motivation and intelligence go hand in hand?

DAPHNE: Yes . . . again it's the trying to learn. If you believe in yourself, you go through it, then your intelligence will show more. It won't be, like, "Oh, let's go get high over the weekend." It'll be "Okay, let's go maybe [volunteer] or go the sporting tournament." Trying to bring yourself to the higher level. Trying to bring yourself up instead of just staying at a plateau or going down. The human wants to strengthen themselves.

For Daphne, a desire to learn and "bring yourself to the higher level" is evidence of a person's high intelligence, which she sees as a natural part of human experience. Yet her description of initiative in schoolwork is not wrapped up in intelligence. While she, Kevin, and Denise share some essential ideas about how intelligence arouses curiosity, enthusiasm, and passion for learning, they do not see initiative in schoolwork as connected to intelligence in the same ways. For Daphne, initiative is separate; she does not articulate a connection at all. Meanwhile, Kevin and Denise see school success as the result of high intelligence plus initiative that depends on that intelligence.

In contrast to Alternative High, the kind of effort that brings success at Elite Charter High seems to come from internal motivation. Whereas Alternative High students rely on classmates, family, and their homeroom teacher for the external "kicks" that keep them on track in school, Elite Charter High students describe initiative as rooted in an internal desire to learn and "challenge themselves," as Rebecca phrases it. Many Elite Charter High students do have families and friends who push them to strive for school success. However, in interviews with me and in the conversations I overheard in classrooms, they did not talk about success as dependent on external encouragement. In her comparative study of two elementary schools, Kathleen Wilcox demonstrates that the middle-class school she observed teaches students to find internal motivation and personal desire to execute their school tasks. In contrast, the working-class school relies on external rules, punishments, and rewards.[5] Thus, we might take the Elite Charter High students' attitudes about initiative as evidence of their socialization in middle- and upper-middle-class schools. Yet they don't simply believe that a person should be self-motivated about schoolwork, which Wilcox suggests is part of how students are trained for future professional occupations. Elite Charter High students also believe that intelligence is a requisite factor for school success.

School Structures Emphasize Intelligence

In the classes I observed, I found that students were seriously engaged with course material. As one might expect, the intensity and pace of the material presented vary according to the track. The AP chemistry class forges through concepts, equations, and lab work at a vigorous pace that is challenging for many students. Denise complains that Mr. Fischer "acts like we should already know it anyway. He teaches like he's teaching review." While this class may be a bit slower than a typical university's introductory class in chemistry, it nonetheless has the rhythm and instruction of a college-level course, true to the AP concept. Mr. Fischer is extremely knowledgeable about chemistry at a level well beyond the concepts he is responsible for in the curriculum.

Mrs. Jones takes a more measured pace with her college-prep class, patiently explaining concepts multiple times. She holds students to high standards, however, and is ready to encourage or chastise them as needed. For example, one morning as the class reviews for the next day's test, she scolds them about a previous test, reminding them that many students "got a basic algebraic formula wrong," solving for x incorrectly in $a = b/x$. "I want to hit the algebra teachers over their heads," she tells the class. Thus, while the content of college-prep chemistry is more fundamental than the content of AP chemistry and the pace is slower, the course still challenges many of the students enrolled in it.

Compared to the other two schools I studied, Elite Charter High is far more focused on academics and achievement. Preparing students for college is a primary goal. Mr. Fischer, who has been teaching here since 1999, comments, "Our school has always been, since I have been there, . . . it has been very college-driven. We have always had 96 percent of the kids go to [college]; 98 percent, that kind of thing, go on to a four-year or a two-year at least. Probably over 90 percent go to a four-year. So it has always been very postsecondary-school–driven." He says that students are "grade-driven," concerned not just about going to college but about "transcript building" so that they will be able to get into a "good" college. They worry tremendously about their grades.

Several structural elements of everyday school life contribute to Elite Charter High's emphasis on academics and achievement. As I mentioned, it uses some of the freedom that charter schools enjoy to structure the educational experience of its students in ways that maximize their engagement with academics. The school is not touted as a place where anyone can learn and succeed, as Alternative High is. Rather, both students and administration are proud that Elite Charter High is a place where intelligent students come to thrive. Although any student who lives in the district can apply for the open lottery to enroll here, the school's brochure encourages students to apply if they are interested in "rigorous curriculum" and "a college focused atmosphere with high expectations."

The school structures AP courses to be a ubiquitous feature of campus life. Receiving high grades in AP courses is considered to be an intellectual accomplishment, and this creates a competitive environment among high-achieving students. As Mr. Fisher remarks, "They compare each other's grades all the time." Students agree. Rebecca says, "Like I said before, I am very competitive. . . . I'm more likely to push myself in the AP class because I'm surrounded by other competitive people. . . . I tend to lean more towards 'Oh, I want to be the smartest person in the class and I have to take all these hard courses to prove that.'" She is certainly not alone. I witnessed many moments when students took opportunities to publicly display and confirm their status as smart and high-achieving.

Often these moments emerged out of structured teaching practices. Mrs. Jones, for example, posts quiz and test scores on the classroom wall where students can not only find their own score but also browse among the scores of classmates to see how they compare. In Mr. Fischer's AP class, students are encouraged to review each other's test results and test papers to see which equations, formulas, and final answers are correct. This also has the effect of making classmates' test results public, particularly when students parade around the classroom "helping" groups of classmates by allowing them to view their test answers.

Likewise, in the AP class I saw many instances when students with correct answers were responsible for explaining their chemistry solutions to classmates. This elevates intelligent, successful students to a status closer to the teacher's. For example, one day I watch as a substitute teacher works through a complicated equation on the board. She asks, "Did everyone see how I did that?"

Several students cry out, "No!"

As the teacher explains the equation, I hear a good deal of mumbling and side discussion throughout the room. Then Steven raises his hand and calls out to her in a respectful voice, interrupting her explanation: "I'm sorry. There was a mistake up there." Jackie quickly follows Steven's lead, explaining to the teacher where the error lies, though she does not know what the correct answer should be. Now Daphne, Adam, James, and Ryan take center stage, loudly talking through the solution together.

"That's it!" Daphne announces and walks over to Jackie's table to explain the problem. Jackie then turns around and explains it to the group of students sitting behind her, and so it is disseminated around the room. The substitute teacher stands quietly to the side while Daphne and the others take over her task.

The pedagogy of both Mrs. Jones and Mr. Fischer encourages student collaboration. Students are routinely told to work in groups and help one another reach and understand solutions. Mr. Fischer often reminds them, "You are each other's resources." Collaboration is often lively in the AP class. In-class homework sessions are filled with cries of "How in the world is *that* the answer?" and hoots of joy when formulas come out right. In the college-prep chemistry class, group work tends to be quieter but no less intense. In both classes, group work allows students to clearly see which classmates are able to tackle problems more quickly than others, and it provides ample opportunities for showing off one's abilities. For example, Adam finishes a worksheet one morning and calls out to Mr. Fischer, "What do we do when we are done?" The question sounds sincere, but it is voiced loudly, making it impossible for his classmates not to recognize that Adam has finished his worksheet more quickly than they have. Mr. Fischer responds equally loudly, "Help other people." Adam then stands up and walks around the room, looking for classmates who might want his help.

In Mrs. Jones's class, competition is similar, though the overall class dynamics are more subdued and students rely more on the teacher to verify correct answers. She often requires collaboration for assignments. One morning students are working in pairs on a task in which they must first solve an equation and then explain it to their partner. Michael sits behind two girls who are working together, and he overhears one give her answer out loud. "That's not right," he says playfully. "I have the right answer right here."

Both girls laugh good-naturedly and return the banter, assuring him that he is wrong. "We have it right, don't worry," one says to him, looking back at his paper. The three decide to call Mrs. Jones over to adjudicate. Although this competitive exchange is friendly, the girls gloat when Mrs. Jones confirms their answer. In this class, it matters who is right and who is wrong.

Both Mr. Fischer and Mrs. Jones strive to make learning engaging. Mrs. Jones designs lab experiments with a "mystery ingredient" that students must figure out and identify through the chemical reactions. Mr. Fischer frequently adds live demonstrations—particularly ones including combustible gases and lit matches—to his lessons. These both reward students with spectacular displays of chemistry and excite them about the world of science. He might say, "Look at the amazing stuff you can do if you just know a few basic properties of helium," as he ignites a controlled explosion in the lab. This helps make chemistry knowledge more appealing to students and diffuses some of the stress they feel about their performance and test scores. Both teachers tell me that students regularly fail their classes despite both teachers' willingness to give partial credit for wrong answers that are good attempts. The courses are demanding, particularly the AP class, where getting an *A* is a coveted achievement.

Jealousy and Heartache over Perfect Grades

Chemistry is just one example of the competitive environment at Elite Charter High, and the theme of grade rivalry emerges throughout my interviews. Several students who take multiple honors/AP courses display a touch of jealousy as they discuss the nearly straight-*A* report card in figure 1.2. Jenny, a white sophomore who is currently in two AP classes, assumes a high-pitched, mocking tone when I hand her the report card. "It's like the perfect little *A* student," she says, batting her eyelashes for dramatic effect. Jenny has a 4.25 GPA this semester but does not consider herself to be wildly successful in school. (An *A* grade in an AP class counts as a 5.0 rather than the usual 4.0.) In her interview, she generally describes herself as content with her grades, but at moments like this she betrays them as an emotional burden. She would like perfect grades but feels they are out of her reach: "I get, like, constant Bs and high Cs in AP chem tests. So even though—like, man! I wish I could get As." When I ask whether her grades give a good picture of how intelligent she is, she says, "I think it's pretty accurate. I'm not, like, a genius, but it's, like, I do pretty well, I guess." I ask what a genius's grades would look like, and her response is immediate: "A 5.0."

At Elite Charter High, a 5.0 GPA would require taking four AP classes and getting straight As in them. Jenny's two AP courses allow her to reach a maximum GPA of 4.5. She tells me that she enjoys school. "I actually do have that 'yearning for learning,'" she laughs. "I really do like it." Yet she is aware that her 4.25 GPA reveals that she is not as successful as she could be. She considers herself an 8 on the 1-to-10 intelligence scale, explaining, "But yeah, I'm not really smart in science."

Elite Charter High's cultural wisdom about what it takes to achieve school success strongly endorses success-through-intelligence, which makes it difficult for someone like Jenny to see herself in any other light. Yet intelligence is not the whole story. For instance, Ryan, a white junior enrolled in three AP classes, leans on initiative, Elite Charter High's modified version of success-through-effort, as he tries to make sense of his less-than-perfect grades. Like Jenny, his immediate response to the high-performance report card is mockery: "Oh, this person is Mr.—uh—Mr. and Mrs. Outstanding." Ryan describes himself as very smart and is proud of his current 4.5 GPA. He seems to have little reason to feel jealous of the report card in figure 1.2. Yet he announces in the interview, almost in a tone of confession, that his overall GPA is only a 4.29. Softly he tells me, "Uh, I have gotten a couple of Bs too." He seems to feel compelled to be forthright about his imperfect grades and volunteers an explanation of his most recent B: "I got, uh, in my math class, uh, I got a B and, and I said a B is a good grade but, like, earlier in pre-calculus, I got two As and I—I know I have the ability to get an A. It's just that I—I might not have, like, looked on specific stuff enough or just certain things that I probably could have done better on."

Ryan's current math class is AP calculus, known around the school as a very difficult course. But unlike Jenny, he blames his B on lack of initiative rather than lack of intelligence. Buying into the logic of success-through-intelligence, Ryan believes that he should have the intelligence required for top grades, so he turns to lack of initiative as an explanation. His disappointment in his B is evident, especially when he contrasts it with his previous As. He is planning to take four AP courses next semester, which will give him a chance to reach a 5.0 GPA, and he seems to look forward to the challenge. He expresses confidence in his ability to attain the highest level of success in school—"I know I have the ability to get an A"—which undoubtedly magnifies his disappointment when his high expectations are not realized.

These displays of jealousy and heartache are further evidence of the competitive AP environment at Elite Charter High. Excellent grades are highly valued, and they inspire envy as well as admiration. Students such as Jenny and Ryan desire perfect grades so deeply that they feel unable to sincerely applaud them on the anonymous report card. In interviews with AP-entrenched students at the school, I repeatedly heard descriptions of student competitions over grades, but only from students who have not triumphed in these competitions. Those who are actually able to earn the best grades, such as James (whom I discuss at length in chapter 6), are much less emotional about the best-grades game.

6

Competitive Classmates
at Elite Charter High

Many students at Elite Charter High believe that they can have a happy, balanced teenage life or straight As, but not both. They are under extreme pressure to achieve high academic success, and they worry that attaining straight As might require them to sacrifice their emotional and mental sanity. Jenny, whom we met in chapter 5, derides her schoolmates' emotional investment in perfect grades: "A lot of people really stress out and are, like, 'I can't believe I got an 89! I'm never ever going to Harvard now!' And kids start crying and stuff. And I'm, like, 'Oh, my gosh. Move on with your life. Go take a walk or something' [she laughs]."

Although he is less sardonic, Mr. Fischer echoes her concern: "[Students say,] 'Am I going to get into a good school? What do I have to do to get into a good school? I can't get a B. If I get a B, I won't get into a good school. If I get a C, I won't get into a school, period.' That mindset has been pounded into kids." He seems genuinely troubled by this attitude. In our 2012 interview, he tells me that in the year after I completed my fieldwork in his classroom he conducted "a study on stress for AP students" as part of his master's degree research. "They sign up for six AP classes [per year]. They think that's what they need to do to get into college. And they are so upset because they can't juggle it all. And they are really succeeding, but they have no idea that they are."

Although Jenny ridicules students who feel devastated when they do not get As, we know that she herself would very much like to have perfect grades (see chapter 5). Still, she asserts, "An A isn't worth giving up your entire life to," expressing an idea that I often heard from students at the school who do not get straight As. According to Jenny, "if you really, like, went really, really, extraordinarily and almost crazy far, you could probably get an A. But if somebody wants to stay just a normal human being, [if that person] just don't like that subject, or that's just not really hitting home with them, then maybe not. They won't get an *A* and will get a *B*-plus or something." In other words, students at Elite Charter High are concerned that initiative can be taken too far: that the pursuit of success can take an unhealthy toll. I did not note this concern at either of the other two schools I studied.

At Alternative High, there is no such thing as trying too hard. Instead, students are concerned about the link between failure and lack of effort, which gives rise to the *smart-but-not-trying* identity story. Alternative High's *cheater* story and Comprehensive High's *trained dog* story embody students' concerns about fraudulent or illegitimate success. But at Elite Charter High there is no similar identity story. Students here are not worried about people who cheat to pass a class. Likewise, the *Average Joe* story does not exist here because being average is an insult. Rather, students' anxieties center on achieving perfect grades in honors and AP classes, something that requires high intelligence and initiative.

The *OCD Overachiever* Identity Story

Kevin tells me, "People who try too hard end up becoming, like, OCD." Many AP students at Elite Charter High use this term to refer to students who exert enormous effort to earn excellent grades. OCD is an acronym for *obsessive-compulsive disorder,* the clinical name of a psychiatric disorder in which a person has obsessive thoughts and impulses. A person who suffers from OCD feels compelled to enact rituals and behaviors in order to stave off some dreaded situation. However, students here use the term less precisely to emphasize the extreme, seemingly obsessive commitment to schoolwork that is required for perfect grades. The term's widespread use at Elite Charter High is a way to link extreme school success with abnormality, a connection that makes sense to students such as Jenny and Ryan, who are envious of and frustrated by classmates who are more academically successful than they are.

Kevin describes an *OCD overachiever* at his school: "It seems kind of crazy. I know people who, like, study all the time, and you can't even hang out with them. It's, like, aghhh!" I ask whether studying so much pays off for these students—that is, whether they are getting all *A*s—and he says that, yes, they do receive excellent grades. "But I guess in the long run, it doesn't really pay off." According to Kevin, *OCD overachievers are* "scared of missing school. . . . They are kind of tied up in this world where they are—where they have a fear of missing something because they are scared that they are going to go all downhill from there. . . . They are too scared. They are scared of having a bad grade. . . . They are crazy." The academic results may be desirable, but the price is sanity.

In my view, students' own frustrated academic aspirations fuel this chastising attitude toward classmates who receive perfect grades. The attitude is remarkably different from the cultural environment at Alternative High, where Reina responds positively to the anonymous high-performance report card, telling me, "It's a good student who overachieves." At Alternative High, overachieving is complimented, whereas at Elite Charter High the *OCD overachiever* identity is ridiculed. Jenny suggests such students need to "go take a walk or something." It is an identity to avoid if one wishes to remain healthy and sane. At each of the three schools I studied, I found a negative identity story that explains school success, and here that identity type is the *OCD overachiever*. Notably, at neither of the other two schools does the scorned-yet-successful identity story involve admirably high intelligence. This difference speaks to how tightly intelligence entwines with all versions of success at Elite Charter High, even negative ones.

The College Strategist Identity Story

The *college strategist* is a student who carefully and conscientiously charts which courses she will take during high school to maximize the likelihood that she will be admitted to an elite (or at least respectable) college or university. Rebecca describes a typical part of this process: "In the beginning of freshman year my parents and I sat down—because they always have the aspirations of me going to Stanford—and so we sat down and we were planning all of my four-year schedule, just to my requirements, and then we were pushing beyond that. So I'm going to be going up to AP Spanish and French, like, French III or IV, and I'm taking all these AP sciences and, like, every AP I can get in, and just crazy stuff." In addition to developing an impressive transcript, the *college strategist* actively seeks out activities that demonstrate qualities she believes are characteristic of desirable college candidates. In our interviews, Elite Charter High students most commonly mention qualities such as being "well rounded," having "leadership abilities," and trying to "do good for greater society." Rebecca's comment demonstrates how easily the high aspirations of a *college strategist* can lead toward the "crazy stuff" of an *OCD averachiever*. Nonetheless, most students I talked to refer to the *college strategist* as a commendable type of student.

During the year of my research, Elite Charter High boasted that 98 percent of its graduating class had immediate plans for college. In other words, just about every student pursues higher education, although some do start at community college rather than a four-year institution. I heard many student conversations about college, and most centered on getting into a "good" four-year school. Importantly, students perceive differences in how well others prepare for a successful college application. They applaud those who strategically develop a transcript and other application materials that demonstrate the character traits they believe college admissions boards most admire. For example, when I show Alexis, a white sophomore who is taking two AP classes this semester, the high-performance report card in figure 1.2, she describes the anonymous student as "very academic, very . . . college-bound, . . . someone who is trying to fit the college profile. Like, they're taking student government in leadership and, like, drama to show that they're—like, this is the kind of thing I can imagine someone planning out their four-year plan."

Many students believe that top colleges are not interested in applicants who focus only on academic excellence but prefer students who lead active and involved lives, pursue talents and interests beyond academics, socialize well with peers, and make contributions to society. Scholarship on admissions to elite colleges supports this assumption, and guidebooks on how to get into such schools also emphasize it.[1] For Alexis and many others at Elite Charter High, the *college strategist* conscientiously embodies this kind of strong college candidate. Mr. Fischer calls such an approach "transcript building," which he describes as including not only "grades" but also "record, community service, . . . just anything that will look good to a school so [the student] can get in. Everybody is freaked out about that right now because there is so much competitiveness to get into college."[2] While Mr. Fischer worries about this behavior, students admire it.

· While students at all of the three schools I studied esteem the idea of going to college after high school, the students at Elite Charter High are particularly committed to this life path. Ryan says, "When [you] are young, you have to go to college." Indeed, for many of the students, there is no other viable option; the only question is which college they will attend. Ryan cannot clearly articulate why young people "have to go to college," perhaps because it has never occurred to him to rationalize it. He tells me, "Especially now when . . . you are in high school and stuff, like, college is such—with AP classes and everything, it, it seems like it's really important. And all of my friends are going to college. And, um, I, I guess it also, like, opens up what I can do, and where I can be hired and such things like that."

Ryan expresses his peers' general attitude that college is valuable, and his focus on future employment is also common. However, Chase articulates a broader sense of the benefits of a college education: "I think it's generally accepted that if you have an education, it betters your chances in life. And most kids—or the vast majority—want to finish high school, and a sizable amount want to go to college because they recognize it could do good for their lives." He sees college as a stepping stone to a good life.

Alexis Admits to "OC" but Not to "D"

We've already heard Alexis praise the owner of the anonymous report card as "very . . . college-bound." Later in our interview, she describes herself in the same way. As she talks about her life and experiences, she draws on both the *OCD overachiever* and the *college strategist* identity stories to characterize herself. However, she does not embrace the two stories equally. Alexis admits to being obsessed with school, even somewhat compulsive about it, yet she does not feel any disorder in her life. That is, she admits to "OC" but not to "D." Overall, she sees herself as a *college strategist*, and she is proud of that identity.

Alexis has straight *A*s. She is currently enrolled in AP history, AP chemistry, Spanish V, and journalism. She holds a 4.5 GPA, the highest possible average for her course load. To others, she is a clear example of an *OCD overachiever*. One of her best friends, Denise, discusses Alexis's impressive score of over 2,000 on the PSAT, which they both recently took during a Kaplan test preparation course: "She remembers little stuff from class. . . . Like, some of the math stuff, they would ask the tiniest little thing, and it's the kind of thing that, if it was mentioned in class, she would write it down just out of fear that it might be on a test. And she would learn it, just in case. Because she can't afford not to get 100 percent on a test." Denise does not hide her aversion to Alexis's tendency to "obsess" over small details of course material, and she describes her friend's efforts as driven by "fear." This is a typical characterization of *OCD overachievers*: that they are "scared" and "nervous" all the time; that they are morbidly afraid of academic imperfection.

Alexis herself admits to obsessing about school: "I've always tried really hard in school, and I've always been, like, obsessed with it. I don't know; it's, like, what I do. . . . My parents aren't even surprised at me anymore." When she compares herself with her closest friends, she again invokes the definition of an *OCD overachiever*. "I think out of all of my friends, I kind of, like, try the hardest. I don't know; that's just how it has always been since I don't know [when]. In the little group, like, I am the one that, like, kills myself for school." Yet Alexis does not see her life as unbalanced, nor does she tell me that she feels overwhelmed by schoolwork. In fact, she says she spends only eight to ten hours on homework each week, which is much less time than most of the students report, even those who claim to be purposely avoiding *OCD*. Denise, for example, tells me she usually spends fifteen hours per week on homework. When I ask Alexis how she feels about her classes this semester, she responds, "I am pretty happy, actually. I was really scared about, like, the AP classes, that they were going to be, like, huge amounts of work and that I wouldn't have time to do anything. But they're not so bad. Like, it's—yeah, I'm pretty happy with the difficulty and the amount of time I'm spending on them."

Rather than feeling that her sanity is destroyed by her dedication to school-work, as is the case with *OCD overachievers*, Alexis is proud of her straight-*A* record: "They are the grades that could get me into a good college. Because colleges look at grades." In our interview, she repeatedly mentions her college future. Although she draws from the *OCD overachiever* identity story when she describes herself, she aligns herself more fully with the *college strategist* story. Denise, however, perceives an imbalance. Even as she confirms Alexis's identity as a *college strategist*, she shakes her head over her friend's homework habits: "Her parents raised her to just be, like, 'Get home from school, start your homework, and do it until you fall asleep in your book.' And she's crazy." In Denise's view, Alexis's life is dominated by her obsession with schoolwork and college admission: "My best friend with the straight *A*s, she just, like, listens to all my music and likes all the same movies as me, and all my friends are her friends, and [she] doesn't really have a life outside of me—except for her charity and volunteer work, which she does for college. [*Denise laughs.*] That's it." Alexis is precisely the kind of person whom Elite Charter High students have in mind when they describe an *OCD overachiever*. Yet Alexis does not see herself in quite the same light. She depicts herself much more favorably as a dedicated *college strategist* who enjoys excellent school success and is happy with school even though she admits to being a little obsessed with it.

Denise Avoids OCD

Like Alexis, Denise is a white sophomore. I met both girls in their AP chemistry class, where they sit next to each other and work together as lab partners. While Denise also draws on the *OCD overachiever* identity story, she does not embrace it but defines herself in opposition to it. She is one of several students whom I interviewed at Elite Charter High who describes herself as capable of receiving excellent grades (defined as straight *A*s in multiple honors/AP classes) but claims that her grades fall short of excellent because she allows herself to live a balanced, healthy, teenage life. Like these other students, Denise is adamant about avoiding OCD.

During our interview I asked her, "Do you agree or disagree with the following statement: 'if students try hard enough, they can get all *A*s in school'?"

DENISE: I definitely disagree!

LISA NUNN: Tell me why. Tell me what seems wrong about that.

DENISE: I haven't gotten straight *A*s since fourth grade—I mean, I kind of agree in the sense that, yes, you can go crazy and you can get straight *A*s, but you still have to go crazy. I mean I *could* have straight *A*s right now if I, after finishing, like, three hours of homework, I then reviewed for my chemistry test that was in two weeks, every night. Okay, so I guess I agree with it, this statement. Just personally, like, I try really hard. People that have an *A* in AP chemistry are not happy people. I mean, they're sad and they're depressed and they're insane. . . . I don't want to be that. That's what I was afraid of for this year, that I would turn into a robot student. And I have, like, all *A*s and one *B*. And I try really hard. I could get that *A*, but there's a certain point, I think. . . . I mean, if you're going to have straight *As* with, like, more than one AP class, then you spend more of your life, like, going the extra limit than you do just, like, working on yourself, kind of. I mean, in high school it seems that the people who do that are more, like, giving in to the system. . . . They're just, like—their own personality is just, like, thin and watery.

Denise's aggressive, disparaging depiction of excellent students helps her see her own imperfect school success as a virtue rather than a failing. Yet in fact, she receives great grades. Her only *B* is in AP chemistry, a difficult course (see chapter 5). She holds *As* in AP history and two non-honors courses. Frequently during our interview she asserts that she is proud of her school success. When I ask whether her GPA worries her, she responds, "It hasn't ever been [a worry], really, except for when I had to get a certain GPA to get a cell phone. I mean, I guess so. I don't really think about it. I don't, like, base my classes around how high I can get my GPA. But I like having a 4.25. It's nice. It's the first—it's always been like a 3.26, and now it's getting up there. . . . Yeah, and I can even get a *C* in one of my classes and still have a 4.0, which is pretty cool. I don't plan on it, but it's secure."

As I've already discussed, college strategists focus on taking classes that maximize their GPA. Yet even though this identity story garners respect at Elite Charter High, Denise claims not to engage in that strategy. She often tries to downplay how much excellent grades mean to her. Still, at many other points during the interview, she gives me the distinct impression that she is indeed obsessed with excellent grades. This ambivalence demonstrates the tension she experiences because she feels unable to achieve straight *As*. For example, less than three minutes into the interview, she volunteers a description of her emotional distress over the fact that her best friend Alexis outperforms her.

DENISE: Like, my best friend sits next to me in both my AP classes, and she blows me out of the park schoolwise.

L. N.: Do you mean in academics? Like, she's better?

DENISE: Yeah, way better. Amazing. And she always has been. That's, like, how she was raised, really, and our parents are good friends. It's, like, an open subject between us. . . . And I started out this year thinking, "I'm going to beat her. I'm going to beat her." And every time I was viciously slapped down. And that gets annoying because I've been best friends with her since kindergarten, and she lives around the block, and we spend every minute together. And it's always, like, I try really hard and I make a big deal about it, because I'm kind of lazy. And she's, like—tries as hard as I do plus does extra credit and just, like, brushes her shoulders off. That brings me down at school.

Although Denise perceives an open rivalry with Alexis over grades, Alexis never mentions academic competition with any of her friends, including Denise. Among my interviews at Elite Charter High, I found that discussions of the tense, competitive atmosphere in AP courses arose much more often with students who are not victorious. Rivalry over grades seems to be more salient in the lives of those who must admit to being in second place.

I show Denise the anonymous report card in figure 1.2, which shows nearly straight *A*s, except for one *A*-minus and one *B*-plus. Denise tells me that she identifies very strongly with this student. She particularly focuses on the *B*-plus as the closest point of association.

DENISE: These are basically my grades and classes. So it's hard not to describe myself.

L. N.: That's okay. Describe yourself.

DENISE: All right. [The student does] try really hard in school and they're one notch below the highest. Not one notch, but you know, just below that one student who every teacher thinks is wonderful.

L. N.: The *A*-plus-plus-plus kid.

DENISE: The *A*-plus-plus-plus student. They're kind of discouraged by those kids and they feel bad for them, but they kind of use that to, like, make themselves feel better.

Here Denise acknowledges that she makes herself feel better about her own performance by feeling bad for classmates who receive excellent grades. At Elite Charter High, the *OCD overachiever* identity story offers a ready framework for disdaining excellent school success. Denise and others like her can justify their own great-but-not-excellent grades by portraying themselves as happy teenagers with a healthy commitment to academics. Denise successfully avoids OCD while claiming to be capable of achieving straight *A*s: "I'm not going to, like, stop listening to music and stuff, going to parties and stuff like that. I will try as hard as I can, but I'm not going to lose myself for school. I still have better grades than most of my friends do, and that's fine. I'm happy with my grades." Nonetheless, her comments throughout our interview consistently carry an undercurrent of disappointment. Clearly she experiences a profound tension between her not-quite-excellent school success and her belief that she is a highly intelligent person who tries hard in school.

James, a *College Strategist* with a Twist

A few of the AP chemistry students I interviewed breeze not just through that class but through high school in general. They seem unconcerned about academic rivalry. Unquestionably intelligent, they do not suffer from anxiety about their grades, as many of their classmates do. Nor do they devote oppressive amounts of time to their schoolwork. Instead, they do as they please outside of school, almost entirely unencumbered by assignments and studying. The *OCD overachiever* identity story never appears in their self-descriptions.

James, a white junior, is one of these students. During our interview, he depicts himself in terms of the *college strategist* identity story. Yet even though he embraces this story, he also modifies it to fit his personal circumstances. In particular, he places a premium on his extracurricular activities. Unlike his peers at Elite Charter High, James does not highlight these activities to show that he is well rounded or has leadership abilities. Instead, he uses extracurricular commitments as a way to show elite college admissions committees that his intelligence surpasses that of other applicants, even those with a comparably high GPA.

James considers himself highly intelligent. During my field observations in his AP chemistry class, I notice that he is often attentive when the teacher is instructing, but I also see him doing other things at his desk, including openly reading a fantasy novel during class time. When I ask how much time he spends on homework, he responds, "I am really lucky, and one of the reasons that math is my favorite subject is because it comes easy to me, so starting last year and continuing to this year, my best friend and I will collaborate. We'll bring the textbooks to school and do the homework during our math class, so homework-wise I technically do an hour to an hour and a half, but it is never done at home. . . . It usually takes me the whole period, but that's with pretty substantial distractions—like, I do have to pay attention every now and then."

James receives straight *A*s, which he believes attest to his high intelligence because his schedule is loaded with three AP courses this semester and four next semester. He tells me that last year in his band class he received a *B* as one quarter's grade because he neglected to turn in "practice reports." He also received a *B*-plus in last year's honors English class. Otherwise, his report cards consistently feature *A*s and a few *A*-minuses. James is quick to explain that "the *B* in English actually wasn't because I struggled in the subject. It was because I didn't read one of the last books, and I was, like, 88 or 89.3 percent in the class, which just wasn't enough to get the *A*." Despite the effort issue in last year's English class, James states several times during our interview that his school success requires minimal effort. Unlike most of his classmates, he does not depend on initiative in order to shine. He describes himself as able to "pick up learning" quickly and easily.

James is not the only student I met at Elite Charter High who soars through school with little effort. However, it is more common for such students to choose a larger number of college-prep courses and fewer honors or AP courses as a strategy to maintain a high GPA with a minimal amount of work. This is how

Julie, a white sophomore whom I met in AP chemistry, manages to do so well at school: "I'm just not a studying kind of person. I just know how to get the *A*." She earns her excellent grades by doing "less than an hour [of homework] every day at home. . . . I try to do most of my homework in class when there's an extra minute." She decided to take AP chemistry this semester "because I kind of felt like I needed some kind of honors class during high school and I thought that might be a good one." She is confident that she has what it takes to succeed in more honors/AP courses. In fact, she tells me that some of her college-prep classes are decidedly unchallenging: "Occasionally I've been in just like a really—just dumb class because I don't take honors. I have really . . . very few honors classes."

Julie's strategy that is not well respected at Elite Charter High. Mrs. Belfry, who teaches both college-prep and remedial English, says she admires students who "take advantage of what the school offers: . . . AP classes, for example. Do they challenge themselves? Or do they take the easy way out?" Mrs. Belfry does not teach any AP courses herself; but when she writes letters of recommendation for her college-prep English students, she emphasizes the initiative of those who "are pushing themselves to go above and beyond the call of duty," and that includes taking AP courses. Julie seems at least somewhat aware of this attitude because she "kind of felt like I needed some kind of honors class during high school." Overall, however, she seems to be comfortable about her curriculum choice.

James's situation is very different. Even though he is relaxed about his grades and his homework, he earns a stellar GPA by excelling in the most challenging academic curriculum that Elite Charter High offers. He explains to me that nowadays he cares a great deal about getting straight *A*s but this was not always the case. In our interview, he recalls the specific moment when he became invested in school success and describes it precisely in terms of the *college strategist* identity story. In sixth grade, he explains, he got a *C* on his report card in writing, which "triggered something": "Like, I used to be fine with *A*s and *B*s, and now I definitely want[ed] to get the straight *A*s." I ask what made him change his attitude, and he tells me,

> Partially because I realized "I'm in middle school now; I have to get to the point where colleges are going to start looking at my transcript." That was a big play because I do want to get into good colleges. . . . I realized that the way the system is judged, you aren't really proving that you're smart at something in the school system unless you get *all* the *A*s when you're in all the honors classes and everything. Now because so many people are trying harder and getting into the honors classes and doing well in them, to prove that you are smarter, you have to do well in *all* of the honors classes; you can't just say, "Oh, I hate English; I can accept a *B* in that."

Throughout our interview James expresses enormous concern about his future college admission. However, he is a *college strategist* with a twist. His concerns do not revolve around being academically qualified for college; his excellent grades and his range of honors/AP classes ensure that he will meet and surpass university prerequisites. Instead, they center on being able to demonstrate to elite college admissions boards that he is not only highly successful in school but also far and away more intellectually talented than other students with equally impressive school records. In other words, he has refined the *college strategist* identity story to better reflect his own personal concerns.

James is frustrated because his *A*s look identical to other people's *A*s, even though he is convinced that they are not as smart as he is. "I'm not sure it's right for them to be able to get an *A* with just effort and not smarts, whether the *A* should only go to the people with the smarts." He feels, however, that he has found a solution to this problem.

JAMES: One of the other ways that you can prove that you're really smart is if you have extracurriculars that go with it.

L. N.: How do extracurriculars signal smarts?

JAMES: Um, basically if [students] have a bunch of extracurriculars and they have a bunch of really hard classes and they are still getting all *A*s, there's only so much time in a day, only so much effort that they could put into each thing. So if you look and they are doing pretty good in their extracurriculars, and they are still getting the *A*s in school, you can kind of make the connection that they are pretty smart and they get the subjects pretty well.

His list of extracurricular activities includes becoming an Eagle Scout at age seventeen, working to earn a black belt in taekwondo, and learning computer programming in his spare time. He expects college admissions personnel to connect his time-intensive extracurricular accomplishments with his transcript "so that, just the fact that I persevered and got the Eagle Scout along with still pulling *A*s in school should—I hope—infer that I'm generally pretty smart in the subjects. And I can—I get the concepts well. . . . I'm doing a lot of stuff that shows that I've done a lot of work to get to certain levels [in taekwondo and Boy Scouts]." This is not a perspective I typically heard in interviews with students at Elite Charter High. Most believe that extracurricular activities are important to list on a college application because they demonstrate that a student is "well rounded" or has "leadership abilities"; they show that the student participates and excels in arenas outside of academics. In contrast, James hopes his extracurricular accomplishments signal that his *A*s prove his high intelligence.

James does not hint that he feels any tension between his cognitive abilities and his school performance. He believes that he is very smart and that his grades reflect his intelligence. Nor does he invoke any elements of the *OCD*

TOURO COLLEGE LIBRARY

overachiever identity story to describe himself. The tension that he mentions is linked to his feelings of superiority over less-talented classmates: "I used to hate my math class sometimes because people would ask so many questions about what to me was the simplest subject. . . . I'm just hating them because I'm irritated, because it's irritating me." He explains that he decided to modify his attentiveness in math class to manage his frustration with classmates. The less attention he pays to the teacher's instruction, the less irritated he feels. Nonetheless, he is well aware that some of his "slower" classmates earn *A*s that look identical to his. He is desperate to make his college application capture his intellectual superiority because he knows his transcript cannot.

Cultural Ideas Are Powerful, and People Are Creative Innovators

At Elite Charter High the cultural wisdom is that intelligence is required for school success and initiative is a particular kind of effort that enhances one's success. As I demonstrated in chapter 5, some students and teachers at the school conceptualize a connection between initiative and intelligence. They believe that highly intelligent people are enthusiastic and curious about learning, which drives them to take initiative in their schoolwork. For students such as Denise, this belief creates tension in their success identities as they struggle to reconcile the fact that they do not feel enthusiastic about some of their schoolwork even though they consider themselves to be intelligent. Although James simply disregards the initiative element of the school's cultural wisdom, most students sound more like Alexis, who has a hard time imagining that excellent grades come without hard work: "Everyone's going to have to study. It's not like people who are really smart are just going to be able to breeze through things. I mean, maybe in some cases, but, like—everyone studies and everyone tries."

Her assumption is not quite accurate. James does "breeze through things." He does not work hard, nor is he conflicted about his lack of effort. His self-confidence illustrates how important it is to understand that cultural ideas are produced and reproduced from both the bottom up and the top down. Elite Charter High may cultivate a particular understanding of school success, but not every student at the school will absorb that understanding into his or her identity in exactly the same way. James is a creative actor in the social world. He is able to modify, adapt, embrace, or dismiss cultural ideas as he sees fit.[3]

Yet the cultural ideas available in a given organizational context are powerful frameworks that guide people's understanding of the world and how they fit into it. Take James's best friend, Adam. Like James, he spends very little time on schoolwork but is still earns perfect grades in AP classes. Whereas Denise says she spends fifteen hours a week on homework, Adam says he spends fifteen minutes a week on it. He gets most of his homework done during school when the teacher is instructing the class on a concept he has already mastered. But even though James feels immune from anxiety about his grades, Adam feels conflicted.

L. N.: What percentage of your grades, would you say, is based on effort and hard work, and how much is based on your intelligence or ability?

ADAM: It's probably 80-percent intelligence, 20-percent effort. I could probably succeed more easily if I put forth more effort. That's a weird statement; I mean, I could go further than I am now with more effort. I think it's because I'm dividing my effort a lot in my life.

L. N.: What do you mean that you could go further?

ADAM: I could get better grades, be esteemed higher by my teachers and peers if I put forth the effort for those higher As.

Adam sounds disappointed in himself as he tells me that he does not push for "higher As," by which he means "98 percent or 99 percent" in his classes instead of the mid-nineties grades that he currently receives. This theme resurfaces multiple times in our interview. When I ask where he would rank his own intelligence on a scale from 1-to-10, he responds, "A 9, I think. It's not perfect. I would consider myself to be much more intelligent if I actually did always do my best."

Throughout our interview Adam confirms the idea that high intelligence is connected to ambition to learn and succeed. Because he has not mustered up the motivation to pursue the highest possible As in his classes, he doubts that he is truly as intelligent as his excellent grades and easy school success would indicate him to be. Clearly, he does not have a low overall opinion of his intelligence, yet he experiences some uncertainty about himself. Currently Adam holds a flawless GPA of 4.75, the highest possible average for his course load. Still, unlike James, who is confident that initiative is simply not required in his case, Adam feels that he "would be esteemed higher" if he took more initiative.

Denise also questions her intelligence, and she uses the same rationale that Adam does. In her case, however, her doubts are confirmed by her less-than-perfect GPA. She acknowledges that she falls short in intelligence when it comes to chemistry: "When I think of intelligence, I think of, like, how knowledge—or how curious you are about one subject. . . . But I don't know. I don't sit at home thinking about chemistry and stuff. I don't, like, look up extra chemistry problems to do on my own and stuff like that. I do okay in the class. I get a B." Here and other moments in the interview Denise indicates that her lackluster approach to chemistry signals a deficiency in her overall intelligence. She does not take initiative in the subject. On the other hand, she takes considerable initiative in her writing, whether for a class assignment or her own pleasure. Both her parents are writers, and her father makes his living at it, so she gets a good deal of encouragement at home for her writing efforts. Denise is able to see her passion for writing as evidence that she is intelligent, and the local beliefs at Elite Charter High support her assumption that passion is an indicator of intelligence. But her confidence is diminished by her relative disinterest in chemistry and math.

When I ask Denise where she would place herself on a 1-to-10 intelligence scale, she responds, "I don't know. A 7? 8?" She explains her rationale: "There's tons of stuff that I don't know about yet that I could expand on and do something that could make me known worldwide and *the* smartest person ever, and I'd say, like, 12 on that scale. But no. I'm fifteen [years old]. I do pretty well in school, try hard, and am pretty interested. I like doing stuff. . . . In English class I would say 10. In math class I would say 7." As we have seen, Denise asserts that she tries hard in school and holds back from greater effort only as a safeguard against becoming OCD. Yet there's a tension in her success identity: she knows she does not want to spend her energy learning more about chemistry or math. Unlike James, she does not breeze through school on intelligence alone. She may describe her approach as a way to avoid OCD, but in fact she simply does not have the internal desire to learn about certain subjects.

Although Alexis achieves excellent school success, she is not free from tensions in her success identity. Denise is sure that Alexis would place herself "at a 9 or 10" and would place Denise at "a 7 or 8" on the 1-to-10 intelligence scale. From Denise's perspective, Alexis sees the intelligence difference between them as black and white: "Yeah. She thinks it's all about grades. It's all about grades to her. She thinks that the other stuff is bullshit. She's all about the cold hard facts. And my grades are one notch below hers, and therefore I'm one notch below her on the 1-to-10 scale." But Alexis is much less certain about her own intelligence level than Denise imagines. Despite her stellar school success, she does not know how much stock she can put into her high school grades as evidence of her intellectually capability. When I ask where she might fall on the 1-to-10 intelligence scale, she hesitates and then falters repeatedly in her response: "I guess, you know—like, I'd be kind of on the upper half, I guess. . . . I think I'm—like, I guess I'd have to say—do I actually have to pick a number? . . . I don't know: 7? 8-ish? 9? I don't know. Just because, like, I get good grades and I understand a lot—I don't know. I can hold a conversation with someone about something—not mindless. So I don't know. It's weird. I've never had to say that before."

At the end of the interview, Alexis asks to return to the subject of the 1-to-10 scale.

ALEXIS: Just the thing we were talking about earlier, asking me to rank myself. Like, I know I get good grades, but I don't—like, I haven't figured out yet, like, how intelligent I really am. I don't know.

L. N.: Well, what would you need to know in order to figure out how smart you are? What kind of information is missing, or what could help you?

ALEXIS: College, really. Because, like, now everyone takes basically the same classes. Like, I guess I am taking more APs than some people might, or I will be. But, like, being challenged more, like, in a situation where you're actually there to—like college. You're in the classes and you're actually—I don't know. I just think you are challenged a lot more probably. And I might be able to see, like, how well I actually do. And I think college is a lot more— it's harder to, like, B. S. your way through. I don't know. I am still trying to figure that out.

It is not that high school has been easy so far. On the contrary, Alexis's success demands hours of dedicated effort. According to the school's cultural wisdom, her motivation, initiative, and excellent school success should allow her to see herself as highly intelligent. However, it fails to confirm her belief in her own high intelligence.

Alexis is another example of how individual students construct their success identities in response to the attitudes and beliefs they encounter in their school settings. Those school-level attitudes and beliefs do not determine an identity. Rather, the individual brings her personal thoughts and perceptions into her interactions with the school organization, and they allow her to filter, dismiss, or embrace the information she encounters. An individual's identity is an ongoing development, a product of the interaction between a person and her social world.[4]

Friendship and Success Identity

In this chapter I have focused on two pairs of best friends: Alexis and Denise, James and Adam. By examining the differences that best friends experience as they construct their success identities, I have demonstrated that each individual's success identity is a discrete product of that person's interaction with the social world. Even best friends process their identities differently.

Literature on peer influence tells us that friendship circles have powerful influence over individuals' attitudes, perceptions, and ambitions. Friends encourage each other to be more alike in attitudes, behavior, and the subjects they enjoy studying.[5] Thus, exploring differences in the tensions that arise in pairs of best friends emphasizes the individual student in the process of identity construction. Further, even best friends do not share identical perspectives on each other's identity. For example, Denise considers Alexis to be an *OCD overachiever,* while Alexis considers herself to be a *college strategist.* Even though they are situated in the same school context and privy to the same identity stories and cultural beliefs about success, students construct their own success identities in their own innovative ways. These pairs of best friends do not share the same kinds of doubts about how intelligent they are, nor do they reconcile their self-doubts in identical ways.

Schools Are More Than a Proxy for Socioeconomic Class

The three schools in this study are different in terms of the socioeconomic levels and ethnoracial backgrounds of the families they serve as well as in the cultural ideas that they endorse. As an inhabited institution, each school modifies the cultural ideas of success-through-intelligence and success-through-effort in its own particular way, creating a unique cultural environment in which individual students construct their success identities. Yet a school's cultural environment cannot be completely disentangled from its neighborhood and families. Certainly families influence how students perceive themselves. Moreover, scholarship on social reproduction suggests that students' aspirations and behaviors are likely to be the result of family rather school influence.[6] Because U.S. schools are typically neighborhood-based, they tend to serve families that are fairly homogenous in terms of socioeconomic class: those who can afford similar housing generally live in the same neighborhoods. Given the complicated overlap between race and socioeconomics, this also means that some schools primarily serve ethnic and racial minorities, while others primarily serve whites.

If family influence were the only explanation for students' understandings of school success, then students from similar socioeconomic and ethnoracial backgrounds should sound a great deal alike, no matter which school they attend. However, my data show that the students who attend the same school are more alike in their beliefs about school success than are students who share class or ethnoracial characteristics. Take Stephanie from Comprehensive High, for example. Her family's income level and her race make her very similar to the majority of students at Elite Charter High. If race, class, or family were a more powerful factor in the formation of her beliefs about school success, then we should expect Stephanie to hold beliefs that are similar to her counterparts at Elite Charter High. Yet this is not the case. She does not say that intelligence makes people feel motivated to learn or that success involves taking initiative in one's schoolwork. She does not mention the importance of strategizing for college, and she certainly does not use OCD or even the concept of overachieving in general as a way to describe successful students. On the contrary, her descriptions of success are steeped in the cultural wisdom and identity stories that are prevalent at her own high school.

Another example is Maria, a low-income Latina student who attends Elite Charter High because she lives within walking distance, not because she is drawn to the high academic mission of the school's charter. Her parents are immigrants from Mexico who speak very little English. Maria will be the first in her family to graduate from high school. Her class position, ethnicity, and family circumstances make her more similar to students at Alternative High than to those at her own school. Yet she does not espouse any of the cultural beliefs about school success that I find at Alternative High. She is convinced that students who receive good grades are smart and that they work hard in school because they "want to learn" and enjoy it. This is the reigning explanation for success at her school. Thus, although the school itself does not determine student beliefs, students can and often do use the school's structure and environment as they work to understand school success.

Identity Stories Are Products of School Environments

Regarding identity stories, there are some important comparisons to be made across schools. For instance, the trained dog story at Comprehensive High is somewhat parallel to the OCD overachiever story at Elite Charter High. AP students at both schools rely on their version of this identity story to justify and legitimize their own less-than-excellent school success. At Comprehensive High, AP students are disdainful about trained dogs, most likely because they are frustrated about having to channel their creative cognitive abilities into the correct-answer teaching formats that students describe as mindless busywork. Recall how Claire asserts that As are based on how well a student "regurgitates" information on tests. In contrast, AP students at Elite Charter High are encouraged to engage in more comprehensive learning endeavors in their classes. As a result of these differences, the parallel identity stories feature different characteristics even though similarly positioned students use these stories in similar ways.

Likewise, an identity story that makes sense in one school environment might not make sense in another. Take the Comprehensive High story of Average Joe, for example. Few students in my sample at Elite Charter High claim that they would be personally satisfied with average grades. In contrast, at Alternative High, students are focused on avoiding failure, not on achieving

mediocrity. Thus, at neither school would the Average Joe identity story resonate with local sensibilities about school success. At Alternative High, Average Joe would contradict the optimistic conviction that hard work results in
school success. At Elite Charter High, an Average Joe would be considered a
"slacker," and his school success would be viewed as disgracefully below par.
Only at Comprehensive High can students such as Mackie embrace Average
Joe with dignity.

7

Beyond Identity

Consequences of School Beliefs on Students' Futures

Beliefs about school success influence not only students' success identities but their future in higher education, and a school's cultural wisdom can boost or compromise students' pursuit of higher education at elite institutions. In this regard, the advantage and disadvantage inherent in the beliefs about school success at Alternative High, Comprehensive High, and Elite Charter High reinforce existing patterns of advantage and disadvantage in American education. Attaining a bachelor's degree is the key to accessing well-paying professional careers in the United States. Moreover, the college one attends also matters because attending an elite college further increases future earnings and job prestige.[1] People from low socioeconomic backgrounds, African Americans, and Latinos are less likely than their white and middle-class counterparts are to complete college degrees, and Latinos as a group are the least likely of all students of color to finish higher education.[2] A main reason for this discrepancy lies in the high schools, which throughout the United States prepare students unequally for advancement to higher education.

Unequal Preparation for College in High School

In a 2003 national study Jay Greene and Greg Forster demonstrate that high schools are disproportionately underpreparing African American and Latino high school students for college futures.[3] Using 2000 data, the authors find that only 70 percent of U.S. high school students graduate and only 32 percent of all students leave high school with the minimum qualifications to attend a four-year college. The figures for African American and Latino students are drastically lower than the national average. Only 51 percent of African American high school students and 52 percent of Latino high school students graduate, meaning that nearly half of these populations drop out and face severely limited economic futures without a high school diploma. Further, a mere 20 percent of African American students and 16 percent of Latino students nationwide leave high school with transcripts that qualify them for four-year colleges. White students, by comparison, graduate at 72 percent nationally, and 34 percent are college-ready upon graduation.

Looking specifically at California, Greene and Forster report that graduation rates for African American and Latino students are slightly higher than the national average (at 58 and 56 percent, respectively, compared to whites at 77 percent). California's college-readiness rates, however, are slightly lower than national rates for Latino students and whites: 15 percent of Latino students leave California high schools with at least minimally college-ready transcripts, as do 30 percent of white students. On the other hand, 22 percent of African American students in California graduate ready for college, a figure that is 2 percent higher than the national average. Thus, overall California is not much different from the nation as a whole.

African Americans, Latinos, and students from low socioeconomic backgrounds are underrepresented on college campuses, even though most colleges actively desire diverse student bodies.[4] Greene and Forster, among others, argue that high school education accounts for the fact that so few African American and Latino students make it into the pool of eligible college applicants.[5] According to these scholars, rather than focusing on the lack of financial aid and affirmative action policies in college admissions, we must look at these students' lack of college preparation. Sociologist James Rosenbaum has also examined students' high school experiences in relation to their college futures. He focuses on the availability of community college as a stepping stone between high school and four-year institutions, whereas Greene and Forster focus on high school graduates' qualifications to attend a four-year institution directly after graduation. Rosenbaum finds that students who receive good grades in high school are most likely to complete a college degree. Further, the better their high school grades, the higher the degree they are likely to complete. Ironically, however, he notes that students believe that their high school success has little or no relevance to their future education and career goals.

Rosenbaum argues that high schools' avid promotion of a "college for all" mantra inadvertently sets up many students for failure in their post-secondary educational pursuits because they are encouraged to set college goals for themselves regardless of their potential for college success.[6] He explains that community colleges' elimination of entrance requirements offers many high school students a false sense of security in their college aspirations. Indeed, there are now relatively few barriers to entering community college after high school, but

Rosenbaum finds that a full 86 percent of seniors with a *C* average or lower and plans to attend college never earn any kind of degree. Similarly, 63 percent of *B*-average seniors with college plans do not complete a degree within ten years. This means that only 37 percent of those students earn a degree. Meanwhile 64 percent of *A*-average seniors with college plans are able to attain a degree within ten years, and the figure is slightly higher for *A*-average seniors who have plans to earn a bachelor's degree or higher (66 percent). Thus, high school grades are a strong indicator of who will finish a college degree.

Scholars and policymakers who are concerned about improving the low numbers of students who transfer from community colleges to four-year institutions tend to focus on improving features of the community colleges themselves.[7] But Rosenbaum emphasizes the importance of the ideas that students have about college while they are still in high school: "The high level of community college dropout arises because high schools offer vague promises of open opportunity for college without specifying the requirements for degree completion."[8] He acknowledges that high schools are not purposely trying to deceive their students. Rather, blanket encouragement to pursue college leads to unintended consequences: "If high school students were informed that they are poorly prepared for community college, they could either increase their efforts to prepare themselves or revise their plans to make them more realistic. In either case, cooling out would not be needed, and youths' plans would be less likely to fail." His study further demonstrates that the students who are already members of disadvantaged groups suffer the highest rates of failed college plans, a finding that other scholars widely support.[9]

Some people continue to argue that schools in general serve as a "great equalizer," helping to minimize inequalities among students from various socioeconomic backgrounds. Nonetheless, students who start their educational experiences in positions of advantage consistently end up on top at the end of high school.[10] This means that we can already expect students like those at Elite Charter High to be better prepared for college than are students like those at Alternative High and Comprehensive High. Part of such college preparation happens inside school by way of courses and curriculum choice, but an important part also happens outside of school in what Patricia McDonough calls college "admissions management," which entails a host of endeavors, including careful preparation for the SAT exam.[11]

The modest percentage of students who do graduate from high school with transcripts that are ready for four-year institutions still face the hurdle of SAT scores before they become well-qualified college applicants. The SAT I is an aptitude test that promises to reveal students' intellectual abilities. We know that the predictive power of the SAT I on college freshmen's grades all but disappears once family income and parents' education are taken into account.[12]

Nevertheless, it is still widely used for college-entrance decisions, in tandem with the SAT II and SAT writing exams. While the SAT II is an achievement test based on mastery of high school curriculum, the SAT I asks test takers questions that are unrelated to their high school courses. This means that students who prepare conscientiously for the SAT I must study additional relevant material on their own; their everyday school experiences will not help them. Not surprisingly, students who come from families with higher incomes and who have parents with higher education are the students who devote greater time, energy, and funds toward familiarizing themselves with the SAT I test. They have the resources and the insider knowledge to participate in this aspect of "admissions management."

As McDonough explains, the college admissions game has dramatically increased in complexity during the past two decades, and the stakes are also much higher. Admissions staffs have grown at unprecedented rates, and U.S. colleges and universities are far more stratified. Students and parents who are aware of the complexities of admission competition must now work harder to ensure admission to elite, selective colleges. These individuals are predominately upper middle class, which is why we would expect them to be more common among Elite Charter High families than among Alternative High and Comprehensive High families. Their efforts include hiring private college counselors to advise them on which college will best fit the student and how to build a strong application. Students enroll in SAT preparation programs, participate in summer experiences such as international travel or wilderness camps that might impress colleges, and so on. Mr. Fischer, the AP chemistry teacher at Elite Charter High, sees this regularly. He calls it "transcript building, . . . just anything that will look good to a school so they can get in." However, he finds it worrisome rather than admirable: "They think: scholarship, AP classes, community service, lots of interests, you know, internships, summer school, whatever you can take. And the kids' lives are dictated by that kind of stuff. I would not want to be a high school student today. Not even remotely." While these endeavors may indeed build a successful college application, Mr. Fischer laments what students lose in the process: "The day they walk in our school, their childhood is gone."

McDonough describes this approach as the "social construction of the college applicant"—that is, the notion that good colleges and universities are looking for a particular type of applicant. Savvy parents and students understand that success in college admissions requires a student to create application materials that depict her as an ideal candidate (or as ideal as possible). These parents and students are also well aware that private college counselors have the best inside information on what selective colleges really want and which colleges are realistic goals for the student.[13] Their professional expertise lies in precisely this knowledge. According to McDonough, the business of buying professional help for college applications is commonplace among upper-middle-class families. In the words of Candy, one of McDonough's high school informants, some students now worry that their glossy applications will "scream private college counseling" to admissions officers.

Elite Colleges Want Students Who "Sparkle"

Elite Charter High's cultural ideas about school success match the expectations of admissions boards at elite colleges. However, the cultural ideas about success at Alternative High and Comprehensive High, both of which serve predominantly low-income and ethnoracial-minority students, are a disadvantage in admission to these colleges. Both Alternative High and Comprehensive High promote attitudes and behaviors that the college-admission process does not recognize as part of the definition of an ideal candidate.

I am using the term *elite colleges* somewhat broadly. In addition to the eight Ivy League universities on the East Coast, which are considered elite by any measure, I include a host of well-respected, highly ranked, selective institutions. All of these schools admit fewer than 50 percent of their applicants, and in the 2005–6 school year approximately eighty-five institutions (some public but most private) fell into this category.[14] To this number, I also add about a hundred well-respected schools with high selectivity, though not quite at the 50-percent threshold. Together, they all comprise what Elite Charter High students and the rest of the higher education world refer to as "good colleges."

How-to books such as *Winning the College Admission Game: Strategies for Students and Parents* by a former dean of admission at Franklin and Marshall College and *Admission Matters: What Students and Parents Need to Know about Getting into College* by an associate chancellor at the University of California paint a clear portrait of the ideal college applicant and offer tips to high school students on how to ensure that they embody this ideal as closely as possible in their application materials. *Admission Matters* explains that admission officers look for evidence that an applicant has "sparkle": "They are looking for someone who is smart, intellectually curious, good hearted, talented, and energetic."[15] Not every book uses the descriptor *sparkle,* but most lay out a similar list of desirable qualities.

Intelligence Sparkles at Elite Charter High

According to *Winning the College Admission Game,* admissions committees want students who are "bright, motivated, high achieving, diverse in background, and 'givers.'" The author, Peter Van Buskirk, goes on to describe each of those qualities in detail.[16] By *bright* he means students "who have the capacity to learn at advanced levels of instruction." But while *motivated* might seem to refer to persistent effort on schoolwork (a quality heavily promoted at Alternative High), Van Buskirk makes it sound like a facet of intelligence rather than dedicated effort: "Colleges want to know how you demonstrate your passion for learning. Do you ask questions and press for greater understanding? Do you 'push the envelope'? Do you stretch yourself beyond the requirements of the classroom? Professors are genuinely excited when students pose questions for which there aren't easy answers. Motivated students energize the classroom." In description, *motivated* sounds nearly identical to Elite Charter High students' idea of initiative.

Recall how Daphne, an AP sophomore at Elite Charter High, explains how she recognizes that another person is intelligent: "If they show a passion for something, then definitely they will have the knowledge of that, and there is intelligence there. . . . [If] they question—that's a big one. Thinking about it can intrigue them enough that they ask about it, then they have the interest and they want to increase their knowledge of that [topic]. So there is intelligence there." Her understanding of intelligence and initiative includes a spirit of ambition. As Rebecca says, highly intelligent people "strive for excellence." At Elite Charter High, students criticize peers for devoting excessive time and emotion to their academic pursuits (as captured in the identity story of the *OCD overachiever*), yet they also see such devotion as evidence that students are highly intelligent. What the former dean of admission at Franklin and Marshall College calls "motivated," students at Elite Charter High call "intelligent"; and as we learned in chapter 5, many students see intelligence as a driving force behind the enthusiasm they associate with initiative.

"High achieving" is the third quality on Van Buskirk's list of desirable traits. As he describes it, this quality is yet another embodiment of academic intelligence. High-achieving students "demonstrate [their] passion for learning. Colleges are always on the lookout for students who love to learn and whose passion takes them to the highest level of challenge and achievement." Van Buskirk explicitly says that a high school transcript is the best way to exhibit one's passion. In other words, by enrolling in advanced courses and receiving top grades in them, students prove that they are passionate about their work. He asserts that most admissions officers look first at a student's transcript and that "an experienced reader can tell within seconds whether you will be competitive." Thus, Elite Charter High students are right to be anxious about their grades if they hope to be competitive college applicants. But this can take a heavy emotional toll on students and their teachers. As

Mr. Fischer tells me with dismay, "I have kids that are *A*-plus students, and they get a *B* on a test and they think, 'Well, I'm going to have to go to community college.'"

Van Buskirk also describes ideal candidates as "diverse in background," a quality that many of Elite Charter High's white students might worry about. *Diverse* is often used as a code word for *ethnoracial* or *not white*. In fact, universities generally seek a wider range of diversity in their students, including religious, sexual, and socioeconomic diversity. Nonetheless, even though ethnoracial diversity is certainly a prime focus, an application will not rise to the top of the admissions pile unless the candidate embodies other ideal traits. An application might be dismissed because of a poor transcript, but it will not be dismissed only because a student is white.

Rounding out his list of traits, Van Buskirk describes the quality he calls a "giver." It turns out that he is not referring to generosity or noble character but about talent. His book cautions students not to run out and participate in every community-service opportunity they can find in order to pad their college applications. Instead, he encourages students to engage in activities that are meaningful to them personally, that are "natural extensions of you and your passions" in ways that "challenge your competencies" and "broaden your perspectives." Thus, the ideal college applicant is "gifted" with a gift that she can share with others and that she has spent her time and energy cultivating through extracurricular activities. Importantly, in an ideal candidate intellectual talent counts as a gift, one that might be evident in "the expression of ideas" or "in laboratories."

In sum, of the five qualities that colleges such as Franklin and Marshall look for in ideal applicants, four can be fulfilled through high intelligence, which, in Van Buskirk's definition, goes hand in hand with ambition, initiative, and passion for learning. While an ideal candidate might possess a talent outside the academic domain—say, dancing—most of his ideal qualities should reveal intellect and enthusiasm demonstrated at high academic levels. This exactly matches the behavior and aspirations of students at Elite Charter High. The goal of Rebecca's four-year plan is admission to Stanford. Alexis says she is happy with her 4.5 GPA because "they're the grades that could get me into a good college." According to Mr. Fischer, his students typically go on to institutions such as "UC San Diego, . . . Stanford, UC Santa Barbara, Berkeley. You know, the UC system is usually their hurdle—UC and then above. The private schools, the big-name private schools." At Elite Charter High, local understandings of school success and the role that intelligence and effort play in it mesh seamlessly with the expectations of elite college admissions boards. The same is not true for Alternative High and Comprehensive High.

Ethnoracial Diversity Alone Is Not Enough Sparkle

Student body diversity is a stated admissions goal at elite colleges, but as I mentioned above, being white does not automatically discount an application. Nonetheless, the ethnoracial diversity of students at Alternative High and Comprehensive High might seem to give them a major admissions advantage. But with the erosion of Affirmative Action mandates, simply being able to check a box other than "Caucasian" does not greatly improve a student's application.[17] As Mitchell Stevens argues, class advantages often influence the process of admissions decisions. In his participant observation study in the admissions office of an elite private college, he finds that staff members work to make thoughtful decisions about acceptances and rejections. This includes careful, individualized readings of applicants' files, a process that should allow personnel to find reasons to accept marginal candidates who would bring valuable ethnoracial diversity to the campus. However, Stevens explains that the process tends to benefit marginal applicants who are upper middle class and usually white. These students often have support from experienced, admissions-savvy adults, including prep school counselors and family friends in high places, who bolster application files with extensive letters of recommendation that provide a compelling, holistic portrait of the applicant as a person.

Because most applicants from comprehensive public high schools do not have access to adults with this kind of institutional know-how, admissions personnel have more trouble constructing a "story" (as Stevens calls it) about who these applicants are as people and how they might enhance the college community. Thus, they are usually rejected. Susan, an admissions officer in Stevens's study, feels powerless about her ability to do anything to amend this inequality: "It is the case that kids from these good private [high] schools do have an edge with these counselors that the public school kids don't have. . . . It just bothers me that here are these kids with so many advantages already, and then they have these counselors who do stuff like this and it works."[18]

Effort at Alternative High Lacks Sparkle

At Alternative High, the local wisdom is that everyone is smart enough to master the demands of school. The difference between those who achieve high academic success and those who do not lies in the amount of effort that each student puts forth. Recall Martín's claim that "actually reading" homework assignments and "putting in answers" leads to effective learning. "Even if you don't understand it thoroughly, over time you will eventually," he says, because effort will bring about comprehension and, by extension, school success. Yet these cultural ideas about school success do not benefit students who aspire to attend elite colleges. Instead, they better align with the expectations of community colleges, the lowest tier of higher education.

The belief that everyone is intellectually capable of succeeding in school sends students a positive and encouraging message. Given that Alternative High students are predominantly from low-performing urban middle schools where many of them struggled academically, the school's mission to build their academic confidence is reasonable and admirable. During my weeks of observation, I regularly saw the principal sit in on lessons and interact with the students one on one. She repeatedly told them that they were "brilliant," "amazing," and "intelligent." The teachers also consistently reinforced the notion that each student is fully capable of achieving school success at as high a level as they are willing to reach for.

Alternative High's teachers and administrators encourage their students to develop college aspirations. For example, beginning in their freshman year, students are required to assemble college binders in which they collect information about a given number of colleges each term. They are graded for this work. The idea is to have students familiarize themselves with the world of higher education by researching different schools in terms of majors, enrollment numbers, tuition costs, social organizations on campus, and so on. The binders help students figure out which sorts of colleges appeal to them. Guidebooks such as *Admission Matters* and *Winning the College Admission Game* advise high school freshman to begin preparing for their college applications by choosing their courses carefully, engaging in meaningful extracurricular activities, pursuing leadership opportunities, and planning a summer of enriching experiences. In contrast, students at Alternative High are just beginning to learn the names of famous and nearby colleges and getting accustomed to the idea that they might one day apply to such a place. Compiling accolades that make their college applications "sparkle" is beyond the scope of all of the freshman and most of the sophomores I talked to at Alternative High.

During the year of my research, Alternative High sophomores were passing the state's exit exam at rates much higher than the state averages for sophomores: over 80 percent in math and over 90 percent in language arts as opposed to state averages of 76 percent in math and 77 percent in language arts. At the same time, they have extremely low scores on some parts of the CST and are slightly under average on other parts. In less than two years' time, these sophomores will take the SAT, including the SAT II achievement test, which is based on high school curricular content that is similar to what appears on the CST. It is difficult to imagine that they will gain enough ground to earn SAT II scores that will make them competitive college applicants.

There is controversy over the usefulness of the SAT I and II in predicting a student's college success. Nonetheless, elite colleges continue to take them very seriously in college admissions. Low scores blemish an application.[19] Van Buskirk explains that many schools have "conceded that your SAT score no longer holds any diagnostic value. It has become, however, a competitive credential," and students should do everything in their power to prepare well for the tests.[20] The ideal candidate has stellar test scores. This presents a serious obstacle for Alternative High students. When I interviewed them, very few were even aware of what the SAT is. Their immediate test concerns revolved around the exit exam, which they were scheduled to take for the first time at the end of tenth grade. As I mentioned in chapter 2, the sophomore class even has a special exit exam teacher who helps prepare them specifically for this test. Thus, unlike sophomores at Elite Charter High, many of whom are already taking SAT preparatory classes, sophomores at Alternative High are focused primarily on the task of graduating from high school. College still seems like a distant dream.

The situation at Alternative High is a good example of what Rosenbaum worries about when he considers the "college for all" ethos that many high schools promote. He argues that without clear guidelines about how to actually succeed in college, many students are inadvertently set up for failure. They are coached to pursue higher education regardless of their potential for success, but when they fail, they feel that they have no one to blame but themselves.[21] Alternative High's cultural belief that school success depends on effort, regardless of one's intelligence level, does not match the beliefs and expectations of admissions officers at elite colleges. This does not mean that the Alternative High is doing something wrong. It means that higher education is rife with inequality.

Selective colleges are looking for "sparkle." They seek students who are "bright," "motivated," and "high achieving"—that is, they want intelligent students with a zest for learning. To catch an admissions officer's attention in the first few seconds of perusing her transcript, an applicant must demonstrate that she is competitive. Do her grades and her course trajectory signal high intellectual capacity parlayed into high academic success? Although effort is certainly part of how a student achieves *As*, the staff member interprets her transcript in terms of an intelligence-based model of academic performance and success, not a strictly effort-based model. Selective colleges do not believe that everyone can master the intellectual demands of school. On the contrary, admissions officers' primary charge is to sort out who is cognitively talented enough to succeed at their school and who is not. Alternative High's belief in effort as the critical ingredient in academic success is a liability on the transcripts and applications of its students. It is an invisible disadvantage. Students are unlikely to build their transcripts and college essays around a demonstration of their intellectual abilities. Rather, they are likely to focus on how hard they work, their responsibility in meeting deadlines, and their perseverance in completing assignments and projects. However, for admissions officers, a demonstration of dogged persistence in school does not equal "bright," "motivated," and "high achieving."

Alternative High Beliefs Match Community College Expectations

Students at all three of the schools in my study have access to California's extensive system of public higher education. As established in the 1960 California Master Plan for Higher Education, three tiers of institutions are available. The top tier is the University of California (UC), whose ten campuses are designed to draw from the top 12.5 percent of high school graduates. The middle tier is the California State University System (CSU), designed to draw from the top 33.3 percent of high school graduates. It has twenty-three campuses. The lowest tier is the community college system, with 110 campuses, which are designed to accept all applicants ages eighteen and older who can benefit from instruction.[22]

Community colleges were founded with the goal of providing higher education for all Americans. They are "the primary source of opportunity for ethnic minorities, immigrants, and low income students. They offer a second chance for students who attended poor high schools, or who did poorly in high school."[23] The necessary model of success in such institutions is effort-based, which exactly fits Alternative High's local beliefs about what it takes to succeed in school.

Community colleges are committed to accessibility, which is made possible through very low fees and open enrollment policies that minimize barriers to success in higher education. One critically important feature of this commitment to accessibility is the wide range of course offerings in developmental studies programs, also known as remediation.[24] Developmental studies programs target students who are underprepared for the demands of college-level academics. They accept students no matter what their academic starting point and educate them for college readiness. Gail Mellow and Cynthia Heelan write that "Developmental Studies is a significant part of helping many groups of students achieve educational success and access to the American Dream. . . . The community college dream is based on the belief that adults can learn, [if] given the right support system and enough time."[25] Nonetheless, Mellow and Heelan acknowledge that a full 60 percent of developmental studies students are under the age of twenty-two. That is, they are traditional college-age students who are beginning their postsecondary educations, but they do not already possess college-ready academic skills.

Alternative High's low-to-average academic performance on the CST indicates that many of its students are unqualified to meet admissions criteria at elite colleges. At a community college, however, they can take advantage of developmental studies offerings that will prepare them for a four-year college.

Some Alternative High students benefit even further. In lieu of AP courses, the school offers its students the opportunity to take community college classes while they are still in high school. With a nearby campus, it has developed a structured program for juniors and seniors, who can take one or two courses there each semester if their homeroom teacher agrees that they are strong enough students. It is an excellent way for Alternative High students to familiarize themselves with college-level academics and to graduate from high school with some college credits to their name. The program should also help them become more competitive applicants to four-year colleges.

As it turns out, many of the Alternative High students I observed and interviewed did gravitate toward community colleges after graduation. When I returned to the school in 2012, Mrs. Williams and Mrs. Greene filled me in on where many of their students had landed. Mrs. Williams's homeroom class had been sophomores when I met them. They had graduated in 2008, and by 2012 some were wrapping up their fourth year in college. Family-like still, most had kept in touch with her. She was able to tell me the whereabouts of all but two of the fourteen students whom I had observed in her class six years earlier. (Two additional students had changed schools before graduating.) Three of these former students had attended four-year colleges—two in the CSU system, one in the more prestigious UC system. None, however, had been able to finish in four years, including Reina, who had been co-valedictorian of her high school class and was the student who was attending a UC campus. Seven members of the cohort were in their fourth year of attending community college. According to Mrs. Williams, two of them planned to transfer to a four-year institution in the near future, one on a sports scholarship. Additionally, two other students had gone on to trade schools.

The outcome was similar for the twenty freshmen in Mrs. Greene's homeroom. Those in college were now finishing their third year. Of the thirteen whose whereabouts she knew (three of the twenty had changed high schools and another three did not keep in touch), four were enrolled in four-year colleges—three at CSUs and one at UC San Diego, which is an elite campus by my definition. Four others were at community colleges or trade schools, and some were working in addition to attending school. Five students were not currently enrolled in college but were married or working in jobs such as construction and security, although a couple of them had started at community college before moving to full-time work. Deshawn attended two years at a UC but was unable to finance it further. He now works full time at a discount retail clothing store.

The principal at Alternative High recognizes that getting into college is only the first obstacle for her students. "We provide all the necessary steps for them to get into a four-year," she says, but finishing college presents another set of difficulties.[26] "With my background and my experience, my biggest fear is: I can get you graduated. I can get you into a four-year. But once you leave me, how are you going to sustain it? Because you are not going to have me and my staff saying, 'You can do this, you can do this,' and [when you don't have the money for a meal card] 'this is what you need to do.'"

During our 2012 interview, the principal invited a guest to sit in on our discussion. Rosario was Alternative High's most celebrated alumna to date. She had completed a bachelor's degree at UC Berkeley, a highly selective elite campus. Rosario was part of Alternative High's first graduating class, and her diploma from Berkeley is not only a major accomplishment for herself but also a feather in the high school's cap. However, her success seems to be the exception that proves the rule: "Out of all of the students that I graduated with, I think there were about seventy-two of us, to my knowledge there are only two of us that graduated from the four-year university track." A later conversation with Mrs. Williams revealed that there is some question as to whether there were in fact two college graduates from that class. Rosario may be the only one.

Some of Alternative High's students have been the first in their families to graduate from high school. Even if the school's cultural wisdom is a disadvantage on their college applications, its belief that effort is the key to success is probably responsible for the positive personal and academic gains the students have made while enrolled there. Alternative High has brought numbers of academically struggling middle schoolers to the point of being interested in college, qualifying for it, and actively pursuing it. Starting one's higher education at a community college is a viable route toward a four-year degree, even one from an elite college. The fact that Alternative High's cultural wisdom resonates with community college expectations does not automatically predict failure. Yet I would be shortsighted not to acknowledge that these students' experiences have not transcended the pattern of social reproduction and that the high school's cultural wisdom plays a part in the complicated, multifaceted dynamics of the process.

Comprehensive High's "Weak Points" Do Not Sparkle

The cultural wisdom about school success at Comprehensive High also creates invisible disadvantages on students' transcripts and in their applications to elite colleges. But rather than aligning students with community colleges, these attitudes match the expectations for success at middle-tier state universities. At Comprehensive High students and teachers do tend to believe that intelligence sets the parameters for school success. As one student, Stephanie, says, "You can try as hard as you can and put in as much effort as you can and still not understand the material." At first glance, this belief might seem to resonate with the logic of admissions officers at elite colleges. But in fact it is a liability on applications to these institutions. Like Stephanie, admissions officers work from the premise that not every applicant is intellectually capable of academic success at their institution. It is the officers' job to determine which students are "bright," "motivated," and "high achieving" enough to be worthy of admission. Yet students at Comprehensive High do not act on their belief about intelligence in a way that attracts the interest of most admissions committees at elite colleges.

Admissions officers use an applicant's transcript as a critical first indicator of whether the student is competitive. As Van Buskirk details, they assess it at multiple points, searching for signs of intelligence, passion for learning, and pursuit of excellence. Both *Winning the College Admission Game* and *Admission Matters* continually emphasize the scope and depth of competition among applicants for admission to selective colleges. Their advice focuses on strategies for demonstrating that one is both highly intelligent and original or unique, and officers expect students to be honing their competitive edge throughout their high school years.

At Elite Charter High, students have a clear sense of the importance of academic competition. This is evident in their *college strategist* identity story and in the intense rivalry over grades. Recall Denise's boiling disappointment over not being able to "beat" her best friend's GPA this year and James's dismay that "slower" classmates are earning *A*s that are identical. But at Comprehensive High, students do not develop similarly competitive academic agendas. While they understand that intelligence is not evenly distributed among students and that higher intelligence gives a person greater potential to excel in school, they do not act on that belief by jockeying for grades and course placements that will set them apart from the competition when they apply to college.

There is no *college strategist* identity story at Comprehensive High because both AP and college-prep students use their beliefs about intelligence to justify the common notion that, in Diana's words, "everyone has a weak point." While students at Alternative High and Elite Charter High also acknowledge that a person may be stronger in, say, math and weaker in, say, English, they do not treat this situation as acceptable or unalterable. At both of those schools, students, especially high-achieving ones, treat their weak points as challenges, areas in which they need to develop skills so that they will succeed across the curriculum.

In contrast, at Comprehensive High, a weak point is a fact of life, and the curriculum structure reinforces this belief. For instance, the way in which the school bundles its AP curriculum contributes to the idea that students are naturally better in some academic subjects than in others. Part of the logic is that people who are good in math are also likely to be good in science but not necessarily good in English.[27] In other words, people have strong suits and weak suits; a left-brain, right-brain split. So students who take AP classes at Comprehensive High tend to choose one bundle rather than overload their schedule with two bundles just to prove that they are good at using both sides of the brain.

How-to guidebooks on college admission warn against this approach. Ideal candidates, they explain, do not have this type of focused AP course work on their transcripts. According to Van Buskirk, selective colleges look for applicants who continually "stretch [themselves] academically across all disciplines."[28] Certainly Comprehensive High students have the option to pursue AP course work in four subjects at once, which would meet these admissions expectations. However, the common understanding that weak points are both expected and accepted deters most of them from pursuing AP courses broadly across disciplines, and this local belief is an invisible liability for students who apply to elite colleges. It promotes complacency about modest success in subjects that are not their strong suit, and this is not part of the profile of an ideal candidate. Such a transcript does not sparkle. Admissions officers interpret limited AP course work as evidence that an applicant might not have the ability and eagerness to succeed at their institution. Yet Comprehensive High students remain confident that excelling in either math/science or language/social science is all that even very intelligent and high-achieving students can expect.

Comprehensive High Beliefs Match
Middle-Tier Public University Expectations

Many Comprehensive High students aim to attend four-year institutions after graduating from high school, though some plan to start at community college and transfer to a four-year school later. Unlike Alternative High, where beliefs about success resonate well with community college expectations, Comprehensive High's assumption that Cs are an acceptable level of success matches expectations in the CSU system, the middle tier of California's higher education hierarchy. General admission to CSU requires a student to complete required high school courses with a grade of C or better, and the applicant's overall GPA must be at least a 2.0, a C average.[29] None of the CSU campuses are elite institutions, unlike some of the UC campuses (in particular, Berkeley, Los Angeles, and San Diego), which have high national status and prestige.[30] Nonetheless, the CSUs are considered to be decent universities where an *Average Joe* can earn a respectable education.

Both the principal and Mrs. Brookings, the AP English teacher, affirm that Comprehensive High students often end up at CSUs—usually a nearby campus in the same county. The school administration and the local community see attending a CSU as respectable and commendable, and in fact the school district recently established a scholarship for all Comprehensive High graduates who attend the local campus. The principal calls it a "pledge" of support to all the students who "grow up in our system" and cross the postsecondary hurdle to a four-year college. By contract with the university, any student who meets the CSU admission criteria is guaranteed admission to this campus. All receive a modest scholarship, enough to at least cover the cost of a semester's books, and the scholarship is renewable for four years of enrollment. Clearly, in the eyes of Comprehensive High students and district administrators, attending a CSU is a worthwhile goal.

Reinforcing Existing Inequalities in Higher Education

One might argue that, for these three schools, admission to elite colleges is not the most relevant point of analysis. If, as is the case at Alternative High, many of the students are the first in their families to seek any higher education, why does it matter how competitive they will be at selective colleges? Shouldn't I focus on whether students at Alternative High and Comprehensive High have access to any college futures at all? Shouldn't I be celebrating the fact that they do indeed have ways into system?

My point is that resting on such a position neglects an important dynamic of higher education in the United States and of young Americans' life chances more broadly. Students do not have equal opportunities to become successful adults. Our nation and its education system are riddled with inequalities, and many are linked to race. African American and Latino students are underrepresented on college campuses across the country, and the imbalance is dramatic at elite colleges. California's three tiers of higher education also embody ethnoracial inequalities. Table 7.1 demonstrates that, in 2003, Latinos and African Americans together made up only 17 percent of the student population on UC campuses, although these two groups comprise 41 percent of the state population.[31] And since 2003, Latinos' share of the California population has grown.

As I discussed early in this chapter, the key to understanding this phenomenon is to look at students' academic experiences during high school. The hierarchy of higher education is a critical mechanism of social reproduction that exacerbates K–12 educational inequalities. How well do students' high school years prepare them for college, and which tier of higher education does that preparation fit them to enter? As Ann Mullen argues in *Degrees of Inequality*, "because of the hierarchical nature of the U.S. higher educational system and the disparities in the rewards that it offers, it is no longer enough to simply look at who goes to college and who does not . . . one needs to examine the opportunities students of different backgrounds have to attend the various institutions

TABLE 7.1.

**Percentage of Racial/Ethnic Minority Enrollment in the
Three Tiers of California Higher Education, 2003**

	University of California	*California State University*	*Community College*	*Percent of California's Population*
Whites	44	43	42	44
Latinos	14	24	29	35
Blacks	3	0.6	8	6
Asian/Pacific Islanders	36	22	17	12
Other	3	5	4	3

Source: Ria Sengupta and Christopher Jepsen, "California's Community College Students," *California Counts: Population Trends and Profiles* 8, no. 2 (2006): 1–24.

within that system. In other words, we need to look not just at *who* goes to college, but who goes *where* to college."[32]

A student who attends an elite college is more likely than other students are to have a prestigious career, higher earnings, and greater life satisfaction.[33] Mullen demonstrates that attending a top college such as Yale confers not only a diploma but also "social superiority and qualifications for leadership" that lower status schools cannot provide. Whereas the less selective public university she studies produces graduates who possess "technical skills" and "a kind of training that sets them apart from those who do not attend college," Yale graduates are "consecrated" as "superior individuals" who "meet the world assured of their own talents, intelligence and worthiness."[34] In other words, the rewards of attending an elite college are go far beyond future advantages on the job market.

Organizational Changes over Time

As I have shown, high schools' cultural ideas about success contribute to why ethnoracial minorities and low socioeconomic students are underqualified for admission to four-year colleges and underprepared for the demands of community college. Much research (for example, in the oppositional culture debate) looks at students' anti-achievement attitudes to explain differences in school performance.[35] But local beliefs also create dissonance between the way in which underrepresented students and the gatekeepers of higher education understand school success. Admissions officers assess the transcripts and applications of Alternative High and Comprehensive High students according to elite colleges' definitions of intelligence and achievement. Given the cultural wisdom about success at these schools, their students are unlikely to be able to build competitive applications around that criteria.

However, organizations are not static entities, and schools are no exception. When I returned to Comprehensive High in 2012, six years after observing and interviewing its students, I was delighted to discover that many of the principal's curricular changes have begun to pay off. Students' standardized scores have risen, as have their college-attendance rates. Today I would no longer describe it as a typical California high school. The principal boasts, "Seven years [after implementing the changes], we are the sixth-highest-performing school in the county. It is a very diverse population, over 50 percent English learners and free and reduced lunch. Kids are going to college at a very high rate—shouldn't really be happening with the population we have if you look at comparative studies with other schools." She tells me that she and her staff have actively worked to improve the image of the school: "We raised the bar everywhere, in everything" to dismantle the impression that it was an "average, mediocre" school. "Many people were getting fake addresses and taking their kids across the hill to [other] schools, so we had to turn that around if were going to have the school grow." She proudly tells me that their efforts have "made a big difference because people started to look at the school and go, 'Wow. Maybe this *is* a place I want to send my kids.'"

Clearly, today's Comprehensive High is different from the Comprehensive High of 2005–6 that I depict and analyze in this book. Such organizational change should come as no surprise; after all, six years is a long time in the life of a school. It also underscores the importance of taking an inhabited institutions approach to studying local culture in organizational environments. Over time the configuration of educational policies, administrative leaders, teachers, students, parents, wider economic conditions, and so on will shift in unpredictable ways. These shifts will alter the concerns that weigh on the people associated with each school, which in turn will alter how they draw on cultural ideas as resources to respond to new concerns. After talking with the principal in 2012, I could not help but wonder if Mackie, for example, would narrate his story as an *Average Joe* if he were attending Comprehensive High today. Does that identity story even matter to the students there now?

While I do not have dramatic changes to report at Elite Charter High, institutional change is also evident than at Alternative High, where student performance over the past six years has increased even more dramatically than it has at Comprehensive High. Walking through the school office at Alternative High, I came across the "college board" of the 2012 graduating class. Here students publicly list all the colleges they apply to, highlight the schools that have accepted them, and star the one they decide to attend. I was fortunate enough to be on campus just a few days before graduation, so the college board was nearly complete. Of the thirty-nine graduating seniors with posts on the board (80 percent of the class), only six had applied exclusively to community colleges. The other thirty-three had aimed at four-year institutions. Six had been accepted to UC campuses, including one to Berkeley. Twenty had applied to CSU campuses along with a smattering of other states' public schools. Of course, students were not accepted at every school to which they applied, yet all were accepted to at least one. The college board was nothing short of impressive. Students focused largely on four-year institutions; and while only four students applied to elite colleges and only one was accepted, the aspirations of the class of 2012 are substantially higher than those of the students whom I met and interviewed in 2006. I was thrilled to see that this class's educational future is so bright.

Interestingly, my 2012 interviews with the principal and Mrs. Williams confirm that the cultural wisdom about school success has not changed much since 2006, at least not from their perspective. They still espouse hard work as the critical ingredient in the recipe for success. However, other changes in the organizational life at Alternative High have helped students improve their academic performance and elevate their college aspirations. (Their CST scores have also markedly increased, far surpassing state averages in some areas.) As I was unable to conduct a thorough study, I cannot say with certainty what factors matter most in the school's current cultural and structural environment. However, I did learn that as the school's reputation in the district has grown, the caliber of incoming students has also increased, meaning that fewer low-performing middle school students now choose Alternative High. This makes me wonder if the pervasive fear of failure that I noted among the students in 2006 is no longer an issue for the students who inhabit the school today. In addition, I conducted my research when Alternative High was a fledgling school. Certainly it now has more institutional experience and has worked out some of the kinks in its system.

Afterword

The ideas that formed this project bgean long before I was an academic sociologist. Freshly out of college, I joined the Peace Corps to teach English in Latvia on
the Baltic Sea. In a small town called Limbaži I set about trying to learn teaching
norms in a Latvian high school. It was not easy. I was faced with an entirely new
set of ideas about how to grade student work. My Latvian colleagues believed
that it was important to assess the knowledge that students carried around in
their heads all the time, not just on test day after they had been cramming ideas
into their short-term memories. This struck me as terribly unfair. Raised in California public schools and steeped in U.S. norms of how to grade schoolwork, I
wanted to grade my Latvian students as I had always been graded. But I gradually
realized that grading, like almost everything else, is culturally relative and that
the American way is not necessarily the best way.

These experiences pushed me to ask questions about the meaning of school
grades that I had not thought about before. If Latvian grades captured the information that you actually retained, those ideas and details that you could pull up
at any moment in a discussion, were those grades better, more holistic measures
of your learning? Did receiving good grades in school in Latvia versus the United
States make students feel different about themselves? What about bad grades?
Growing up, I understood that good grades conferred positive moral status on
a student, a status I enjoyed throughout my educational career. Not only were
straight As a signal to the world that you were smart, they also meant you were a
good kid. Conversely, bad grades signaled a moral failing. Someone who got Ds
and Fs was not just a bad student but also a bad person. Now I started to wonder
if this was everyone's understanding of grades in the United States or if it might
be limited to people like me who got straight As. These questions stayed with
me after I returned from the Peace Corps and began graduate work in sociology.

I wanted to study grades from students' perspectives. What did grades say about who they were as people?

As my project developed, I learned that high school students' success identities are often tied to their future aspirations for college. This was uncertain territory for me because I realized that my own college-going experience had been shamefully uninformed. Although I had attended a lovely small liberal arts college and received an excellent education, I had actually stumbled upon that happy outcome instead of carefully and purposely pursuing my best college options as most other people apparently had. My decisions were not haphazard; they made the most sense at the time, given the college knowledge that I had access to. I simply did not have any people in my life to guide me. Yet I was not the first person in my family to go to college. My mother has a bachelor's degree and my older sister was a sophomore on a UC campus. As a high-achieving student in a middle-class neighborhood school, I was surrounded by friends and classmates who were planning to go to college. Yet somehow I missed all the insider knowledge that (I found out later) my friends all knew. For example, no one explained the importance of visiting college campuses. It sounded expensive and difficult to arrange, so I did not do it. Applications were also expensive, so I applied to only three schools: UC San Diego and Stanford (both based on reputation) and Whittier College, which I had never heard of before but which sent me great promotional material and really seemed to want me there.

No one helped me with my applications. This was a mistake. I was rejected from UC San Diego because I did not submit a transcript. My guidance counselor (whom I had never met before that day) pulled me out of class to tell me that she had found out about the missing transcript and was faxing one over right away. I stood in her office, watching as she frantically stamped the school seal onto a large blue paper. I was too embarrassed to tell her that I did not know what a transcript was. I just nodded and thanked her. The application had undoubtedly instructed me to include one, but I had not understood what I needed to do. Even at that late stage, with the counselor's help, I very likely could have appealed my rejection and successfully been admitted to UC San Diego. I know that now. At that time, however, I had never heard of an appeal, so I did not know it was possible.

A letter came from Stanford in the dreaded thin envelope. I was surprised to discover that I had not been rejected but placed on its wait list. When I tell people now that I was wait-listed at Stanford, their eyes brighten, and they treat me as if I have just won an award. "Wow, that's impressive," they say. At the time it did not feel like an award. I did not know that the wait list was a perfectly respectable avenue into a competitive school. My eyes interpreted the letter as saying that Stanford did not want me but was willing to tolerate me if its top-choice students decided not to come. I was sure that if I ended up at Stanford, my professors and classmates would somehow all know that I was a "wait-list kid," that I did not really belong there. Plus, my family could not afford Stanford. I was sure that scholarships were given only to students whom the school was trying to woo into acceptance. Being on the wait list must mean I had no chance at financial help. Of course, I now know that this is absolutely not the case. As a high school senior, however, I simply did not have the right information. No one told me, and I did not ask. I declined the spot on Stanford's wait list, thinking I was protecting my dignity and avoiding impossible debt.

Luckily, the letter from Whittier College came in a thick envelope. UC San Diego and Stanford were both lost, but I was going to college after all. The letter offered me a generous scholarship, proving that Whittier truly wanted me to join its incoming freshman class. It validated my sense of self as a valuable person with intellectual talents and great potential. I accepted immediately.

I am not sorry that I did not go to Stanford or UC San Diego. I thrived at Whittier College. I offer this story of my college application experience only to position myself as a researcher analyzing the college-going trajectories of public high school students in California. I did not come to this project from a perspective of great privilege. Instead, I came with a great deal of empathy for students who are facing their futures and making decisions based on the ideas and information they have available to them. In this book I emphasize the benefits of attending an elite college even though I did not attend one myself. In my analysis I make judgments about how well each school is positioning its students for acceptance to elite colleges, but I do not believe that elite colleges are the only places that create rewarding life futures for students. My own life story disavows that idea. Nonetheless, overwhelming evidence demonstrates that meaningful rewards come with attending an elite university. I would be remiss to argue that access to any college is all that matters, just as any of us would be wrong to assume that every definition of success pays off equally well in the college admissions game.

APPENDIX A:
IDENTITY THEORY AND
INHABITED INSTITUTIONALISM

Investigating student success identities offers a useful bridge between the work on identity done in social psychology and cultural sociology. As Tim Hallett, David Shulman, and Gary Alan Fine show, symbolic interactionism (one important strain of social psychology) lays a foundation for inhabited institutionalism's focus on "the constitutive role of people in organizations."[1] Similarly, Judson Everitt's recent work on teachers links symbolic interactionism's concern with how individuals make sense of their interactions and experiences with inhabited institutionalism's interest in identifying "social mechanisms through which people's sense-making and interaction drive institutional functioning."[2] Yet little scholarship explicitly discusses how inhabited institutionalism might expand theoretical approaches to understanding identity.

Though cultural sociologists and social psychologists do not often directly engage with one another, they share common conceptualizations of identity, primarily through narrative. This overlap is precisely where inhabited institutionalism can intervene in both literatures. Using identity stories as an analytic framework adds a critical organizational layer to social psychology analyses, just as emphasizing organization-level modifications of larger cultural schemas adds important nuance to cultural sociology analyses of how individuals make sense of themselves and their place in the world.

Social psychology is a vast field of study with two distinct realms: one rooted in psychology and another rooted in sociology.[3] The latter best aligns with cultural sociology and has been heavily influenced by symbolic interactionism as developed in the Chicago School under George Herbert Mead.[4] Even this subset of social psychologists offers myriad approaches to studying identity.[5] Some draw on Erving Goffman to look at identity through performances of self.[6] Some draw on Sigmund Freud to look at identity through psychoanalysis as a "way to understand the non-conscious, non-rational, emotional elements of identity."[7] Some draw on Michel Foucault to look at identities through the discourses that produce them, for example, Foucault characterizes identity through "technologies of the self" that allow individuals to "know" and "take care of" themselves.[8] Some draw on Ulrich Beck or Anthony Giddens to look at identity as a product of the postmodern condition. In this work identity is a reflexive process in which individuals continually assess and make sense of themselves and their choices in "a world of plural, but ambiguous, options."[9] Still others look at identity through cognitive schemas that pattern our ideas about the world and ourselves.[10]

Meanwhile, cultural sociologists typically refer to symbolic interactionism or a particular theorist such as Goffman to support the basic premise that identities are socially constructed; arise from interaction between agentic, strategic individuals; and are continually in flux. Beyond a brief reference, cultural sociologists usually feel little need to detail how they know what they know about identity, not because they are uninterested in theoretical frameworks of identity formation but because they take these ideas as established understandings of the self that lie behind the cultural analysis at hand.

One notable exception is cultural sociologists' treatment of Pierre Bourdieu, whose conceptualization of habitus has been influential in their study of how identity works in people's lives and whom they often directly engage and challenge. Bourdieu theorizes that the things we say, do, and think about the world are automatic and unconsciously formulated by our social dispositions. We acquire these dispositions from the sensibilities of the people who shape and influence us, such as our family, who also unwittingly reinforce them throughout our lives.

Many cultural sociologists (among others) believe that this dispositional framework offers a limited understanding of identity.[11] Wendy Bottero argues that individuals are reflexive about themselves and their place in the world at more moments than Bourdieu allows for. In his explanation, individuals become reflexive about their identity when they experience dissonance between their habitus and a particular field. Generally these are moments of crisis when an individual is confronted by expectations that do not match her habitus. They are exceptional rather than everyday moments.

Bottero disagrees. She sees reflexivity as a routine part of life: "It is important to retain a sense that the encounter between habitus and field is also an encounter between agents."[12] She argues that we should view identity as "situated intersubjectivity." This refinement of Bourdieu's ideas takes us closer to symbolic interactionist understandings of how identities work. According to Bottero, "framing the 'socialized subjectivity' of the habitus as a situated intersubjectivity means exploring the *links* between dispositions, the monitoring and coordination of conduct, agents' reflexive accounts of their activity, and the mobilization of groups of agents into collectivities, as *component* features of the collective accomplishment of practices."[13]

What Bottero refers to as "agents' reflexive accounts of their activity," social psychologists refer to as "self narratives."[14] James Holstein and Jaber Gubrium's articulation is arguably closest to cultural sociologists' approaches:

> We tell the story of the self at the crossroads of narrative, social interaction, culture, and institutional life. . . . We are more deeply concerned with the resources and conditions of self construction than is typical of ethnomethodology. While certainly appreciating the *hows* of self construction, we are equally interested in the various *whats* that bear on the process—*whats* that extend to discourse and surrounding institutional environments of talk and social interaction.[15]

In other words, they pay close attention to the available cultural resources and the constraints on individuals as they craft their personal identities, which is precisely what cultural sociologists tend to explore when they take up the thorny question of how culture works in individuals' lives.

Using Claude Lévi-Strauss's metaphor of the *bricoleur,* Holstein and Gubrium argue that, "as a bricoleur, the self constructor is involved in something like an interpretive salvage operation, crafting selves from the vast array of available resources, making do with what he or she has to work with in the circumstances at hand, all the while constrained, but not completely controlled, by the working conditions of the moment."[16] Along with symbolic interactionists, these scholars see identity as situational, specific to the moment of interaction and evolving over time. Equally important to Holstein and Gubrium (but less so to some other sociological psychologists) is that we view ourselves as having a coherent, core self that is relatively stable even as it undergoes change. Yes, the self is a "social construction" but one that "we both assemble and live out as we take up or resist the varied demands of everyday life."[17] We do not think of ourselves as completely different people from one context to the next, even if we do recognize that we behave differently in one situation than in another or talk differently with one group of people than with another. We are continually at work making meaning out of our interactions (with both other people and institutions) and crafting our identity in response to those meanings.

Holstein and Gubrium argue that "narrative practice lies at the heart of self construction."[18] Thus, by listening to individuals talk about themselves, their experiences, and their lives, researchers can hear how "locally available" institutional and cultural resources shape those identities.[19] This is what I did in the study I describe this book.[20] Like other cultural sociologists, I have sought to reveal the implicit cultural frameworks that individuals draw on to make sense of themselves and their options for action. Mary Blair-Loy takes a similar approach in her study of high-level female executives who experience a dilemma between two cultural expectations, or schemas: that one should be devoted to either work or child rearing.[21] The way in which the individual women in her study navigate these "competing devotions" varies because each woman makes her own sense out of who she is and what she wants. Yet at the same time Blair-Loy finds patterns in women's responses to their cultural dilemma, partly because only a limited number of choices are available to them. This is one example of how culture drives human action.

Blair-Loy's study offers insight into the "whats" of identity construction, as Holstein and Gubrium call them. Schemas of devotion are the available cultural resources, and they shape and constrain the women's understandings of their options: for example, the option to be a devoted mother. By listening to self-narratives, Blair-Loy hears how each woman makes sense of herself in light of these schemas. Importantly, she also hears how individuals creatively rework the schemas, altering them to accommodate their own understandings of their place in the world.

Although both cultural sociologists and sociological psychologists use self-narratives to study personal identities, the two groups do not treat them in identical ways. Sociological psychologists also emphasize identity as the discrete result of narrative. As Leslie Irvine argues, "selfhood is a narrative accomplishment. The self is the premise and the result of the stories people tell about themselves."[22] While people experience themselves as having a core, coherent self that they can describe through narrative, social psychologists recognize that that the version of self-identity that a researcher hears in an interview is created precisely in that moment of storytelling. It is not a description of a permanent and stable identity. Cultural sociologists tend not to engage in identity theory at this level, but they do not completely disregard the importance of situational interactions. Indeed, this is precisely what Nina Eliasoph and Paul Lichterman emphasize as "culture in interaction."[23]

Beyond the question of the ephemeral versus stable nature of identity, the two groups share many central concerns. For instance, both recognize the reciprocal influence of actors and structures. Holstein and Gubrium argue, "It is important to remember that narrative practice does not simply unfold within the interpretive boundaries of [institutions], but contributes to the definitions of those boundaries in its own right."[24] Cultural sociologists focus on the cultural resources that form those "interpretive boundaries," while sociological psychologists concentrate on the identities that are constructed from the cultural resources.

My empirical analysis shows how inhabited institutionalism can inter-vene in both literatures. Using this framework, I work to expand cultural soci-ology's understanding of how cultural schemas shape identity. Schools adapt and modify the cultural schemas of success-through-intelligence and success-through-effort in a way that mediates individual students' understandings of themselves. Unlike the women Blair-Loy interviewed, who seem to draw directly on nationwide work-devotion and family-devotion schemas in their self-narratives, the students I interviewed draw on the local versions of the cultural schemas of success, which are modified by their particular school environment. As I demonstrate ways in which individuals construct their identities in response to identity stories, I use the framework of inhabited institutionalism to expand social psychology's understandings of identity for-mation though narrative. Identity stories are cultural constructs, an important institutional resource that supplies an available model of a possible self that exists in a particular organizational context at a particular moment. Holstein and Gubrium argue,

> Local culture offers ways of constructing self that are reflexively both productive of and responsive to everyday interpretive circumstances. It doesn't force particular self definitions upon participants; rather it makes them accountable in the local scheme of things. It does not dictate how persons see or convey themselves, but provides shared-in-common resources to a community that, in turn, comes to identify itself in terms that the culture provides. Always crafted to the circumstances at hand, the stock of salient, accountable resources provided by settings, commu-nities, organizations, or institutions comprises self-defining images and vocabularies that are realized in locally storied selves.[25]

Identity stories easily fit Holstein and Gubrium's description of "images and vocabularies" that are available for individuals to use to define themselves. Certainly they appear in "locally storied selves," which is precisely where I found them when I listened to students who attend the same schools. Inhab-ited Institutionalism agrees that it is critical for researchers to have a nuanced understanding of the local meanings assigned to relevant objects, actions, and identities in the organizational (cultural) environment in which individuals operate. Holstein and Gubrium refer to this as the "organizational embedded-ness" of self-construction and recognize that "localized configurations of mean-ing are mediated by organizational conditions."[26] Seeing schools as inhabited institutions helps us understand how local actors collectively make sense out of larger cultural ideas about success and allows us to readily recognize the iden-tity stories that surface in students' narrative accounts.

Social psychologists do not often use identity stories, though I borrow the concept from Ann Westenholz, a scholar of organizations, whose work directly interrogates the postmodern condition of decentered and reflexive identities. In her research, which intersects both social psychology and scholarship on organizations, Westenholz shows that recognizing what she calls field stories is critical to understanding the work-related identities of individuals who are engaged in the practices of a particular field.[27] In particular, she helps us understand the process by which a person shifts between one identity and another in a work environment.

My study elaborates on Westenholz's concept in two important ways. First, I show the distinctive character of identity stories that arise within a single organization. While she, too, looks for these stories within a closed arena (in her case, the field of software development), hers span multiple companies rather than being specific to the environment of each organization. This is useful to her analysis because she focuses on individuals who move through multiple organizations as they work. Observing how colleagues negotiate emerging identities for each other based on their work practices, she demonstrates that they draw on available field stories as source material for these identity negotiations. In contrast, my project shows that looking at the identity stories generated in each organizational environment increases our understanding of the raw material that individuals have available to them. The identity stories at each of the three high schools in my study reflect the specific concerns of the students at that school; they are not shared across the schools.

Second, I elaborate Westenholz's use of field stories by investigating how individuals creatively use identity stories. Recall Alexis, who admits to being "OC" but not "D," and René and Stephanie, who both define themselves in opposition to a *trained dog*. Whereas Westenholz focuses on the identity that a worker's colleagues attribute to her, I show how individuals negotiate the meanings of identity stories as they apply those stories to themselves. My work also emphasizes the tensions, dilemmas, and emotional consequences of these identity negotiations.

APPENDIX B: METHODOLOGY

During the 2005–6 school year, I conducted in-depth, one-on-one interviews with fifty-seven students, approximately nineteen at each school.[1] The interviews ranged from about forty minutes to more than two hours long, but most lasted about an hour and a half. I recorded and transcribed each of them verbatim. My interview respondents were students in classrooms in which I had observed for three consecutive weeks before the interviews took place.[2] I limited my study to ninth, tenth, and eleventh graders. In 2012, I collected a second wave of interviews with five teachers and two principals from across the three schools, all of whom were also part of my earlier observations.[3] These interviews were also conducted one on one. Their length ranged from twenty-five minutes to slightly more than an hour, and I recorded and transcribed them verbatim.

Throughout this book I discuss the various cultural ideas about success that I found at the three schools. I do not mean to imply that every comment made by every student I interviewed at each school perfectly resonated with each other. Naturally, students' descriptions of what it takes to succeed varied somewhat. What I describe as prevalent cultural ideas at each school are just that: prevalent, not universal.[4] They are patterns of thought that I found to be common or typical in each context, ideas that surfaced and resurfaced in interviews with students, teachers, and principals.

One component of the interview that I mention throughout the book is students' reactions to anonymous report cards. To learn about identity types and cultural ideas at each school, I wanted my respondents to describe other people in addition to themselves. I did not want them to talk about specific classmates whom they know well; rather, I wanted to hear them describe character types and rationales for school success more generally. To this end, I asked each to look at a high-performance and a low-performance report card, which I handed to them during the interview. I asked them to imagine that the report card owners were students at their school and to describe what they thought these anonymous students might be like. The report cards elicited responses that characterized students' beliefs about the type of person who receives excellent grades versus the type of person who receives poor grades. These responses offered insight into the relationship students perceive between identity and school success as well as the links among intelligence, effort, and school success. If students did not volunteer comments on, say, intelligence, I asked them directly for their impression of how intelligent the anonymous students might be.

Of course, I also wanted students to talk about themselves and their own identities. Throughout the interviews, I invited them to discuss their school success in a number of concrete and abstract ways. The data in this book include responses to questions about students' own grades, their experiences with teachers, their opinions of what constitutes fair and unfair grading practices, the differences between learning inside and outside of school, their perceptions of the effort-to-intelligence ratio required for school success, and so on.

While students required little prompting to talk about their effort in school, they sometimes were reluctant to discuss their own intelligence, probably because intelligence is not only a highly valued trait but also widely seen as beyond an individual's control. There is a sense of shame in admitting that one does not have enough of it.[5] In an effort to broach this topic respectfully, I included a question in the interview guide in which I asked each respondent to rank herself on a 1-to-10 intelligence scale. I was less interested in the number that the student ascribed to herself than in her description of why she thought that particular number fit her. I followed up the intelligence-scale question with "What was going through your mind that made you decide that was the right number?" To clarify vague or confusing answers, I sometimes also added, "How do you know you are not a 10?"

In this book, I present student responses to these questions as an opportunity to reveal the explanations and rationales behind their self-rankings. I also use them as a point of comparison with two other questions in the interview: (1) where would their friends rank them on the same intelligence scale? and (2) where would their closest family members rank them? I used these questions to elicit student perceptions of how others see their intelligence in relation to how they themselves see their intelligence. They also gave students a chance to explain how others view them.

Like all human beings, the students I interviewed expressed contradictory ideas at various moments in our discussion. Some changed their minds mid-sentence when answering a question and then changed it again upon further reflection. My job in analyzing the interview data was to listen carefully to their ideas, whether they were consistent or not. I saw contradictions in student answers as evidence of the tensions and dilemmas that they feel when they think about school success and where they fit into the world as intelligent, hardworking, successful people.

NOTES

INTRODUCTION

1. Deshawn is not his real name. I use pseudonyms for all students, teachers, and schools mentioned in this book.

2. On achievement ideology, see Jay MacLeod, *Ain't No Makin' It: Leveled Aspirations in a Low-Income Neighborhood* (Boulder: Westview, 1987); and Hugh Mehan, Lea Hubbard, and Irene Villanueva. "Forming Academic Identities: Accommodation without Assimilation among Involuntary Minorities," *Anthropology and Education Quarterly* 25, no. 2 (1994): 91–117. On American dream ideology, see Jennifer L. Hochschild, *Facing Up to the American Dream: Race, Class, and the Soul of the Nation* (Princeton, N.J.: Princeton University Press, 1995); Jennifer L. Hochschild and Nathan Scovronick, *The American Dream and the Public Schools* (New York: Oxford University Press, 2003); Heather Beth Johnson, *The American Dream and the Power of Wealth: Choosing Schools and Inheriting Inequality in the Land of Opportunity* (New York: Routledge, 2006); and Steven Brint and Jerome Karabel, *The Diverted Dream: Community Colleges and the Promise of Educational Opportunity in America, 1900–1985* (New York: Oxford University Press, 1989).

3. For scholarship that shows school cultures' local meanings, see Gerald Grant, *The World We Created at Hamilton High* (Cambridge, Mass: Harvard University Press, 1988); Reba Page, "The Uncertain Value of School Knowledge: Biology at Westridge High," *Teachers College Record* 100, no. 3 (1999): 554–601; and Julie McLeod and Lyn Yates, *Making Modern Lives: Subjectivity, Schooling, and Social Change* (Albany: State University of New York Press, 2006). See also Amy Binder and Kate Wood, *Becoming Right: How Campuses Shape Young Conservatives* (Princeton, N.J.: Princeton University Press, 2012), which demonstrates how school culture shapes students' ideological discourse and political action.

4. For an introduction to inhabited institutions scholarship, see Tim Hallett, "The Myth Incarnate: Recoupling Processes, Turmoil, and Inhabited Institutions in an Urban Elementary School," *American Sociological Review* 75, no. 1 (2010): 52–74; Amy Binder, "For Love and Money: Organizations' Creative Responses to Multiple Environmental Logics," *Theory and Society* 36, no. 6 (2007): 547–72; and Ann Westenholz, Jesper Pedersen, and Frank Dobbin, "Introduction: Institutions in the Making: Identity, Power, and the Emergence of New Organizational Forms," *American Behavioral Scientist* 49, no. 7 (2006): 889–96.

5. For work that analyzes how teachers make sense out of their classroom experiences and pedagogical training in ways that shape the institutional functioning of their schools, see Judson G. Everitt, "Teacher Careers and Inhabited Institutions: Sense Making and Arsenals of Teaching Practice in Educational Institutions," *Symbolic Interaction* 35, no. 2 (2012): 203–20; and his "Inhabitants Moving In: Prospective Sense

Making and the Reproduction of Inhabited Institutions in Teacher Education," *Symbolic Interaction* 36, no. 2 (2013): 177–96. .

6. Tim Hallett and Marc Ventresca, "Inhabited Institutions: Social Interactions and Organizational Forms in Gouldner's Patterns of Industrial Bureaucracy," *Theory and Society* 35 (2006): 229.

7. Organizational scholars from both traditions have recently engaged one another directly in dialogue on how the two perspectives might be bridged. See the extensive set of paired conversations published in the *Journal of Management Inquiry* 21, no. 1, which includes Karen Aten, Jennifer Howard-Grenville, and Marc Ventresca; Mary Jo Hatch; Tammar Zilber; Bob Hinings; Maijken Schultz; and Calvin Morill. Inhabited institutionalism in general, and my study in particular, establish the kinds of links that these scholars call for in their dialogue.

8. See Hallett, "The Myth Incarnate"; Tim Hallett, "Between Deference and Distinction: Interaction Ritual through Symbolic Power in an Educational Institution," *Social Psychology Quarterly* 70, no. 2 (2007): 148–71; John Meyer and Brian Rowan, "Institutionalized Organization: Formal Structure As Myth and Ceremony," *American Journal of Sociology* 83 (1977): 340–63; Charles Bidwell, "Analyzing Schools As Organizations: Long-Term Permanence and Short-Term Exchange," *Sociology of Education,* extra issue (2001): 100–14; Everitt, "Teacher Careers and Inhabited Institutions"; Everitt, "Inhabitants Moving In"; Janice Danielle Aurini, "Patterns of Tight and Loose Coupling in a Competitive Marketplace: The Case of Learning Center Franchises," *Sociology of Education* 85, no. 4 (2012): 373–87; as well as Heinz-Dieter Meyer and Brian Rowan, eds., *The New Institutionalism in Education* (Albany: State University of New York, 2006).

9. Hallett, "The Myth Incarnate."

10. Everitt, "Teacher Careers and Inhabited Institutions."

11. Mary Blair-Loy, *Competing Devotions: Career and Family among Women Executives* (Cambridge, Mass.: Harvard University Press, 2003), 5.

12. See William Sewell, Jr., "Theory of Structure: Duality, Agency, and Transformation," *American Journal of Sociology* 98, no. 1 (1992): 1–29; and Roger Friedland and John Mohr, "The Cultural Turn in American Sociology," in *Matters of Culture: Cultural Sociology in Practice,* ed. Roger Friedland and John Mohr, 1–68 (Cambridge: Cambridge University Press, 2004.) Sewell's conceptualization is a response to the rigid notion of social structure previously used by sociologists and anthropologists. Sewell seeks a definition of structure that allows for human agency and transformation of structures. Drawing on and modifying the theories of Anthony Giddens and Pierre Bourdieu, Sewell presents social structure as a duality of cultural schemas on the one hand and resources on the other. He defines *cultural schemas* as patterns and assumptions that guide individuals' actions, and he often refers to them as rules. He defines *resources* as the material and human effects generated by the enactment of those schemas—in other words, material resources that are defined by and reinforced by the rules of schemas. Agents (people) generally follow the schemas and generally reproduce existing social structure, according to Sewell, but they are able to transpose schemas to new situations—one way in which human agency can bring change. Although his conceptualization has been criticized, Sewell's work lays the groundwork for contemporary cultural sociology's understanding of structure as stable yet transformable and agency as a necessary part of the process of structuration.

13. That is not to say that Sewell and Blair-Loy ignore organizations. Sewell sees schemas as instantiated within patterns of resources, and organizations can be seen as a type of resource. Blair-Loy studies schemas that are specified by particular institutions: the

family and the firm. For example, she shows how individuals negotiate their personal dedication to their careers against the work-devotion schema that is cultivated by capitalist firms, which are organizations. However, her study focuses on cultural ideas (schemas) that are understood to be shared across many organizations and many families.

14. My data show that students generally do not draw on a cultural idea of success directly from the cultural atmosphere of American society writ large, such as the American dream ideology that Hochschild describes in her work. Rather, they tend to draw it from the cultural atmosphere of their own high schools.

15. See note 2.

16. For a history of IQ-based educational tests, see Nicholas Lemann, *The Big Test: The Secret History of American Meritocracy* (New York: Farrar, Straus, and Giroux, 1999). For an explanation of IQ tests and the normal curve, see Stephen Stigler, *The History of Statistics: The Measurement of Uncertainty before 1900* (Cambridge, Mass: Belknap/Harvard University Press, 1986.)

17. This is evidenced by many aspects of U.S. culture—notably, the wide popularity of books for testing and improving one's IQ (for example, Phillip Carter, *The Complete Book of Intelligence Tests: 500 Exercises to Improve, Upgrade and Enhance Your Mind Strength* [Chichester, England: Wiley, 2005]; and Richard E. Nisbett, *Intelligence and How to Get It: Why Schools and Cultures Count* [New York: Norton, 2009]). On the popularity of IQ-offshoot theories such as multiple intelligences, see Howard Gardner, *Frames of Mind: The Theory of Multiple Intelligences* (New York: Basic Books, 1983); Daniel Goleman, *Emotional Intelligence* (New York: Bantam, 1995); and Sabrina Zirkel, "Social Intelligence: The Development and Maintenance of Purposive Behavior," in *The Handbook of Emotional Intelligence*, ed. Rueven Bar-On and Stephen Parker, 3–27 (San Francisco: Jossey-Bass, 2000). For a wider discussion of IQ-ism in the United States, see Robert Sternberg, "Myths, Countermyths, and Truths about Intelligence," *Educational Researcher* 25, no. 2 (1996): 11–16; John Richardson and Karen Bradley, "The Moral Career of Intelligence and the Construction of Educational Psychology," paper presented at the annual meeting of the American Sociological Association, Philadelphia, 2005; and N. J. Mackintosh, *I.Q. and Human Intelligence* (Oxford: Oxford University Press, 1998). IQ has also been used to legitimate racist claims regarding U.S. populations in education and immigration. See Stephen Gould, *The Mismeasure of Man* (New York: Norton, 1981); and Richard Herrnstein and Charles Murray, *The Bell Curve: Intelligence and Class Structure in American Life* (New York: Free Press, 1994).

18. See Annette Lareau, *Unequal Childhoods: Class, Race, and Family Life* (Berkeley: University of California Press, 2003); and Karolyn Tyson, *Integration Interrupted: Tracking, Black Students, and Acting White after Brown* (Oxford: Oxford University Press, 2011).

19. For a discussion of the theoretical debates that gave rise to this line of inquiry, see Brooke Harrington and Gary Alan Fine, "Where the Action Is: Small Groups and Recent Developments in Sociological Theory," *Small Group Research* 37, no. 1 (2006): 4–19; Westenholz, Pedersen, and Dobbin, "Introduction"; John Meyer and W. Richard Scott, eds., *Organizational Environments: Ritual and Rationality* (Beverly Hills, Calif.: Sage, 1983); Paul Hirsch and Michael Lounsbury, "Ending the Family Quarrel: Toward a Reconciliation of 'Old' and 'New' Institutionalisms," *American Behavioral Scientist* 40, no. 4 (1997): 406–18; Ronald Jepperson, "Institutions, Institutional Effects, and Institutionalism," in *The New Institutionalism in Organizational Analysis*, ed. Walter W. Powell and Paul J. Dimaggio, 143–63 (Chicago: University of Chicago Press, 1991); and Meyer and Rowan, "Institutionalized Organization." For descriptions of other empirical cases

of organizations that refine and adapt widely held cultural ideas to fit the needs and sensibilities of the actors in particular organizational settings, see Binder, "For Love and Money"; Hallett, "The Myth Incarnate"; Heather Haveman and Rao Hayagreeva, "Hybrid Forms and the Evolution of Thrifts," *American Behavioral Scientist* 49, no. 7 (2006): 974–86; Gerardo Patriotta and Giovan Lanzara, "Identity, Institutions, and New Work Roles: The Case of a Green Field Automotive Factory," *American Behavioral Scientist* 49, no. 7 (2006): 987–99; Renate Meyer and Gerhard Hammerschmid, "Changing Institutional Logics and Executive Identities: A Managerial Challenge to Public Administration in Austria," *American Behavioral Scientist* 49, no. 7 (2006): 1000–1014; Ann Westenholz, "Identity Work and Meaning Arena: Beyond Actor/Structure and Micro/Macro Distinctions in an Empirical Analysis of IT Workers," *American Behavioral Scientist* 49, no. 7 (2006): 1015–29; and Silva Dorado, "Small Groups As Context for Institutional Entrepreneurship: An Exploration of the Emergence of Microfinance in Bolivia," *Organization Studies* 34, no. 4 (2013): 533–57.

20. Schools are a common site of inhabited institutionalist inquiry. In addition to the foundational studies already cited, recent work on schools include Everitt, "Teacher Careers and Inhabited Institutions"; Everitt, "Inhabitants Moving In"; and Aurini, "Patterns of Tight and Loose Coupling."

21. This debate began with James S. Coleman's *Equality of Educational Opportunity* (Washington, D.C.: U.S. Department of Health, Education, and Welfare, 1966), which found that educational inequality in public schools is explained by differences in parents' income and education rather than actual differences among schools. More recent contributions to this debate include W. Norton Grubb, *The Money Myth: School Resources, Outcomes, and Equity* (New York: Russell Sage Foundation, 2009); Charles M. Payne, *So Much Reform, So Little Change: The Persistence of Failure in Urban Schools* (Cambridge, Mass: Harvard Education Press, 2008); Gerald Grant, *Hope and Despair in the American City* (Cambridge, Mass: Harvard University Press, 2009); Grant, *The World We Created at Hamilton High;* and Hochschild and Scovronick, *American Dream and Public Schools.* Scholarship on elite private education also contributes to this debate; see Mitchell Stevens, *Creating a Class: College Admission and the Education of Elites* (Cambridge, Mass: Harvard University Press, 2007); and Shamus Rahman Kahn, *Privilege: The Making of an Adolescent Elite at St. Paul's School* (Princeton, N.J.: Princeton University Press, 2011).

22. This term comes from Horace Mann, who in the 1880s advocated for the United States to adopt public education because of its potential to be the "great equalizer" in American society.

23. An important set of research in this area follows Bourdieu's understandings of schools as institutions that legitimate the cultural habits and sensibilities of elites. See Pierre Bourdieu and Jean-Claude Passeron, *Reproduction in Education, Society, and Culture* (Beverly Hills, Calif.: Sage, 1977).

24. See Michael A. Haedicke, "'Keeping Our Mission, Changing Our System': Translation and Organizational Change in Natural Foods Co-Ops," *Sociological Quarterly* 53, no. 1 (2012): 44–67; Dorado, "Small Groups As Context"; Hallett, "The Myth Incarnate"; and Binder, "For Love and Money."

25. Everitt, "Inhabitants Moving In," 195.

26. I do not mean to imply that all students at a particular school say identical things regarding school success and identity stories. Real life and real people are more complicated and varied. Here and throughout the book, I emphasize the patterns that I found at each school and focus on recurring themes in interviews with different students at a given school. I am highlighting the similarities as opposed to claiming that all students were uniform or homogenous in the ways in which they described these ideas to me.

27. See Thomas J. Espenshade and Alexandra Walton Radford, *No Longer Separate, Not Yet Equal: Race and Class in Elite College Admission and Campus Life* (Princeton, N.J.: Princeton University Press, 2009); and Jay P. Greene and Greg Forster, "Public High School Graduation and College Readiness Rates in the United States," in *Education Working Paper 3* (New York: Manhattan Institute, Center for Civic Innovation, 2003). For examples of schools that overcome these patterns and successfully prepare low-income minority youth for college, see Hugh Mehan, Gordon C. Chang, Makeba Jones, and Season S. Mussey, *In the Front Door: Creating a College-Going Culture of Learning* (Boulder, Colo.: Paradigm, 2012).

28. There is some debate over the magnitude of these effects. For a review of this literature, see Theodore P. Gerber and Sin Yi Cheung, "Horizontal Stratification in Postsecondary Education: Forms, Explanations, and Implications," *Annual Review of Sociology* 34 (2008): 299–318.

29. For a thorough treatment of the advantages of attending a selective, elite institution of higher education, see Ann Mullen, *Degrees of Inequality: Culture, Class, and Gender in American Higher Education* (Baltimore: Johns Hopkins University Press, 2010).

CHAPTER 1   ALTERNATIVE HIGH

1. School reform efforts characterize our current educational era, though few U.S. states or districts agree on which reforms work best. For recent scholarship on this topic, see Charles M. Payne, *So Much Reform, So Little Change: The Persistence of Failure in Urban Schools* (Cambridge, Mass: Harvard Education Press, 2008); Anthony Bryk, Penny Bender Sebring, Elaine Allensworth, Stuart Luppeschu, and John Easton, *Organizing Schools for Improvement: Lessons from Chicago* (Chicago: Chicago University Press, 2010); and David Labaree, *Someone Has to Fail: The Zero-Sum Game of Public Schooling* (Cambridge, Mass: Harvard University Press, 2010).

2. My observations at Alternative High are fixed in the 2005–2006 school year, when it was inhabited by a relatively low-performing student body and the school was in its early years of operation. In that year, the school's English and math scores were only slightly lower than state averages, but science and social science scores were 25 to 30 percent lower. In subsequent years, the school's scores steadily improved to well above state averages in English and science, while hovering at the state average in math and social science. Thus, the low performance I describe in this chapter is somewhat specific to a fledgling school and may be due to the low academic preparation of these early student cohorts. In my 2012 interviews I learned that the caliber of incoming students has risen over the years as Alternative High has gained status in the district. This has likely contributed to improved standardized test scores. However, I did not find any differences in the attitudes of the teachers and the principal toward hard work and success.

3. *Socioeconomically disadvantaged* is defined by the state of California as annual earned income less than 35,798 dollars for a family of four (in 2005–2006).

4. See Kathleen Wilcox, "Differential Socialization in the Classroom: Implications for Equal Opportunity," in *Doing the Ethnography of Schooling: Educational Anthropology in Action*, ed. George Spindler, 270–309 (New York: Holt, Rinehart, and Winston, 1982); Michael Apple, *Ideology and Curriculum* (London: Routledge and Kegan Paul, 1979); Michael Apple, *Education and Power* (Boston: Routledge and Kegan Paul, 1982); Jonathan Kozol, *Savage Inequalities: Children in America's Schools* (New York: Harper Perennial, 1991); Jean Anyon, *Ghetto Schooling: A Political Economy of Urban Educational Reform* (New York: Teachers College Press, 1997); Jean Anyon, "Social Class and School

Knowledge," *Curriculum Inquiry* 11, no. 1 (1981): 3–42; John Devine, *Maximum Security: The Culture of Violence in Inner-City Schools* (Chicago: University of Chicago Press, 1996); and Judith N. DeSena and George Ansalone, "Gentrification, Schooling, and Social Inequality," *Educational Research Quarterly* 33, no. 1 (2009): 60–74.

5. See Jeanne Oakes, *Keeping Track: How Schools Structure Inequality* (New Haven, Conn.: Yale University Press, 1985); Jeanne Oakes, Adam Gamoran, and Reba Page, "Curriculum Differentiation: Opportunities, Outcomes and Meanings," in *Handbook of Research on Curriculum*, ed. P. W. Jackson, 570–608 (Washington, D.C.: American Educational Research Association, 1992); James E. Rosenbaum, *Making Inequality: The Hidden Curriculum of High School Tracking* (New York: Wiley, 1976); and Maureen Hallinan, "Tracking: From Theory to Practice," *Sociology of Education* 67, no. 2 (1994): 79–84.

6. See Samuel Bowles and Herbert Gintis, *Schooling in Capitalist America: Educational Reform of Economic Life* (London: Routledge and Kegan Paul, 1976); and Apple, *Education and Power*.

7. See Rosenbaum, *Making Inequality*; Apple, *Ideology and Curriculum*; Apple, *Education and Power*; and Lois Weis, Cameron McCarthy, and Greg Dimitriadis, eds., *Ideology, Curriculum, and the New Sociology of Education: Revisiting the Work of Michael Apple* (New York: Routledge, 2006).

8. Apple, *Education and Power*, 13.

9. For a discussion of how schools can untrack students, see Hugh Mehan, Lea Hubbard, Irene Villanueva, and Angela Lintz, *Constructing School Success: The Consequences of Untracking Low Achieving Students* (New York: Cambridge University Press, 1996). For a critique of the pitfalls of untracking efforts, see Susan Yonezawa and Amy Stuart Wells, "Reform As Redefining the Spaces of Schools: An Examination of Detracking by Choice," in *Beyond Silenced Voices: Class, Race, and Gender in United States Schools*, ed. Lois Weis and Michelle Fine, 47–61 (Albany: State University of New York Press, 2005).

10. See James E. Rosenbaum, *Beyond College for All: Career Paths for the Forgotten Half* (New York: Russell Sage Foundation, 2001).

11. For classic examples of working-class and low-income youth who disbelieve the promise that doing well in school will improve their life chances, see Paul Willis, *Learning to Labor: How Working Class Kids Get Working Class Jobs* (New York: Columbia University Press, 1977); and Jay MacLeod, *Ain't No Makin' It: Leveled Aspirations in a Low-Income Neighborhood* (Boulder, Colo.: Westview, 1987). A related line of scholarship shows how some (but not all) ethnoracial minorities similarly reject school success because they see it as "acting white." Key studies on this debate include Signithia Fordham and John Ogbu, "Black Students' School Success: Coping with the Burden of 'Acting White,'" *Urban Review* 18, no. 3 (1987): 1–31; Karolyn Tyson, William Darity, Jr., and Domini Castellino, "It's Not a Black Thing: Understanding the Burden of Acting White and Other Dilemmas of High Achievement," *American Sociological Review* 70, no. (2005): 582–605; Karolyn Tyson, *Integration Interrupted: Tracking, Black Students, and Acting White after Brown* (Oxford: Oxford University Press, 2011); Philip Cook and Jens Ludwig, "The Burden of 'Acting White': Do Black Adolescents Disparage Academic Achievement?," in *The Black-White Test Score Gap*, ed. Christopher Jencks and Meredith Phillips, 375–400 (Washington, D.C.: Brookings Institution Press, 1998); and James Ainsworth-Darnell and Douglas Downey, "Assessing the Oppositional Culture Explanation for Racial/Ethnic Differences in School Performance," *American Sociological Review* 63 (1998): 536–53.

12. Other scholars have also investigated ways in which school environments shape students' understandings of their personal or social identities and their futures. See

Valerie Walkerdine, Helen Lucey, and June Melody, *Growing up Girl: Psychosocial Explorations of Gender and Class* (London: Palgrave, 2001); Julie McLeod, Julie and Lyn Yates, *Making Modern Lives: Subjectivity, Schooling, and Social Change* (Albany: State University of New York Press, 2006); Steven Wortham, *Learning Identity: The Joint Emergence of Social Identification and Academic Learning* (Cambridge: Cambridge University Press, 2006); and Wendy Luttrell, *Schoolsmart and Motherwise: Working-Class Women's Identity and Schooling* (New York: Routledge, 1997).

13. Curriculum tracking is common in public schools; yet scholarship shows mixed results in terms of its effectiveness on student learning, and many studies show that it disproportionately disadvantages non-white and low-income students. For further reading on the controversy over curriculum tracking, see Oakes, *Keeping Track;* Rosenbaum, *Making Inequality;* Adam Gamoran, *The Variable Effects of High School Tracking* (Madison, Wisc.: Center on Organization and Restructuring of Schools, 1992); Hallinan, "Tracking"; William Carbonaro, "Tracking, Students' Effort, and Academic Achievement," *Sociology of Education* 78, no. 1 (2005): 27–49; Tyson, *Integration Interrupted;* and Mehan et al., *Constructing School Success.*

14. See Lisa M. Nunn, "Classrooms As Racialized Spaces: Dynamics of Collaboration, Tension, and Student Attitudes in Urban and Suburban High Schools," *Urban Education* 46, no. 6 (2011): 1226–55.

15. Median home values based on 2000 U.S. Census data are available on http://factfinder.census.gov.

16. See James S. Coleman, *The Adolescent Society: The Social Life of the Teenager and Its Impact on Education* (New York: Free Press of Glencoe, 1961).

17. See the introduction for a discussion of this line of theory.

CHAPTER 2   FEARING FAILURE AT ALTERNATIVE HIGH

1. As I explain in appendix B, I interviewed Mrs. Williams in the second phase of data collection in 2012.

2. For detailed ethnographic accounts of how families can pave the way to children's academic success, see Annette Lareau, *Unequal Childhoods: Class, Race, and Family Life* (Berkeley: University of California Press, 2003); and Peter Demerath, *Producing Success: The Culture of Personal Advancement in an American High School* (Chicago: Chicago University Press, 2009).

3. Research shows that low-income, African American, and Latino students drop out of high school at disproportionately high rates. Based on demographics, Alternative High students are likely to drop out themselves, so it is not surprising that they personally know other people who have not completed high school. See Jay P. Greene and Greg Forster, "Public High School Graduation and College Readiness Rates in the United States," *Education Working Paper 3* (New York: Manhattan Institute, Center for Civic Innovation, 2003); and Michelle Fine, *Framing Dropouts: Notes on the Politics of an Urban High School* (Albany: State University of New York Press, 1991). For a wider discussion of schools' roles in perpetuating these inequalities, see David Labaree, *Someone Has to Fail: The Zero-Sum Game of Public Schooling* (Cambridge, Mass: Harvard University Press, 2010).

4. See Ann Westenholz, "Identity Work and Meaning Arena: Beyond Actor/Structure and Micro/Macro Distinctions in an Empirical Analysis of IT Workers," *American Behavioral Scientist* 49, no. 7 (2006): 1015–29; and her "Emerging Identities beyond Organizational Boundaries," in *Identity in the Age of the New Economy: Life in Temporary and Scattered*

Work Practices, ed. Ann Westenholz and Torben Elgaard Jensen, 122–46 (Cheltenham, England: Elgar, 2004). I use *identity stories* rather than Westenholz's *identity field stories* to simplify the terminology for nonspecialist readers.

5. See Jenny M. Stuber, "Class Dismissed? The Social-Class Worldviews of Privileged College Students," in *Educating Elites: Class Privilege and Educational Advantage*, ed. Adam Howard and Rubén A. Gaztambide-Fernandez (Lanham, Md.: Rowman and Littlefield Education, 2010), 140.

6. See the introduction for an explanation of cultural schemas and cultural ideas.

7. See Jeanne Oakes, *Keeping Track: How Schools Structure Inequality* (New Haven, Conn: Yale University Press, 1985), 90.

8. Scholarship on teachers' expectations demonstrates that is common for teachers to expect African American students to have low academic performance and to misbehave. See Jacqueline Jordan Irvine, *Black Students and School Failure: Policies, Practices, and Prescriptions* (Westport, Conn.: Greenwood, 1990); Ronald F. Ferguson, "Teachers' Perceptions and Expectations and the Black-White Test Score Gap," *Urban Education* 38, no. 4 (2003): 460–507; Angel Harris, *Kids Don't Want to Fail: Oppositional Culture and the Black-White Achievement Gap* (Cambridge, Mass: Harvard University Press, 2011); and Ann Arnett Ferguson, *Bad Boys: Public Schools in the Making of Black Masculinity* (Ann Arbor: University of Michigan Press, 2001).

9. See John Richardson and Karen Bradley, "The Moral Career of Intelligence and the Construction of Educational Psychology," paper presented at the annual meeting of the American Sociological Association, Philadelphia, 2005.

10. See the introduction for a discussion of inhabited institutionalism theory.

CHAPTER 3   COMPREHENSIVE HIGH

1. The state of California defines *socioeconomically disadvantaged* as annual earned income less than 35,798 dollars (based on a family of four in 2005–6).

2. Median home values based on 2000 U.S. Census data are available at http://factfinder .census.gov.

3. See Burton Clark, *The Distinctive College: Antioch, Reed, and Swarthmore* (Chicago: Aldine, 1970).

4. The distinct classroom atmospheres I found in college-prep and AP curricula align with the findings of scholars who study curriculum tracks. See Jeanne Oakes, *Keeping Track: How Schools Structure Inequality* (New Haven, Conn: Yale University Press, 1985); and Mary Metz, *Classrooms and Corridors: The Crisis of Authority in Desegregated Secondary Schools* (Berkeley: University of California Press, 1978). Also see Lisa M. Nunn, "Classrooms As Racialized Spaces: Dynamics of Collaboration, Tension, and Student Attitudes in Urban and Suburban High Schools," *Urban Education* 46, no. 6 (2011): 1226–55.

5. See Metz, *Classrooms and Corridors*.

6. Education is also gendered, although that dynamic is beyond the scope of my analysis here.

7. I did not have the opportunity to continue observations after the AP exams were completed. However, I had the firm impression that correct-answer–orientation was the standard format of instruction.

8. This discussion with the principal took place during our 2012 interview, and her focus on CST scores since 2004–5 has been paying off. She says, "Seven years later, we are the sixth-highest-performing school in the county." That ranking is based on annual Academic Performance Index (API) scores.

CHAPTER 4   SEPARATE WORLDS, SEPARATE CONCERNS

1. The API index ranges from 200 to 1,000 points.
2. The genius identity type is similar to what Stuber calls a "mythical figure." See Jenny M. Stuber, "Class Dismissed? The Social-Class Worldviews of Privileged College Students," in *Educating Elites: Class Privilege and Educational Advantage*, ed. Adam Howard and Rubén A. Gaztambide-Fernandez (Lanham, Md.: Rowman and Littlefield Education, 2010), 140.
3. See James E. Rosenbaum, *Beyond College for All: Career Paths for the Forgotten Half* (New York: Russell Sage Foundation, 2001).

CHAPTER 5   ELITE CHARTER HIGH

1. Median home values are based on 2000 U.S. Census data. See http://factfinder.census .gov.
2. The state of California defines *socioeconomically disadvantaged* as annual earned income less than 35,798 dollars (based on a family of four in 2005–6).
3. See Murray Milner, Jr., *Freaks Geeks and Cool Kids: American Teenagers, Schools and the Culture of Consumption* (New York: Routledge, 2004).
4. Not all public high schools are places where being smart and getting good grades are antithetical to popularity. For an example of a high-performing public high school in which students strive for academic accomplishments and the bragging rights that go along with being seen as intelligent, see Peter Demerath, *Producing Success: The Culture of Personal Advancement in an American High School* (Chicago: Chicago University Press, 2009).
5. See Kathleen Wilcox, "Differential Socialization in the Classroom: Implications for Equal Opportunity," in *Doing the Ethnography of Schooling: Educational Anthropology in Action*, ed. George Spindler 270–309 (New York: Holt, Rinehart, and Winston, 1982).

CHAPTER 6   COMPETITIVE CLASSMATES AT ELITE CHARTER HIGH

1. For scholarly literature and journalists' accounts of admission processes in elite colleges, see Mitchell Stevens, *Creating a Class: College Admission and the Education of Elites* (Cambridge, Mass: Harvard University Press, 2007); Jerome Karabel, *The Chosen: The Hidden History of Admission and Exclusion at Harvard, Yale, and Princeton* (New York: Houghton Mifflin, 2005); Daniel Golden, *The Price of Admission: How America's Ruling Class Buys Its Way into Elite Colleges—and Who Gets Left Outside the Gates* (New York: Three Rivers Press, 2006); and Jacques Steinberg, *The Gatekeepers: Inside the Admissions Process of a Premier College* (New York: Penguin, 2002). For guidebooks on how to get admitted to good colleges, see Sally Springer and Marion Franck, *Admission Matters: What Students and Parents Need to Know about Getting into College* (San Francisco: Jossey-Bass, 2005); and Peter Van Buskirk, *Winning the College Admission Game: Strategies for Students and Parents* (Lawrenceville, N.J.: Peterson, 2007).
2. This conversation took place during our 2012 interview, and I was careful to ask Mr. Fischer whether he thought it was true for the group of students I had observed and interviewed in 2005 and 2006. He affirmed that it was.
3. See the Introduction for a discussion of these dynamics in relation to inhabited institutionalism theory at both the meso and micro levels.
4. See appendix A for a discussion of identity formation theories.

5. See Joyce Levy Epstein, "The Influence of Friends on Achievement and Affective Outcomes," in *Friends in School: Patterns of Selection and Influence in Secondary Schools*, ed Joyce Levy Epstein and Nancy Karweit, 177–200 (New York: Academic Press, 1983); Maureen Hallinan and Richard Williams, "Students' Characteristics and the Peer-Influence Process," *Sociology of Education* 63 (1990): 122–32; Catherine Riegle-Crumb, George Farkas, and Chandra Muller, "The Role of Gender and Friendship in Advanced Course Taking," *Sociology of Education* 79, no. 3 (2006): 206–28; and James Daniel Lee, "More Than Ability: Gender and Personal Relationships Influence Science and Technology Development," *Sociology of Education* 75 (2002): 349–73.

6. Prominent theorist Pierre Bourdieu emphasizes family sensibilities as the primary mechanism for social reproduction. See Pierre Bourdieu and Jean-Claude Passeron, *Reproduction in Education, Society, and Culture* (Beverly Hills, Calif.: Sage, 1977). For empirical studies in education that draw on Bourdieu's theory, see Jay MacLeod, *Ain't No Makin' It: Leveled Aspirations in a Low-Income Neighborhood* (Boulder, Colo.: Westview, 1987); Annette Lareau, *Unequal Childhoods: Class, Race, and Family Life* (Berkeley: University of California Press, 2003); and Tiffany Chin and Meredith Phillips, "Social Reproduction and Child-Rearing Practices: Social Class, Children's Agency, and the Summer Activity Gap," *Sociology of Education* 77, no. 3 (2004): 185–210.

CHAPTER 7   BEYOND IDENTITY

1. See Ann Mullen, *Degrees of Inequality: Culture, Class, and Gender in American Higher Education* (Baltimore: Johns Hopkins University Press, 2010).

2. See Gail O. Mellow and Cynthia Heelan, *Minding the Dream: The Process and Practice of the American Community College* (Lanham, Md.: Rowman and Littlefield, 2008); and Anne-Marie Nuñez, "Latino Students' Transitions to College: A Social and Intercultural Capital Perspective," *Harvard Educational Review* 79, no. 1 (2009): 22–49. Even in college, Latinos are marginal populations in STEM majors such as engineering. See Michelle Madsen Camacho and Susan M. Lord, *The Borderlands of Education: Latinas in Engineering* (Lanham, Md.: Lexington, 2013).

3. See Jay P. Greene and Greg Forster, "Public High School Graduation and College Readiness Rates in the United States," *Education Working Paper 3* (New York: Manhattan Institute, Center for Civic Innovation, 2003).

4. See Eric Grodsky, "Compensatory Sponsorship in Higher Education," *American Journal of Sociology* 112, no. 6 (2007): 1662–712; Mitchell Stevens, *Creating a Class: College Admission and the Education of Elites* (Cambridge, Mass: Harvard University Press, 2007); Karl Alexander, Robert Bozick, and Doris Entwisle, "Warming up, Cooling out, or Holding Steady? Persistence and Change in Educational Expectations after High School," *Sociology of Education* 81, no. 4 (2008): 371–96; Daniel Golden, *The Price of Admission: How America's Ruling Class Buys Its Way into Elite Colleges—and Who Gets Left Outside the Gates* (New York: Three Rivers Press, 2006); Peter Sacks, *Tearing Down the Gates: Confronting the Class Divide in American Education* (Berkeley: University of California Press, 2007); Douglas S. Massey, Camille Z. Charles, Garvey F. Lundy, and Mary J. Fischer, *The Source of the River: The Social Origins of Freshmen at America's Selective Colleges and Universities* (Princeton, N.J.: Princeton University Press, 2003); Jerome Karabel, *The Chosen: The Hidden History of Admission and Exclusion at Harvard, Yale, and Princeton* (New York: Houghton Mifflin, 2005); and Thomas J. Espenshade and Alexandria Walton Radford, *No Longer Separate, Not Yet Equal: Race and Class in Elite College Admission and Campus Life* (Princeton, N.J.: Princeton University Press, 2009).

5. See also Thomas Bailey and Vanessa Smith Morest, "The Community College Equity Agenda in the Twenty-First Century: Moving from Access to Achievement," in *Defending the Community College Equity Agenda*, ed. Thomas Bailey and Vanessa Smith Morest, 246–70 (Baltimore: Johns Hopkins University Press, 2006)"; Colleen Moore and Nancy Shulock, *Divided We Fail: Improving Completion and Closing Racial Gaps in California's Community Colleges* (Sacramento: Institute for Higher Education Leadership and Policy, 2010); and Robert Waassmer, Colleen Moore, and Nancy Shulock, *California Community College Transfer Rates: Policy Implications and a Future Research Agenda* (Sacramento: California State University, Senate Office of Research, 2003).

6. See James E. Rosenbaum, *Beyond College for All: Career Paths for the Forgotten Half* (New York: Russell Sage Foundation, 2001).

7. See W. Norton Grubb, "'Like, What Do I Do Now?' The Dilemmas of Guidance Counseling," in *Defending the Community College Equity Agenda*, ed. Bailey and Morest, 195–222; Bailey and Morest, "The Community College Equity Agenda"; Penelope E. Herideen, *Policy, Pedagogy, and Social Inequality: Community College Student Realities in Post-Industrial America* (Westport, Conn.: Bergin and Garvey, 1998); Nancy Shulock and Colleen Moore, "Diminished Access to the Baccalaureate for Low-Income and Minority Students in California: The Impact of Budget and Capacity Constraints on the Transfer Function," *Educational Policy* 19, no. 2 (2005): 418–42; Mellow and Heelan, *Minding the Dream;* and Nuñez, "Latino Students' Transition to College."

8. See Rosenbaum, *Beyond College for All*, 56–57

9. See Steven Brint and Jerome Karabel, *The Diverted Dream: Community Colleges and the Promise of Educational Opportunity in America, 1900–1985* (New York: Oxford University Press, 1989); Alexander et al., "Warming Up, Cooling Out, or Holding Steady?"; Kevin Dougherty, *The Contradictory College* (Albany: State University of New York Press, 1994); Nuñez, "Latino Students' Transition to College"; Moore and Shulock, "Divided We Fail"; Jerry Trusty, "High Educational Expectations and Low Achievement: Stability of Educational Goals across Adolescence," *Journal of Educational Research* 93 (2000): 356–65; and William Bowen, Matthew Chingos, and Michael McPherson, *Crossing the Finish Line: Completing College at America's Public Universities* (Princeton, N.J.: Princeton University Press, 2009).

10. For studies that argue that schools act as a great equalizer, see Barbara Heyns, *Summer Learning and the Effects of Schooling* (New York: Academic Press, 1978); and Douglas B. Downey, Paul T. von Hippel, and Breckett Broh, "Are Schools the Great Equalizer? School and Non-School Sources of Inequality in Cognitive Skills," *American Sociological Review* 69, no. 5 (2004): 613–35. For studies arguing that students who are born with advantages tend to end up on the top of the educational hierarchy, see Peter W. Cookson and Caroline Hodges Persell, *Preparing for Power: America's Elite Boarding Schools* (New York: Basic Books, 1985); Karabel, *The Chosen;* Stevens, *Creating a Class;* Heather Beth Johnson, *The American Dream and the Power of Wealth: Choosing Schools and Inheriting Inequality in the Land of Opportunity* (New York: Routledge, 2006); and Nicholas Lemann, *The Big Test: The Secret History of American Meritocracy* (New York: Farrar, Straus, and Giroux, 1999).

11. See Patricia M. McDonough, "Buying and Selling Higher Education: The Social Construction of the College Applicant," *Journal of Higher Education* 65, no. 4 (1994): 427–46.

12. See Richard C. Atkinson, "Achievement versus Aptitude Tests in College Admissions," *Issues in Science and Technology* 18, no. 2 (2002): 31–36. For a comprehensive discussion of how the SAT and other standardized tests have "reflected, reproduced and

transformed social inequalities," see Eric Grodsky, John Robert Warren, and Erika Felts, "Testing and Social Stratification in American Education," *Annual Review of Sociology* 34 (2008): 385–404.

13. See also Stevens, *Creating a Class.*

14. Sally Springer and Marion Franck, *Admission Matters: What Students and Parents Need to Know about Getting into College* (San Francisco: Jossey-Bass, 2005), 6.

15. Ibid., 35.

16. All guidebook quotations in this and the following paragraph come from Peter Van Buskirk, *Winning the College Admission Game: Strategies for Students and Parents* (Lawrenceville, N.J.: Peterson, 2007), 72–73. In the section "Intelligence Sparkles at Elite Charter High," the long quotations are from pp. 60, 94, and 77.

17. See Springer and Franck, *Admission Matters.*

18. Stevens, *Creating a Class,* 206.

19. See Golden, *The Price of Admission;* Stevens, *Creating a Class;* and Sacks, *Tearing Down the Gates.*

20. Van Buskirk, *Winning the College Admission Game,* 55.

21. See Rosenbaum, *Beyond College for All.*

22. See University of California, Educational Relations Department, "Major Features of the California Master Plan," 2007.

23. James E. Rosenbaum, Regina Deil-Amen, and Ann E. Person, *After Admission: From College Access to College Success* (New York: Russell Sage Foundation, 2006), 1. On the mission of community colleges to provide broad access to higher education, see also Brint and Karabel, *The Diverted Dream;* Mellow and Heelan, *Minding the Dream;* and Thomas Bailey and Vanessa Smith Morest, "Introduction: Defending the Community College Equity Agenda," in *Defending the Community College Equity Agenda,* ed. Bailey and Morest, 1–27.

24. See Dolores Perin, "Can Community Colleges Protect Both Access and Standards? The Problem of Remediation," *Teachers College Record* 108, no. 3 (2006): 339–73; Dolores Perin and Kerry Charron, "Lights Just Click on Every Day, in *Defending the Community College Equity Agenda,* ed. Bailey and Morest, 155–94; Mellow and Heelan, *Minding the Dream;* and Moore and Shulock, "Divided We Fail."

25. Mellow and Heelan, *Minding the Dream,* 174.

26. For a thorough discussion of the issues surrounding college completion, which is particularly daunting for minority and low-income students, see Bowen et al., *Crossing the Finish Line.*

27. In 2012 the principal explained that the administration's goal in implementing bundled AP courses was to improve students' skills in the humanities, and she is pleased with the outcomes of the program seven years later: "It has increased their ability to read, write, and analyze because that's what they have to do in the humanities. There is a strong emphasis on those skills. Those skills are also the ones that they need to get into college. They end up with a lot more AP classes than other students because they are linked." However, she was the only person I heard talk like this about course bundling. Both students and teachers discussed its rationale in terms of left-brain versus right-brain strengths in which humanities are only one possible avenue of study.

28. Van Buskirk, *Winning the College Admission Game,* 60.

29. See California State University, "Eligibility Index Table for Residents of California or Graduates of California High Schools," 2009, http://www.csumentor.edu.

30. For sources that discuss California college rankings, see Fern Oram, ed. *440 Colleges for Top Students* (Lawrenceville, N.J.: Peterson, 2007); Springer and Franck, *Admission*

Matters; Robert Teranishi, Walter R. Allen, and Daniel G. Solorzano, "Opportunity at the Crossroads: Racial Inequality, School Segregation, and Higher Education in California," *Teachers College Record* 106, no. 11 (2004): 2224–45; Andrea Venezia, "Connecting California's K–12 and Higher Education Systems: Challenges and Opportunities," in *Crucial Issues in California Education 2000,* 153–76 (Berkeley, Calif.: Policy Analysis for California Education, 2000); and John T. Yun and Jose F. Moreno, "College Access, K–12 Concentrated Disadvantage, and the Next 25 Years of Education Research," *Educational Researcher* 35, no. 12 (2006): 12–19.

31. See Ria Sengupta and Christopher Jepsen, "California's Community College Students," *California Counts: Population Trends and Profiles* 8, no. 2 (2006): 1–24.

32. Mullen, *Degrees of Inequality,* 5.

33. See Dominic Brewer, Eric Eide, and Ronald Ehrenberg, "Does It Pay to Attend an Elite Private College? A Cross-Cohort Evidence on the Effects of College Type on Earnings," *Journal of Human Resources* 34, no. 1 (1999): 104–23; and Linda Datcher Loury and David Garman, "College Selectivity and Earnings," *Journal of Labor Economics* 13, no. 2 (1995): 289–308. On the debate over the strength of the effects of attending an elite college, see Theodore P. Gerber and Sin Yi Cheung, "Horizontal Stratification in Postsecondary Education: Forms, Explanations, and Implications," *Annual Review of Sociology* 34 (2008): 299–318; and Mitchell Stevens, Elizabeth A. Armstrong, and Richard Arum, "Sieve, Incubator, Temple, Hub: Empirical and Theoretical Advances in the Sociology of Higher Education," *Annual Review of Sociology* 34 (2008): 127–51. For qualitative accounts of the benefits of elite education, see Shamus Rahman Kahn, *Privilege: The Making of an Adolescent Elite at St. Paul's School* (Princeton, N.J.: Princeton University Press, 2011); and Mullen, *Degrees of Inequality.*

34. Mullen, *Degrees of Inequality,* 212.

35. Extensive literature exists on the debate over whether or not African American (and other "involuntary minority") students hold cultural attitudes that oppose school success, based on the notion that academic achievement is "acting white." See Signithia Fordham and John Ogbu, "Black Students' School Success: Coping with the Burden of 'Acting White," *Urban Review* 18, no. 3 (1987): 1–31; Nilda Flores-Gonzales, "Puerto Rican High Achievers: An Example of Ethnic and Academic Identity Compatibility," *Anthropology and Education Quarterly* 30, no. 3 (1999): 343–62; James Ainsworth-Darnell and Douglas Downey, "Assessing the Oppositional Culture Explanation for Racial/Ethnic Differences in School Performance," *American Sociological Review* 63 (1998): 536–53; Hugh Mehan, Gordon C. Chang, Makeba Jones, and Season S. Mussey, *In the Front Door: Creating a College-Bound Culture of Learning* (Boulder, Colo.: Paradigm, 2012); and Maria Eugenia Matute-Bianchi, "Ethnic Identities and Patterns of School Success and Failure among Mexican-Descent and Japanese-American Students in a California High School: An Ethnographic Analysis," *American Journal of Education* 95, no. 1 (1986): 233–55. Recent contributions to this debate include Karolyn Tyson, William Darity, Jr., and Domini Castellino, "It's Not a Black Thing: Understanding the Burden of Acting White and Other Dilemmas of High Achievement," *American Sociological Review* 70, no. (2005): 582–605; Douglas B. Downey, James Ainsworth, and Zhenchao Qian, "Rethinking the Attitude-Achievement Paradox among Blacks," *Sociology of Education* 82, no. 1 (2009): 1–19; Karolyn Tyson, *Integration Interrupted: Tracking, Black Students, and Acting White after Brown* (Oxford: Oxford University Press, 2011); and Angel Harris, *Kids Don't Want to Fail: Oppositional Culture and the Black-White Achievement Gap* (Cambridge, Mass: Harvard University Press, 2011).

APPENDIX A: IDENTITY THEORY AND INHABITED INSTITUTIONALISM

1. See Tim Hallett, David Shulman, and Gary Alan Fine, "Peopling Organizations: The Promise of Symbolic Interactionism for an Inhabited Institutionalism," in *The Oxford Handbook of Organizational Studies: Classical Foundations,* ed. Paul S. Adler (New York: Oxford University Press, 2009), 488.

2. Judson G. Everitt, "Teacher Careers and Inhabited Institutions: Sense Making and Arsenals of Teaching Practice in Educational Institutions," *Symbolic Interaction* 35, no. 2 (2012): 204. For more work that ties inhabited institutionalism to social interactionism, see Judson G. Everitt, "Inhabitants Moving In: Prospective Sense Making and the Reproduction of Inhabited Institutions in Teacher Education," *Symbolic Interaction* 36, no. 2 (2013): 177–96; and Tim Hallett, "Between Deference and Distinction: Interaction Ritual through Symbolic Power in an Educational Institution," *Social Psychology Quarterly* 70, no. 2 (2007): 148–71.

3. This camp is often referred to as psychological social psychology. Its concerns center on processes that happen inside an individual's head, such as cognition, emotion, perception, and motivation; and its scholarship interrogates how an individual's behavior is influenced by various aspects of self—for instance, personality. Quantitative methods are common, including psychometric testing and laboratory experiments. See the preface in John DeLamater, ed., *Handbook of Social Psychology* (New York: Kluwer Academic/Plenum, 2003).

4. The work of the Chicago School was refined and elaborated by the postwar Second Chicago School, taught by Herbert Blumer, himself a student of Mead's (see Gary Alan Fine, ed., *A Second Chicago School? The Development of a Postwar American Sociology* [Chicago: University of Chicago Press, 1995]). This camp is often referred to as sociological social psychology, sociological psychology, or microsociology (see Andrew Weigert, J. Smith Teitge, and Dennis W. Teitge, *Society and Identity: Toward a Sociological Psychology* [Cambridge, U.K.: Cambridge University Press, 1986]). Its concerns center on how individuals' behavior is influenced by social life and the reciprocal influences between social life and individuals' behavior. Qualitative methods are common, particularly observation in the "actual places where everyday social life is lived" as opposed to laboratory settings (see Spencer Cahill, ed. *Inside Social Life: Readings in Sociological Psychology and Microsociology* [New York: Oxford University Press, 2007], ix).

5. On those who bridge the two social psychologies, see Karen S. Cook, Gary Alan Fine, and James S. House, eds., *Sociological Perspectives on Social Psychology* (Boston: Allyn and Bacon, 1995); and DeLamater, *Handbook of Social Psychology.* This interdisciplinary group of scholars draws partly on symbolic interactionism, often a version known as structural symbolic interactionism (see Sheldon Stryker, "From Mead to a Structural Symbolic Interactionism and Beyond," *Annual Review of Sociology* 34 [2008]: 15–31). Scholars sometimes combine it with a second framework for understanding behavior—for example, perceptual control theory (see Peter J. Burke and Jan E. Stets, *Identity Theory* [New York: Oxford University Press, 2009]; social exchange theory (see Linda D. Molm and Karen S. Cook, "Social Exchange and Exchange Networks," in Cook et al., *Sociological Perspectives on Social Psychology,* 209–35); or social cognition theory (see Judith A. Howard, "Social Psychology of Identities," *Annual Review of Sociology* 26 (2000): 367–93).

6. See the introduction to Cahill, *Inside Social Life.*

7. Steph Lawler, *Identity: Sociological Perspectives* (Cambridge, U.K.: Polity, 2008), 83. See also Anthony Elliot and Paul du Gay, eds., *Identity in Question.*(London: Sage, 2009).

8. See Luther H. Martin, Huck Gutman, and Patrick Hutton, eds., *Technologies of the Self: A Seminar with Michel Foucault* (Amherst: University of Massachusetts Press, 1988); Ian Hacking, "Between Michel Foucault and Erving Goffman: Between Discourse in the Abstract and Face-to-Face Interaction," *Economy and Society* 33, no. 3 (2004): 277–302; and Lawler, *Identity*.

9. Giddens, *Modernity and Self-Identity*, 81. See also Elliot and du Gay, eds., *Identity in Question*.

10. Social psychologists who draw on social cognition theory use a distinct set of cognitive schemas in their work: role schemas, event schemas, content-free schemas, and person schemas (see Judith A. Howard, "Social Cognition," in Cook et al., *Sociological Perspectives on Social Psychology*, 90–117). Howard, for instance, uses two types of person schemas (self schemas and group schemas) as "abstract and organized packages of information [that] are the cognitive versions of identity" (Howard, "Social Psychology of Identities," 368). Social cognition theory's parameters for understanding person schemas include defining one's own identity traits, such as "political activism" or "religiosity" (Howard, "Social Cognition," in Cook et al., *Sociological Perspectives on Social Psychology*, 93). This is not quite the same as cultural sociologists' approach to understanding the role that widely shared cultural schemas play in identity formation. Also see Judith A. Howard and Daniel G. Renfrow, "Social Cognition," in DeLamater, *Handbook of Social Psychology*,) 259–82.

11. See Matthew Adams, "Hybridizing Habitus and Reflexivity: Towards an Understanding of Contemporary Identity?" *Sociology* 40, no. 3 (2006): 511–28; Wendy Bottero, "Intersubjectivity and Bourdieusian Approaches to 'Identity,'" *Cultural Sociology* 4, no. 1 (2010): 3–22; Steven Threadgold, "Reflexivity of Contemporary Youth, Risk and Cultural Capital," *Current Sociology* 57, no. 1 (2009): 47–68; Craig Calhoun, "Habitus, Field, and Capital: The Question of Historical Specificity," in *Bourdieu: Critical Perspectives*, ed. Craig Calhoun, Edward Li Puma, and Moishe Postone 61–88 (Chicago: University of Chicago Press, 1993); and Richard Shusterman, ed. *Bourdieu: A Critical Reader* (Oxford: Blackwell, 1999).

12. Bottero, "Intersubjectivity and Bourdieusian Approaches," 15.

13. Ibid.

14. Unlike social psychologists, cultural sociologists generally do not use the term *narrative* to describe a process to construct a self, although they do use the concept as a cultural construct. For a thorough discussion, see Francesca Polletta, Pang Ching Bobby Chen, Beth Gharrity Gardner, and Alice Motes, "The Sociology of Storytelling," *Annual Review of Sociology* 37 (2011): 109–30.

15. James Holstein and Jaber Gubrium, *The Self We Live By: Narrative Identity in a Postmodern World* (New York: Oxford University Press, 2000), 96–97.

16. Ibid., 153. Here, identity construction is reminiscent of Swidler's toolkit metaphor for cultural repertoires, which individuals access to make sense of their lives and construct "strategies of action" (see Ann Swidler, "Culture in Action: Symbols and Strategies," *American Sociological Review* 51 [1986]: 273–86). Her emphasis on the situational and ephemeral nature of individuals' uses of available meanings has been criticized (see the introduction in Jeffrey C. Alexander, Ronald N. Jacobs, and Philip Smith, eds., *The Oxford Handbook of Cultural Sociology* [New York: Oxford University Press, 2012]).

17. Holstein and Gubrium, *The Self We Live By*, 10.

18. Ibid., 104.

19. Ibid., 161.

20. My discussion is limited to personal identity as opposed to collective identity or social identity, which both cultural sociologists and social psychologists also study.

21. Mary Blair-Loy, *Competing Devotions: Career and Family among Women Executives* (Cambridge, Mass.: Harvard University Press, 2003).

22. Leslie Irvine, "Even Better Than the Real Thing: Narratives of the Self in Codependency," *Qualitative Sociology* 23 (2000): 9.

23. Nina Eliasoph and Paul Lichterman, "Culture in Interaction," *American Journal of Sociology* 108, no. 4 (2003): 735–94.

24. Holstein and Gubrium, *The Self We Live By*, 107.

25. Ibid., 163.

26. Ibid., 165.

27. Ann Westenholz, "Identity Work and Meaning Arena: Beyond Actor/Structure and Micro/Macro Distinctions in an Empirical Analysis of IT Workers," *American Behavioral Scientist* 49, no. 7 (2006): 1015–29.

APPENDIX B   METHODOLOGY

1. Due to constraints of the human-subjects guidelines that governed the research, the sample of students I drew from each classroom was not random but was comprised of students who volunteered to be interviewed for the project. The respondents were solicited directly from each of the eight classrooms in which I conducted observations. The principal of each school assigned these classes to me, choosing them to accommodate my request to observe in one advanced curriculum class and one general curriculum class. (Alternative High was an exception because it does not practice curriculum tracking.) In each of the original six classes that the principals offered me, I observed class meetings for three consecutive weeks. At Elite Charter High and Comprehensive High, I then requested an additional classroom to expand my exposure to their curriculum. In both of those classes, observations lasted for one week.

2. I selected classrooms that would allow me to highlight differences among and within the three schools. In this I followed the example of Amy Binder, *Contentious Curricula: Afrocentrism and Creationism in American Public Schools* (Princeton, N.J.: Princeton University Press, 2002).

3. I interviewed all three Elite Charter High teachers in the study, but the principal had moved on, and I was unable to contact her. At Comprehensive High, I interviewed the AP English teacher and the principal. However, in 2007, a year after my first wave of research, she became a high-level administrator in the same school district and thus was no longer the principal when I interviewed her in 2012. At Alternative High, I interviewed the principal and the sophomore homeroom teacher. The freshman homeroom teacher had left to teach at a traditional high school and was unavailable for an interview. Nonetheless, she relayed the current whereabouts of her 2005–6 students to the sophomore homeroom teacher, who shared them with me (see chapter 7).

Although six years is a long time in the life of a school, the ideas about success that the teachers and principals expressed in our 2012 interviews were, for the most part, highly consistent with my 2005–6 observations and informal interview notes. Conducting this second wave of interviews allowed me to both confirm and refine various conclusions I had drawn about each school site based on the first wave of data collection.

4.   The variation I find is similar to the variation Binder and Wood find in dominant and submerged styles of discourse between the student groups at the two universities in their study. See Amy Binder and Kate Wood, *Becoming Right: How Campuses Shape Young Conservatives* (Princeton, N.J.: Princeton University Press, 2012).

5. See Stephen Gould, *The Mismeasure of Man* (New York: Norton, 1981); and John Richardson and Karen Bradley, "The Moral Career of Intelligence and the Construction of Educational Psychology," paper presented at the annual meeting of the American Sociological Association, Philadelphia, 2005

BIBLIOGRAPHY

Adams, Matthew. "Hybridizing Habitus and Reflexivity: Towards an Understanding of Contemporary Identity?" *Sociology* 40, no. 3 (2006): 511–28.

Ainsworth-Darnell, James, and Douglas Downey. "Assessing the Oppositional Culture Explanation for Racial/Ethnic Differences in School Performance." *American Sociological Review* 63 (1998): 536–53.

Alexander, Jeffrey C., Ronald N. Jacobs, and Philip Smith, eds. *The Oxford Handbook of Cultural Sociology*, edited by Jeffrey C. Alexander, Ronald N. Jacobs and Philip Smith. New York: Oxford University Press, 2012.

Alexander, Karl, Robert Bozick, and Doris Entwisle. "Warming up, Cooling out, or Holding Steady? Persistence and Change in Educational Expectations after High School." *Sociology of Education* 81, no. 4 (2008): 371–96.

Anyon, Jean. *Ghetto Schooling: A Political Economy of Urban Educational Reform*. New York: Teachers College Press, 1997.

———. "Social Class and School Knowledge." *Curriculum Inquiry* 11, no. 1 (1981): 3–42.

Apple, Michael. *Education and Power*. Boston: Routledge & Kegan Paul, 1982.

———. *Ideology and Curriculum*. London: Routledge & Kegan Paul, 1979.

Aten, Karen, and Jennifer Howard-Grenville. "Encouraging Trade at the Boundary of Organizational Culture and Institutional Theory." *Journal of Management Inquiry* 21, no. 1 (2012): 114–17.

Aten, Karen, Jennifer Howard-Grenville, and Marc Ventresca. "Organizational Culture and Institutional Theory: A Conversation at the Border." *Journal of Management Inquiry* 21, no. 1 (2012): 78–83.

Atkinson, Richard C. "Achievement versus Aptitude Tests in College Admissions." *Issues in Science and Technology* 18, no. 2 (2002): 31–36.

Aurini, Janice Danielle. "Patterns of Tight and Loose Coupling in a Competitive Marketplace: The Case of Learning Center Franchises." *Sociology of Education* 85, no. 4 (2012): 373–87.

Bailey, Thomas, and Vanessa Smith Morest, eds. *Defending the Community College Equity Agenda*. Baltimore: Johns Hopkins University Press, 2006.

Bidwell, Charles. "Analyzing Schools As Organizations: Long-Term Permanence and Short-Term Exchange." *Sociology of Education* Extra Issue (2001): 100–14.

Binder, Amy. *Contentious Curricula: Afrocentrism and Creationism in American Public Schools*. Princeton, N.J.: Princeton University Press, 2002.

———. "For Love and Money: Organizations' Creative Responses to Multiple Environmental Logics." *Theory and Society* 36, no. 6 (2007): 547–72.

Binder, Amy, and Kate Wood. *Becoming Right: How Campuses Shape Young Conservatives*. Princeton, N.J.: Princeton University Press, 2012.

Blair-Loy, Mary. *Competing Devotions: Career and Family among Women Executives.* Cambridge, Mass.: Harvard University Press, 2003.

Bottero, Wendy. "Intersubjectivity and Bourdieusian Approaches to 'Identity.'" *Cultural Sociology* 4, no. 1 (2010): 3–22.

Bourdieu, Pierre, and Jean-Claude Passeron. *Reproduction in Education, Society, and Culture.* Beverly Hills, Calif.: Sage, 1977.

Bowen, William, Matthew Chingos, and Michael McPherson. *Crossing the Finish Line: Completing College at America's Public Universities.* Princeton, N.J.: Princeton University Press, 2009.

Bowles, Samuel, and Herbert Gintis. *Schooling in Capitalist America: Educational Reform of Economic Life.* London: Routledge & Kegan Paul, 1976.

Brewer, Dominic, Eric Eide, and Ronald Ehrenberg. "Does It Pay to Attend an Elite Private College? A Cross-Cohort Evidence on the Effects of College Type on Earnings." *Journal of Human Resources* 34, no. 1 (1999): 104–23.

Brint, Steven, and Jerome Karabel. *The Diverted Dream: Community Colleges and the Promise of Educational Opportunity in America, 1900–1985.* New York: Oxford University Press, 1989.

Bryk, Anthony, Penny Bender Sebring, Elaine Allensworth, Stuart Luppeschu, and John Easton. *Organizing Schools for Improvement: Lessons from Chicago.* Chicago: Chicago University Press, 2010.

Burke, Peter J., and Jan E. Stets. *Identity Theory.* New York: Oxford University Press, 2009.

Cahill, Spencer, ed. *Inside Social Life: Readings in Sociological Psychology and Microsociology.* New York: Oxford University Press, 2007.

Calhoun, Craig. "Habitus, Field, and Capital: The Question of Historical Specificity." In *Bourdieu: Critical Perspectives,* edited by Craig Calhoun, Edward Li Puma and Moishe Postone, 61–88. Chicago: University of Chicago Press, 1993.

California State University. "Eligibility Index Table for Residents of California or Graduates of California High Schools." 2009. http://www.csumentor.edu.

Camacho, Michelle Madsen, and Susan M. Lord. *The Borderlands of Education: Latinas in Engineering.* Lanham, Md.: Lexington, 2013.

Carbonaro, William. "Tracking, Students' Effort, and Academic Achievement." *Sociology of Education* 78, no. 1 (2005): 27–49.

Carter, Phillip. *The Complete Book of Intelligence Tests: 500 Exercises to Improve, Upgrade and Enhance Your Mind Strength.* Chichester, England: Wiley, 2005.

Chin, Tiffany, and Meredith Phillips. "Social Reproduction and Child-Rearing Practices: Social Class, Children's Agency, and the Summer Activity Gap." *Sociology of Education* 77, no. 3 (2004): 185–210.

Clark, Burton. *The Distinctive College: Antioch, Reed, and Swarthmore.* Chicago: Aldine, 1970.

Coleman, James S. *The Adolescent Society: The Social Life of the Teenager and Its Impact on Education.* New York: Free Press of Glencoe, 1961.

————. *Equality of Educational Opportunity.* Washington, D.C.: U.S. Department of Health, Education, and Welfare, 1966.

Cook, Karen S., Gary Alan Fine, and James S. House, eds. *Sociological Perspectives on Social Psychology.* Boston: Allyn and Bacon, 1995.

Cook, Philip, and Jens Ludwig. "The Burden of 'Acting White': Do Black Adolescents Disparage Academic Achievement?" In *The Black-White Test Score Gap,* edited by Christopher Jencks and Meredith Phillips, 375–400. Washington, D.C.: Brookings Institution Press, 1998.

Cookson, Peter W., and Caroline Hodges Persell. *Preparing for Power: America's Elite Boarding Schools.* New York: Basic Books, 1985.

DeLamater, John, ed. *Handbook of Social Psychology*. New York: Kluwer Academic/Plenum, 2003.

Demerath, Peter. *Producing Success: The Culture of Personal Advancement in an American High School*. Chicago: Chicago University Press, 2009.

DeSena, Judith N., and George Ansalone. "Gentrification, Schooling, and Social Inequality." *Educational Research Quarterly* 33, no. 1 (2009): 60–74.

Devine, John. *Maximum Security: The Culture of Violence in Inner-City Schools*. Chicago: University of Chicago Press, 1996.

Dorado, Silva. "Small Groups As Context for Institutional Entrepreneurship: An Exploration of the Emergence of Microfinance in Bolivia." *Organization Studies* 34, no. 4 (2013): 533–57.

Dougherty, Kevin. *The Contradictory College*. Albany: State University of New York Press, 1994.

Downey, Douglas B., James Ainsworth, and Zhenchao Qian. "Rethinking the Attitude-Achievement Paradox among Blacks." *Sociology of Education* 82, no. 1 (2009): 1–19.

Downey, Douglas B., Paul T. von Hippel, and Breckett Broh. "Are Schools the Great Equalizer?: School and Non-School Sources of Inequality in Cognitive Skills." *American Sociological Review* 69, no. 5 (2004): 613–35.

Eliasoph, Nina, and Paul Lichterman. "Culture in Interaction." *American Journal of Sociology* 108, no. 4 (2003): 735–94.

Elliot, Anthony, and Paul du Gay, eds. *Identity in Question*. London: Sage Publications, 2009.

Epstein, Joyce Levy. "The Influence of Friends on Achievement and Affective Outcomes." In *Friends in School: Patterns of Selection and Influence in Secondary Schools*, edited by Joyce Levy Epstein and Nancy Karweit, 177–200. New York: Academic Press, 1983.

Espenshade, Thomas J., and Alexandria Walton Radford. *No Longer Separate, Not Yet Equal: Race and Class in Elite College Admission and Campus Life*. Princeton, N.J.: Princeton University Press, 2009.

Everitt, Judson G. "Inhabitants Moving In: Prospective Sense Making and the Reproduction of Inhabited Institutions in Teacher Education." *Symbolic Interaction* 36, no. 2 (2013): 177–96.

———. "Teacher Careers and Inhabited Institutions: Sense Making and Arsenals of Teaching Practice in Educational Institutions." *Symbolic Interaction* 35, no. 2 (2012): 203–20.

Ferguson, Ann Arnett. *Bad Boys: Public Schools in the Making of Black Masculinity*. Ann Arbor: University of Michigan Press, 2001.

Ferguson, Ronald F. "Teachers' Perceptions and Expectations and the Black-White Test Score Gap." *Urban Education* 38, no. 4 (2003): 460–507.

Fine, Gary Alan, ed. *A Second Chicago School? The Development of a Postwar American Sociology*. Chicago: University of Chicago Press, 1995.

Fine, Michelle. *Framing Dropouts: Notes on the Politics of an Urban High School*. Albany: State University of New York Press, 1991.

Flores-Gonzales, Nilda. "Puerto Rican High Achievers: An Example of Ethnic and Academic Identity Compatibility." *Anthropology and Education Quarterly* 30, no. 3 (1999): 343–62.

Fordham, Signithia, and John Ogbu. "Black Students' School Success: Coping with the Burden of 'Acting White.'" *Urban Review* 18, no. 3 (1987): 1–31.

Friedland, Roger, and John Mohr. "The Cultural Turn in American Sociology." Chap. 1 In *Matters of Culture: Cultural Sociology in Practice*, edited by Roger Friedland and John Mohr, 1–68. Cambridge: Cambridge University Press, 2004.

Gamoran, Adam. *The Variable Effects of High School Tracking*. Madison, Wisc.: Center on Organization and Restructuring of Schools, 1992.

Gardner, Howard. *Frames of Mind: The Theory of Multiple Intelligences.* New York: Basic Books, 1983.

Gaztambide-Fernandez, Rubén A. *The Best of the Best: Becoming Elite at an American Boarding School.* Cambridge, Mass: Harvard University Press, 2009.

Gerber, Theodore P., and Sin Yi Cheung. "Horizontal Stratification in Postsecondary Education: Forms, Explanations, and Implications." *Annual Review of Sociology* 34 (2008): 299–318.

Giddens, Anthony. *Modernity and Self-Identity: Self and Society in the Late Modern Age.* Stanford: Stanford University Press, 1991.

Golden, Daniel. *The Price of Admission: How America's Ruling Class Buys Its Way into Elite Colleges—and Who Gets Left Outside the Gates.* New York: Three Rivers Press, 2006.

Goleman, Daniel. *Emotional Intelligence.* New York: Bantam, 1995.

Gould, Stephen. *The Mismeasure of Man.* New York: Norton, 1981.

Grant, Gerald. *Hope and Despair in the American City.* Cambridge, Mass: Harvard University Press, 2009.

———. *The World We Created at Hamilton High.* Cambridge, Mass: Harvard University Press, 1988.

Greene, Jay P., and Greg Forster. Public High School Graduation and College Readiness Rates in the United States." *Education Working Paper 3.* New York: Manhattan Institute, Center for Civic Innovation, 2003.

Grodsky, Eric. "Compensatory Sponsorship in Higher Education." *American Journal of Sociology* 112, no. 6 (2007): 1662–712.

Grodsky, Eric, John Robert Warren, and Erika Felts. "Testing and Social Stratification in American Education." *Annual Review of Sociology* 34 (2008): 385–404.

Grubb, W. Norton. "'Like, What Do I Do Now?' The Dilemmas of Guidance Counseling." In *Defending the Community College Equity Agenda,* edited by Thomas Bailey and Vanessa Smith Morest, 195–222. Baltimore: Johns Hopkins University Press, 2006.

———. *The Money Myth: School Resources, Outcomes, and Equity.* New York: Russell Sage Foundation, 2009.

Hacking, Ian. "Between Michel Foucault and Erving Goffman: Between Discourse in the Abstract and Face-to-Face Interaction." *Economy and Society* 33, no. 3 (2004): 277–302.

Haedicke, Michael A. "'Keeping Our Mission, Changing Our System': Translation and Organizational Change in Natural Foods Co-Ops." *The Sociological Quarterly* 53, no. 1 (2012): 44–67.

Hallett, Tim. "Between Deference and Distinction: Interaction Ritual through Symbolic Power in an Educational Institution." *Social Psychology Quarterly* 70, no. 2 (2007): 148–71.

———. "The Myth Incarnate: Recoupling Processes, Turmoil, and Inhabited Institutions in an Urban Elementary School." *American Sociological Review* 75, no. 1 (2010): 52–74.

Hallett, Tim, David Shulman, and Gary Alan Fine. "Peopling Organizations: The Promise of Symbolic Interactionism for an Inhabited Institutionalism." In *The Oxford Handbook of Organizational Studies: Classical Foundations,* edited by Paul S. Adler, 486–509. New York: Oxford University Press, 2009.

Hallett, Tim, and Marc Ventresca. "Inhabited Institutions: Social Interactions and Organizational Forms in Gouldner's Patterns of Industrial Bureaucracy." *Theory and Society* 35 (2006): 213–36.

Hallinan, Maureen. "Tracking: From Theory to Practice." *Sociology of Education* 67, no. 2 (1994): 79–84.

Hallinan, Maureen, and Richard Williams. "Students' Characteristics and the Peer-Influence Process." *Sociology of Education* 63 (1990): 122–32.

Harrington, Brooke, and Gary Alan Fine. "Where the Action Is: Small Groups and Recent Developments in Sociological Theory." *Small Group Research* 37, no. 1 (2006): 4–19.

Harris, Angel. *Kids Don't Want to Fail: Oppositional Culture and the Black-White Achievement Gap.* Cambridge, Mass: Harvard University Press, 2011.

Hatch, Mary Jo. "Bringing Culture Back from Institutional Siberia." *Journal of Management Inquiry* 21, no. 1 (2012): 84–87.

Hatch, Mary Jo, and Tammar Zilber. "Conversation at the Border between Organizational Culture Theory and Institutional Theory." *Journal of Management Inquiry* 21, no. 1 (2012): 94–97.

Haveman, Heather, and Rao Hayagreeva. "Hybrid Forms and the Evolution of Thrifts." *American Behavioral Scientist* 49, no. 7 (2006): 974–86.

Herideen, Penelope E. *Policy, Pedagogy, and Social Inequality: Community College Student Realities in Post-Industrial America.* Westport, Conn.: Bergin and Garvey, 1998.

Herrnstein, Richard, and Charles Murray. *The Bell Curve: Intelligence and Class Structure in American Life.* New York: Free Press, 1994.

Heyns, Barbara. *Summer Learning and the Effects of Schooling.* New York: Academic Press, 1978.

Hinings, Bob. "Connections between Institutional Logics and Organizational Culture." *Journal of Management Inquiry* 21, no. 1 (2012): 98–101.

Hirsch, Paul, and Michael Lounsbury. "Ending the Family Quarrel: Toward a Reconciliation of 'Old' and 'New' Institutionalisms." *American Behavioral Scientist* 40, no. 4 (1997): 406–18.

Hochschild, Jennifer L. *Facing Up to the American Dream: Race, Class, and the Soul of the Nation.* Princeton, N.J.: Princeton University Press, 1995.

Hochschild, Jennifer L., and Nathan Scovronick. *The American Dream and the Public Schools.* New York: Oxford University Press, 2003.

Holstein, James, and Jaber Gubrium. *The Self We Live By: Narrative Identity in a Postmodern World.* New York: Oxford University Press, 2000.

Howard, Judith, A. and Daniel G. Renfrow "Social Cognition." In *Handbook of Social Psychology,* edited by John DeLamater, 259–82. New York: Kluwer Academic / Plenum, 2003.

———. "Social Cognition." In *Sociological Perspectives on Social Psychology,* edited by Karen S. Cook, Gary Alan Fine and James S. House, 90–117. Boston: Allyn and Bacon, 1995.

———. "Social Psychology of Identities." *Annual Review of Sociology* 26 (2000): 367–93.

Irvine, Jacqueline Jordan. *Black Students and School Failure: Policies, Practices, and Prescriptions.* Westport, Conn.: Greenwood, 1990.

Irvine, Leslie. "Even Better Than the Real Thing: Narratives of the Self in Codependency." *Qualitative Sociology* 23 (2000): 9–28.

Jepperson, Ronald. "Institutions, Institutional Effects, and Institutionalism." In *The New Institutionalism in Organizational Analysis,* edited by Walter W. Powell and Paul J. Dimaggio, 143–63. Chicago: University of Chicago Press, 1991.

Johnson, Heather Beth. *The American Dream and the Power of Wealth: Choosing Schools and Inheriting Inequality in the Land of Opportunity.* New York: Routledge, 2006.

Kahn, Shamus Rahman. *Privilege: The Making of an Adolescent Elite at St. Paul's School.* Princeton, N.J.: Princeton University Press, 2011.

Karabel, Jerome. *The Chosen: The Hidden History of Admission and Exclusion at Harvard, Yale, and Princeton.* New York: Houghton Mifflin, 2005.

Kozol, Jonathan. *Savage Inequalities: Children in America's Schools.* New York: Harper Perennial, 1991.

Labaree, David. *Someone Has to Fail: The Zero-Sum Game of Public Schooling.* Cambridge, Mass: Harvard University Press, 2010.

Lareau, Annette. *Unequal Childhoods: Class, Race, and Family Life.* Berkeley: University of California Press, 2003.

Lawler, Steph. *Identity: Sociological Perspectives.* Cambridge: Polity Press, 2008.

Lee, James Daniel. "More Than Ability: Gender and Personal Relationships Influence Science and Technology Development." *Sociology of Education* 75 (2002): 349–73.

Lemann, Nicholas. *The Big Test: The Secret History of American Meritocracy.* New York: Farrar, Straus, and Giroux, 1999.

Loury, Linda Datcher, and David Garman. "College Selectivity and Earnings." *Journal of Labor Economics* 13, no. 2 (1995): 289–308.

Luttrell, Wendy. *Schoolsmart and Motherwise: Working-Class Women's Identity and Schooling.* New York: Routledge, 1997.

Mackintosh, N. J. *I.Q. and Human Intelligence.* Oxford: Oxford University Press, 1998.

MacLeod, Jay. *Ain't No Makin' It: Leveled Aspirations in a Low-Income Neighborhood.* Boulder, Colo.: Westview, 1987.

Martin, Luther H., Huck Gutman, and Patrick Hutton, eds. *Technologies of the Self: A Seminar with Michel Foucault.* Amherst: University of Massachusetts Press, 1988.

Massey, Douglas S., Camille Z. Charles, Garvey F. Lundy, and Mary J. Fischer. *The Source of the River: The Social Origins of Freshmen at America's Selective Colleges and Universities.* Princeton, N.J.: Princeton University Press, 2003.

Matute-Bianchi, Maria Eugenia. "Ethnic Identities and Patterns of School Success and Failure among Mexican-Descent and Japanese-American Students in a California High School: An Ethnographic Analysis." *American Journal of Education* 95, no. 1 (1986): 233–55.

McDonough, Patricia M. "Buying and Selling Higher Education: The Social Construction of the College Applicant." *The Journal of Higher Education* 65, no. 4 (1994): 427–46.

McLeod, Julie, and Lyn Yates. *Making Modern Lives: Subjectivity, Schooling, and Social Change.* Albany: State University of New York Press, 2006.

Mehan, Hugh, Gordon C. Chang, Makeba Jones, and Season S. Mussey. *In the Front Door: Creating a College-Bound Culture of Learning.* Boulder, Colo.: Paradigm, 2012.

Mehan, Hugh, Lea Hubbard, and Irene Villanueva. "Forming Academic Identities: Accommodation without Assimilation among Involuntary Minorities." *Anthropology and Education Quarterly* 25, no. 2 (1994): 91–117.

Mehan, Hugh, Lea Hubbard, Irene Villanueva, and Angela Lintz. *Constructing School Success: The Consequences of Untracking Low Achieving Students.* New York: Cambridge University Press, 1996.

Mellow, Gail O., and Cynthia Heelan. *Minding the Dream: The Process and Practice of the American Community College.* Lanham, Md.: Rowman and Littlefield, 2008.

Metz, Mary. *Classrooms and Corridors: The Crisis of Authority in Desegregated Secondary Schools.* Berkeley: University of California Press, 1978.

Meyer, Heinz-Dieter, and Brian Rowan, eds. *The New Institutionalism in Education.* Albany: State University of New York, 2006.

Meyer, John, and Brian Rowan. "Institutionalized Organization: Formal Structure As Myth and Ceremony." *American Journal of Sociology* 83 (1977): 340–63.

Meyer, John, and W. Richard Scott, eds. *Organizational Environments: Ritual and Rationality.* Beverly Hills, Calif.: Sage, 1983.

Meyer, Renate, and Gerhard Hammerschmid. "Changing Institutional Logics and Executive Identities: A Managerial Challenge to Public Administration in Austria." *American Behavioral Scientist* 49, no. 7 (2006): 1000–14.

Milner, Murray, Jr. *Freaks Geeks and Cool Kids: American Teenagers, Schools and the Culture of Consumption.* New York: Routledge, 2004.

Molm, Linda D, and Karen S. Cook. "Social Exchange and Exchange Networks." In *Sociological Perspectives on Social Psychology,* edited by Karen S. Cook, Gary Alan Fine, and James S. House, 209–35. Boston: Allyn and Bacon, 1995.

Moore, Colleen, and Nancy Shulock. *Divided We Fail: Improving Completion and Closing Racial Gaps in California's Community Colleges.* Sacramento: Institute for Higher Education Leadership and Policy, 2010.

Morill, Calvin. "From Bridges to Trading Zones in Organizational Culture and Institutional Research." *Journal of Management Inquiry* 21, no. 1 (2012): 109–13.

Mullen, Ann. *Degrees of Inequality: Culture, Class, and Gender in American Higher Education.* Baltimore: Johns Hopkins University Press, 2010.

Nisbett, Richard E. *Intelligence and How to Get It: Why Schools and Cultures Count.* New York: Norton, 2009.

Nuñez, Anne-Marie. "Latino Students' Transitions to College: A Social and Intercultural Capital Perspective." *Harvard Educational Review* 79, no. 1 (2009): 22–49.

Nunn, Lisa M. "Classrooms As Racialized Spaces: Dynamics of Collaboration, Tension, and Student Attitudes in Urban and Suburban High Schools." *Urban Education* 46, no. 6 (2011): 1226–55.

Oakes, Jeannie. *Keeping Track: How Schools Structure Inequality.* New Haven, Conn: Yale University Press, 1985.

Oakes, Jeannie, Adam Gamoran, and Reba Page. "Curriculum Differentiation: Opportunities, Outcomes and Meanings." In *Handbook of Research on Curriculum,* edited by P. W. Jackson, 570–608. Washington, D.C.: American Educational Research Association, 1992.

Oram, Fern, ed. *440 Colleges for Top Students.* Lawrenceville, N.J.: Peterson, 2007.

Page, Reba. "The Uncertain Value of School Knowledge: Biology at Westridge High." *Teachers College Record* 100, no. 3 (1999): 554–601.

Patriotta, Gerardo, and Giovan Lanzara. "Identity, Institutions, and New Work Roles: The Case of a Green Field Automotive Factory." *American Behavioral Scientist* 49, no. 7 (2006): 987–99.

Payne, Charles M. *So Much Reform, So Little Change: The Persistence of Failure in Urban Schools.* Cambridge, Mass: Harvard Education Press, 2008.

Perin, Dolores. "Can Community Colleges Protect Both Access and Standards? The Problem of Remediation." *Teachers College Record* 108, no. 3 (2006): 339–73.

Perin, Dolores, and Kerry Charron. "Lights Just Click on Every Day." In *Defending the Community College Equity Agenda,* edited by Thomas Bailey and Vanessa Smith Morest, 155–94. Baltimore: Johns Hopkins University Press, 2006.

Polletta, Francesca, Pang Ching Bobby Chen, Beth Gharrity Gardner, and Alice Motes. "The Sociology of Storytelling." *Annual Review of Sociology* 37 (2011): 109–30.

Richardson, John, and Karen Bradley. "The Moral Career of Intelligence and the Construction of Educational Psychology." Paper presented at the annual meeting of the American Sociological Association. Philadelphia, 2005.

Riegle-Crumb, Catherine, George Farkas, and Chandra Muller. "The Role of Gender and Friendship in Advanced Course Taking." *Sociology of Education* 79, no. 3 (2006): 206–28.

Rosenbaum, James E. *Beyond College for All: Career Paths for the Forgotten Half.* New York: Russell Sage Foundation, 2001.

———. *Making Inequality: The Hidden Curriculum of High School Tracking.* New York: Wiley, 1976.

Rosenbaum, James E., Regina Deil-Amen, and Ann E. Person. *After Admission: From College Access to College Success.* New York: Russell Sage Foundation, 2006.

Sacks, Peter. *Tearing Down the Gates: Confronting the Class Divide in American Education.* Berkeley: University of California Press, 2007.

Schultz, Maijken. "Relationships between Culture and Institutions: New Interdependencies in a Global World?." *Journal of Management Inquiry* 21, no. 1 (2012): 102–06.

Schultz, Maijken, and Bob Hinings. "A Comment on the Border between Institutional and Organizational Culture Theories." *Journal of Management Inquiry* 21, no. 1 (2012): 107–08.

Sengupta, Ria, and Christopher Jepsen. "California's Community College Students." *California Counts: Population Trends and Profiles* 8, no. 2 (2006): 1–24.

Sewell, William Jr. "Theory of Structure: Duality, Agency, and Transformation." *American Journal of Sociology* 98, no. 1 (1992): 1–29.

Shulock, Nancy, and Colleen Moore. "Diminished Access to the Baccalaureate for Low-Income and Minority Students in California: The Impact of Budget and Capacity Constraints on the Transfer Function." *Educational Policy* 19, no. 2 (2005): 418–42.

Shusterman, Richard, ed. *Bourdieu: A Critical Reader.* Oxford: Blackwell Publishers, 1999.

Springer, Sally, and Marion Franck. *Admission Matters: What Students and Parents Need to Know about Getting into College.* San Francisco: Jossey-Bass, 2005.

Steinberg, Jacques. *The Gatekeepers: Inside the Admissions Process of a Premier College.* New York: Penguin, 2002.

Sternberg, Robert. "Myths, Countermyths, and Truths about Intelligence." *Educational Researcher* 25, no. 2 (1996): 11–16.

Stevens, Mitchell. *Creating a Class: College Admission and the Education of Elites.* Cambridge, Mass: Harvard University Press, 2007.

Stevens, Mitchell, Elizabeth A. Armstrong, and Richard Arum. "Sieve, Incubator, Temple, Hub: Empirical and Theoretical Advances in the Sociology of Higher Education." *Annual Review of Sociology* 34 (2008): 127–51.

Stigler, Stephen. *The History of Statistics: The Measurement of Uncertainty before 1900.* Cambridge, Mass: Belknap/Harvard University Press, 1986.

Stryker, Sheldon. "From Mead to a Structural Symbolic Interactionism and Beyond." *Annual Review of Sociology* 34 (2008): 15–31.

Stuber, Jenny M. "Class Dismissed? The Social-Class Worldviews of Privileged College Students." In *Educating Elites: Class Privilege and Educational Advantage*, edited by Adam Howard and Rubén A. Gaztambide-Fernandez, 131–51. Lanham, Md.: Rowman and Littlefield Education, 2010.

Swidler, Ann. "Culture in Action: Symbols and Strategies." *American Sociological Review* 51 (1986): 273–86.

Teranishi, Robert, Walter R. Allen, and Daniel G. Solorzano. "Opportunity at the Crossroads: Racial Inequality, School Segregation, and Higher Education in California." *Teachers College Record* 106, no. 11 (2004): 2224–45.

Threadgold, Steven. "Reflexivity of Contemporary Youth, Risk and Cultural Capital." *Current Sociology* 57, no. 1 (2009): 47–68.

Trusty, Jerry. "High Educational Expectations and Low Achievement: Stability of Educational Goals across Adolescence." *Journal of Educational Research* 93 (2000): 356–65.

Tyson, Karolyn. *Integration Interrupted: Tracking, Black Students, and Acting White after Brown.* Oxford: Oxford University Press, 2011.

Tyson, Karolyn, William Darity, Jr., and Domini Castellino. "It's Not a Black Thing: Understanding the Burden of Acting White and Other Dilemmas of High Achievement." *American Sociological Review* 70, no. (2005): 582–605.

University of California, Educational Relations Department. "Major Features of the California Master Plan for Higher Education." 2007.

Van Buskirk, Peter. *Winning the College Admission Game: Strategies for Students and Parents.* Lawrenceville, N.J.: Peterson, 2007.

Venezia, Andrea. "Connecting California's K–12 and Higher Education Systems: Challenges and Opportunities." In *Crucial Issues in California Education 2000*, 153–76. Berkeley, CA: Policy Analysis for California Education, 2000.

Waassmer, Robert, Colleen Moore, and Nancy Shulock. *California Community College Transfer Rates: Policy Implications and a Future Research Agenda.* Sacramento: California State University, Senate Office of Research, 2003.

Walkerdine, Valerie, Helen Lucey, and June Melody. *Growing up Girl: Psychosocial Explorations of Gender and Class.* London: Palgrave, 2001.

Weigert, Andrew, J. Smith Teitge, and Dennis W. Teitge. *Society and Identity: Toward a Sociological Psychology.* Cambridge, U.K.: Cambridge University Press, 1986.

Weis, Lois, Cameron McCarthy, and Greg Dimitriadis, eds. *Ideology, Curriculum, and the New Sociology of Education: Revisiting the Work of Michael Apple.* New York: Routledge, 2006.

Westenholz, Ann. "Emerging Identities beyond Organizational Boundaries." In *Identity in the Age of the New Economy: Life in Temporary and Scattered Work Practices*, edited by Ann Westenholz and Torben Elgaard Jensen, 122–46. Cheltenham, England: Elgar, 2004.

———. "Identity Work and Meaning Arena: Beyond Actor/Structure and Micro/Macro Distinctions in an Empirical Analysis of IT Workers." *American Behavioral Scientist* 49, no. 7 (2006): 1015–29.

Westenholz, Ann, Jesper Pedersen, and Frank Dobbin. "Introduction: Institutions in the Making: Identity, Power, and the Emergence of New Organizational Forms." *American Behavioral Scientist* 49, no. 7 (2006): 889–96.

Wilcox, Kathleen. "Differential Socialization in the Classroom: Implications for Equal Opportunity." In *Doing the Ethnography of Schooling: Educational Anthropology in Action*, edited by George Spindler, 270–309. New York: Holt, Rinehart, and Winston, 1982.

Willis, Paul. *Learning to Labor: How Working Class Kids Get Working Class Jobs.* New York: Columbia University Press, 1977.

Wortham, Steven. *Learning Identity: The Joint Emergence of Social Identification and Academic Learning.* Cambridge: Cambridge University Press, 2006.

Yonezawa, Susan, and Amy Stuart Wells. "Reform As Redefining the Spaces of Schools: An Examination of Detracking by Choice." In *Beyond Silenced Voices: Class, Race, and Gender in United States Schools*, edited by Lois Weis and Michelle Fine, 47–61. Albany: State University of New York Press, 2005.

Yun, John T., and Jose F. Moreno. "College Access, K-12 Concentrated Disadvantage, and the Next 25 Years of Education Research." *Educational Researcher* 35, no. 12 (2006): 12–19.

Zilber, Tammar. "The Relevance of Institutional Theory for the Study of Organizational Culture." *Journal of Management Inquiry* 21, no. 1 (2012): 88–93.

Zirkel, Sabrina. "Social Intelligence: The Development and Maintenance of Purposive Behavior." In *The Handbook of Emotional Intelligence*, edited by Rueven Bar-On and Stephen Parker, 3–27. San Francisco: Jossey-Bass, 2000.

INDEX

ABOUT THE AUTHOR

LISA M. NUNN is an assistant professor of sociology at the University of San Diego.

CPSIA information can be obtained at www.ICGtesting.com
Printed in the USA
BVOW04s1352240314

348596BV00001B/1/P

9 780813 563619